UPANISHADS

Gateways of Knowledge

SRI M.P. PANDIT

PUBLISHER:
LOTUS LIGHT PUBLICATIONS
P.O. Box 2
Wilmot, WI 53192 U.S.A.

FIRST U.S. EDITION NOVEMBER 24, 1988

Published by Lotus Light Publications
by arrangement with Sri M.P. Pandit

COVER: MINA YAMASHITA GRAPHIC DESIGN

ISBN: 0-941524-44-2

Library of Congress Catalog Card Number 88-83077

Printed in the United States of America

FOREWORD

This short treatise is very welcome. There is no dearth of books on the Upanishads by scholars. They give only partial intellectual views that ignore or fail to appreciate the deeper spiritual meanings of many things which appear to be gross or fantastic or obscure. Even most Indian scholars have only tried to present those aspects which would be acceptable to the West. Sri Aurobindo, with his deeper knowledge of the West and an increased appetite for the complete Truth, tries to grasp the Upanishadic wisdom in its entirety by diving back into the spiritual vision of the Seers who uttered the truths; and then applying his quickened and purified intellect and his profound scholarship, he presents the philosophy of the secret wisdom in conceptual terms. His integral view also re-asserts the traditional belief that the Vedas and the Upanishads, which modern scholars find to be antagonistic, really form a continuous culture. His disciple and follower, the great Vedic scholar, Sri Kapali Sastry, corroborates his view in his many scholarly writings, including his Sanskrit Commentary on the Vedas.

Sri M. P. Pandit has been carrying on the study of the Vedas and the Upanishads in this integral perspective. In the present work he gives a brief but complete view of the Upanishads as explained by Sri Aurobindo and Sri Kapali Sastry, justifying his position with profuse quotations from some neglected parts of the Vedas and the Upanishads, and meeting also the possible objections of the Western or Westernised scholars.

This book will, therefore, be not only a critical and scholarly introduction to Upanishadic thought, but also a good guide to the understanding of some of the basic but abstruse concepts of Sri Aurobindo's *The Life Divine*, like 'supermind', 'supramental', 'truth-consciousness', etc. which are traced back to their concrete setting.

Shantiniketan   D. M. DATTA

PREFACE

For a people who seek to be reborn out of a decadent past into a dynamic present, it is indispensable to know and safeguard the genius of its heritage. Each society develops a particular truth of life and it is that that marks out its individuality and justifies its existence. Whatever the changing moulds of expression suited to the needs of the time, it must keep alive this fount of life within; for after all, it is that which fertilises and enlivens all currents of thought and activity without. In a word, the people has to recover its own soul and tend its growth. For it is only around a living soul that the body can gather and develop strength and progress.

In India, the soul of the nation has been — it is universally recognised — the Truth of the Spirit. There are countries whose career has been motivated and shaped by other truths, those of Beauty, Strength, Harmony and Order and others. They made their contribution to the sum total of human progress in their respective fields and passed. But not so India. India knows no death. There is no country, barring perhaps China, with such a long continuous past as hers. That is because the inspiration that governs her life is immortal: it is the Truth of God, an eternal Verity of verities, *Sanātana Dharma*. What is this spiritual truth that decays not, and what the Dharma that expresses it?

It goes without saying that this Dharma is not the rule of Ritual or Social hierarchy that have encrusted the way of life known as Hinduism. It is the formulation of an impulsion from the depths of evolving humanity. It is this native spring of the soul that has still kept the people awake in spirit and vigorous in thought, however exhausted in vitality. And of those, in modern times, who have sought to seize and use this key to the renaissance of the nation, Sri Aurobindo is the foremost.

With the unerring eye of the Seer he plumbed deep into the profounds of the past dating back to prehistoric origins and traced a continuous, a meaningful tradition from the recorded times of the Veda down to the present day. He examined and weighed the achievement in each sphere of the national endeavour—Religion, Spirituality, Sociology, Polity, Art, Painting, Sculpture, Literature, Science, Philosophy ; he explored the extent to which they fulfilled the aspirations of the developing Soul of the people, in the measure of their faithfulness to the central guiding spirit, and also the reasons why they failed to move further. He reinterpreted the Wisdom that has been handed down the millenniums, in terms of the modern intellect and sought to apply its light and power to the solution of the problems of the current age. To this end he took up for exposition the central body of the Books of Knowledge — the Veda, the Upanishad, the Gita — which have been the acknowledged sources of India's tradition, religious and secular, and laid bare their core of dynamic Wisdom for the men of today to draw upon.

It is fashionable to regard the Upanishads as the first awakenings of the Indian mind which attained full maturity in the age of the Darshanas ; the Vedas, anterior to them, as liturgies of a primitive people yet in infancy of development, and the Puranas and Tantras, posterior to the Upanishads, decaying

overgrowths of myth, mummery and magic. Sri Aurobindo does not accept this view. He sees throughout
one tradition, and one Truth basing that fundamental
tradition, viz. the universe is a manifestation of God,
Man an emanation from Him, and all life an unveiling
of the Divine. The Vedas give expression to this
sublime vision of the Ancient Fathers, *pūrve pitarah*, as it
impressed itself on their early intuitive mentality and
record a sustained endeavour to live it in their daily
life. The Upanishads coming long after the passing of
this Dawn of Indian civilisation, seek to reclaim, verify
and present this Knowledge in terms suited to their
later age. They are veritable gateways of knowledge.

What is the message of the Upanishads? How far
do they represent a continuity and in what manner a
change from the Vedic tradition? Are they merely
interesting pages in the history of Indian Religion or do
they have a larger significance and even a relevance to
the man of today? Are they only philosophical treatises or
are they also manuals of Sadhana? Do they preach the
unreality of the world and counsel flight from life to the
Beyond or do they rather proclaim the eternal truth of
life, emphasise the unity of creation in a common
underlying Divinity and enjoin upon man to realise his
highest state here and now, *ihaiva?*

Such are the pertinent and topical questions that
are raised and dealt with in Sri Aurobindo's writings on
the Upanishads. The present study has for its aim a
convenient presentation of this approach to the subject
and it is hoped that it would, in its own way, help
towards a truer understanding and appreciation of the
significance of this bequest of Indian tradition at a time
like the present when spiritual values are the most
needed but the least in evidence. May it join its voice

to the imperative Call of Mother India to her children to awake to their responsibilities as the custodians of the most opulent, mature and potent Culture on earth, to live up to the high Ideals they have inherited, and take the lead that is naturally theirs, in guiding humanity out of the twilight of the half-gods of mind and life into the luminous reign of the plenary Spirit.

Sri Aurobindo Ashram,
   Pondicherry

M. P. PANDIT

CONTENTS

A GENERAL SURVEY OF
THE UPANISHADS

THE UPANISHADS

It is a kind of poetry—word of vision and rhythm of spirit—that has not been written before or after.

SRI AUROBINDO

INTRODUCTORY

The number of texts claiming to be Upanishads is large, more than two hundred at least. Traditionally, a hundred and eight of them are recognised as genuine Upanishads and out of these again, only twelve or thirteen texts are accepted as authentic, ancient scripture. The Isha, Kena, Katha, Prashna, Mundaka, Mandukya, Taittiriya, Aitareya, Chhandogya and Brihadaranyaka are the ten major Upanishads of unchallenged authority. The Kaushitaki and the Shvetashvatara Upanishads are also recognised as important inasmuch as they are frequently referred to in the *Brahma Sutras*.

The Upanishads are some of them in prose, some in verse and some in both. Most of the older ones like the Brihadaranyaka, Chhandogya, Taittiriya, Aitareya, Kaushitaki and the Prashna are in prose ; Isha, Katha, Mundaka and Shvetashvatara are in verse ; the Kena is partly in prose and partly in verse.

Each Upanishad belongs to one of the Vedas. Excepting the Isha which forms a direct part of the Shukla Yajur Veda Samhita (the final chapter), all the others form part of either a Brahmana or an Aranyaka of their respective Veda Samhitas. Thus :

The Aitareya and Kaushitaki belong to the Rig Veda; the Katha or Kathaka belongs to the Katha school of the Yajur Veda, the Shvetashvatara and the Taittiriya to the Krishna Yajur Veda and the Brihadaranyaka to the Shukla Yajur Veda.

The Kena, known by its first word (*kena*, by whom), also called the Talavakara, is of the

Sama Veda; so too does the Chhandogya belong to the Sama.

The Prashna, Mundaka and Mandukya belong to the Atharva Veda.

CHAPTER I

THE WESTERN APPROACH

THE popularity enjoyed by the Upanishads among the western Orientalists of the last century and the modern scholars of Indian thought and philosophy is something truly phenomenal. Alone among the large number of the sacred texts of Hindu Religion, they have been held aloft as specimens of Indian Thought at its highest[1], records that can stand comparison with the products of the Greek mind which provided the first moulds for the efflorescence of the western civilisation. As a rule, to these scholars who took to the study of the Indian heritage from a dateless past, the Vedas are little more than liturgical texts for use in ceremonial functions of the primitive communities steeped in animistic ignorance, the Brahmanas clever annotations of wily priests to perpetuate their hold on the superstitious masses ; the Puranas are mythology, picturesque perhaps, but nothing more, the Tantras fabrications of a degenerate mentality indulging in black magic, necromancy, dissipation and trading on the credulity of an innately religious minded people. The Upanishads alone are entitled to represent the true Indian spirit in the sphere of religion, philosophy and spirituality. They are the natural reactions from the religious hedonism

---

[1] "On the tree of Indian wisdom there is no fairer flower than the Upanishads." *Deussen.*

"The Upanishads are the oftiest utterances of Indian intelligence... Whatever value the reader may assign to the ideas they represent, they are the highest product of the ancient mind, and almost the only element of interest in Indian literature, which is at every stage replete with them to saturation." *Gough.*

of the Vedic society. In keeping with the pattern
of progress of humanity everywhere, the Indian mind
gradually releases itself from the holds of the exclusive
demands of the physical life of the body, even reacts
violently against that excessive preoccupation, and
begins to speculate and soar—in a word, begins the
mental life proper. It starts thinking seriously about
the nature of the world and its constituents, of God and
of the destiny of man. The Upanishads represent this
phase of Indian evolution and record the results of these
exercises of the mind ; the later philosophical systems—
the Darshanas — are only metaphysical developments
and systematisations of the philosphical ideas and
concepts arrived at by the thinkers of the Upanishads.

No doubt there is much that baffles the modern
reader in these texts. Many of them are made up of
'detached statements'[1], i.e. disjointed utterances in which
it is difficult to trace any thread of connection. There
is no such logical arrangement and sequence as we find
in their Greek counterparts. "The teaching of the Upanishads is not a homogeneous, self-contained system,
but lacks unity and completeness" (A. Schweitzer).
From sublime speculations on the nature of the Highest
Reality they abruptly pass to the most elementary
details of biological reproduction ; most glorious
descriptions of the being of man in its suprasensuous
statuses are found side by side with unabashed eulogy
and childish exaltations of food. They are so uneven—
at times mutually contradictory also — that even the
more 'sympathetic' interpreters are obliged to protest :
"We are often vexed with their unstable, contradictory
and partly foolish statements" (Bloomfield); "By the

---

[1] Schopenhauer,

side of so much that is fresh, natural, simple, beautiful and true, (they) contain so much that is not only unmeaning, artificial and silly, but even hideous and repellant" (Max Muller). But all the same, we are assured, the Upanishads are notable departures from the traditional Indian penchant for mysticism and sacerdotalism and are important because of the new orientation in thought and outlook which they denote, the many 'errors of innocence' of their authors notwithstanding, and because of their embryonic store of 'flashing truths and inspired ideas' which base, in one way or other, all the later Systems in Indian Philosophy including heterodox Buddhism. And historically they are important because they are the expression of a vigorous revolt of the Kshatriya class against the dominance of the Brahmin in the Vedic age. If there is no consistent philosophy in them, it is because they are works of different authors, at different periods, of men who have not yet attained a sufficient maturity of mind.

This in brief is the position of the occidental Indologists in regard to the Upanishads, generally. And barring a few exceptions, Indian scholars trained in the western tradition have accepted their view viz.:

"We find in the Upanishads an advance on the Samhita mythology, Brahmana hair-splitting, and even Aranyaka theology, though all these stages are to be met with. The authors of the Upanishads transform the past they handle, and the changes they effect in the Vedic religion indicate the boldness of the heart that beats only for freedom . . Tentative solutions of metaphysical questions are put forth in the form of dialogues and disputations . . . Not being systematic philosophy, or the production of a single author, or even of the same

age, they contain much that is inconsistent and un-
scientific." "The Upanishads are regarded as a class of
literature independent of the Vedic hymns and the
Brahmanas . . . They attempt to moralise the religion of
the Vedas without disturbing their form . . . (they are) a
protest against the externalism of the Vedic practices
and an indifference to the sacredness of the Veda. The
religion of the Vedas certainly was more joyous, but it
was a lower form of religion . . . the attitude of the Upanishads is not favourable to the sacredness of the Vedas."
(Dr. Radhakrishnan)[1]

The tenor of these conclusions, however, is contrary
to the spirit of the Indian tradition according to which
the Upanishads are not only the natural terminus, the
close but also the final word, the crown and summit of
the Vedas, *veda-anta*. The Knowledge that is proclaimed
to be enshrined in the Revealed Scripture that is the
Veda is here brought out to the fuller view; what is in
the Upanishads is derived from and rests upon the
kernel in the Veda.[2] That is why the Rishis of these
texts so frequently invoke the authority of the Vedic
seers in confirmation of what they say e.g. *tadetadṛcā-
bhyuktam*, "this is said by the Rik," *taduktam ṛṣiṇā*,
"that is said by the Rishi" etc., or quote a whole Rik in
clinching their pronouncement. The Upanishads are
throughout conscious of their Vedic origin and background and freely draw from it. That is why we find
that not only many of the ideas in the Upanishads are
to be found in some germ form or other in the Vedas,
but at times even the images and similes are the same
e.g., fire from tinders, spokes and the wheel, dry

---

[1] *Indian Philosophy*, Vol. I.

[2] *Vedaguhyopaniṣatsu*, Upanishads which are the secret of the Veda
(Shvetashvatara Up. V. 6).

coconut and the kernel, boat and the waters, to choose
a few at random. The symbols they use are essentially
the symbols we find in the Vedas, albeit here with an
extended significance viz., birds, waters, swan, the Tree
Inverted (with roots above and branches downward)
etc. The Vedic spirit pervading the Upanishads is unmistakable and not a few of the unbiassed minds have
been slow to recognise it. Both the Vedas and the Upanishads are of the same origin — SHRUTI, the Revealed
Word.

Sri Aurobindo accepts and upholds this ancient
tradition.

CHAPTER II

THE INDIAN TRADITION

Who verily knows and who can here declare it,
Whence it was born and whence comes this
    creation?
The Gods are later than this world's production.
Who knows then whence it first came into being?
He, the first origin of this creation,
Whether he formed it all or did not form it,
Whose eye controls this world in highest heaven,
He verily knows it, or perhaps he knows not.[1]

Who is this mighty personage who beholds in his titanic
vision the entire spread of creation, measures as it were,
the stature of the very Gods in a single sweep of his look
and knocks at the Gates of the Creator Himself to
fathom the greatest Mystery of all? He is no ordinary
poet or philosopher, to be sure; the audacity of his
spirit is too overwhelming to be contained in such human
bounds. He is Prajapati Parameshtin, one of the
patriarchs of the old Aryan society in the Vedic Age,
one of the galaxy of the leaders who moulded and
shaped the Indian civilisation in its earliest apogee of
spiritual progress and advancement, the sole surviving
records of which are to be found in the Rig Veda. For,
as Sri Aurobindo points out, the Rishis of the Rig Veda

---

[1] को अद्धा वेद क इह प्र वोचत्कुत आजाता कुत इयं विसृष्टि: ।
अर्वाग्देवा अस्य विसर्जनेनाथा को वेद यत आवभूव ॥
इयं विसृष्टिर्यंत आवभूव यदि वा दधे यदि वा न ।
यो अस्यध्यक्ष: परमे व्योमन्त्सो अङ्ग वेद यदि वा न वेद ॥

    Rig Veda X. 129. 6, 7 (translated by Griffith).

are neither the simple priests nor the bards of a primitive
society in the infant stages of human progress, nor are
the hymns of the Samhita mere chants of liturgy for use
in ceremonies of a nature-worshipping community, as
concluded by European scholars and their Indian
following. The Vedic Age represents the rising curve
of a remarkable cycle of civilisation governed by a
predominantly symbolic mentality. It was essentially
a religious, a mystic spirit that suffused the lives and
thoughts of its people. A happy, natural intuition was
their guide even as it is observed to be elsewhere where
men have not yet cultivated the rule of Reason. They
were aware that the physical world of objects that is
seen before the eyes is not the whole truth of everything.
They felt the Presence of Something behind and above,
informing and moving the external objects and
phenomena. Thus indeed were the Natural elements,
Physical objects endowed, to their vision and feeling,
with a life and power which was Supraphysical. A
strong religious imagination and symbolic mentality
ordered their life and thought. In fact, "Symbolism
and widespread imaginative or intuitive religious feeling
go together...the symbol is of something which man
feels to be present behind himself and his life and his
activities — the Divine, the Gods, the Vast and the deep
unnameable, a hidden, living and mysterious nature of
things. All his religious and social institutions, all the
moments and phases of his life are to him symbols in
which he seeks to express what he knows or guesses of
the mystic influences which are behind them and shape
and govern them" (Sri Aurobindo).[1]

The Rishis were the mentors and leaders of such a
society who had struck out their own lines of inner

---

[1] *The Human Cycle*, Chap. I.

development and growth towards the Higher Godheads and the Truths embodied in them. Having perceived the existence and the living influence of the Higher Powers and divinities, they made it their one supreme purpose in life to imbibe and grow into those higher verities of existence. It is this their journey up the hill of their Being, the Knowledge that was vouchsafed to them on the higher or deeper levels of the soul, their inspired chants of call to the Gods, that found inspired expression in human language and are preserved for posterity in the Mantras of the Veda. No doubt, to the common folk the Mantras were only litanies for use in religious ceremonies. But to the initiates, their fuller content was revealed by the Mystics. To them the Mantra was a living vehicle of the spiritual power and truth that was active in the Rishi who gave them the sound-form and it served always as a dynamo with which each seeker could charge the battery of his own flame of aspiration and progress. Sri Aurobindo points out that like everything else, even the ceremonies, the Sacrifice for example, had a symbolic significance. The outer form which was meant for the lay society always concealed a deeper truth which had meaning only for the qualified. The very rituals of worship were arranged with a view to this end viz. to promote and assist the initiate in his inner Yajna. The hymns of the Rig Veda represent but a fragment that has survived of the records of this unique Age.

In time, like all ages in the march of the history of human progress, this Age of the Vedic Mystics came to an end. The vigour with which they pursued their search after Truth was on the wane and a natural fatigue set in. The externals of the rituals gradually lost the breath of the life within them and the luminous

truths of the ancient hymns went under an obscuration.
Nobody knows how long this eclipse continued.
However, certain it is that at some time a powerful
movement of revival took place and this had a twin
aspect. One was the movement towards the recovery
and resuscitation of the forms of the Vedic Religion and
Sacrifice, the rituals: this was represented by the
Brahmanas. The other was for the reclamation and
revelation of the soul of the Vedic religion, the treasure
of Knowledge embedded in the sacred Mantras: the
stir and movement of the Upanishads. Both of these
were among the notable expressions of the fresh outburst
of a spiritual and material prosperity that characterised
the renaissance of the Aryan Spirit in that epoch.

It was not to be expected that the Rishis of the
Upanishads would be content merely to restate or
re-inculcate the utterances of the seers of the Veda,
however authentic in themselves. These intrepid
voyagers of the Unknown sought to re-live the truths
embedded in the hymns, in their own lives and in their
own ways, to invest them with the imprimatur of their
own personal realisation of their verity, make them
freshly alive and give them an expression in terms more
suited to the mentality of their time which was so distant
from the mystic age of the Vedas. Or, they took the
perceptions of the ancient seers as their starting-
point and launched upon their own adventure —
taking care every now and then to refer to the
cumulative Wisdom of the older Fathers for confirmation
— arriving at other, if not higher, summits of Realisation.
The Upanishads are the "records of many methods of
approach to the ultimate Reality, inspired utterances of
seers who, by disciplined effort, by whole-souled devotion
to their subject, by subtler and higher faculties revelatory

and intuitional, developed by spiritual means, penetrated into and broke open the seals of the secrets of subtle psychological and spiritual truths and lived the life of the Spirit. In their effort they were, as a rule, aided by the tradition of the Vedic Rishis, by the achievements of others who had gone before them, or by the help — not unoften — proferred by the Higher Intelligences and Powers of the Universal Spirit itself."[1] "The thinkers and sages of the Upanishads have certainly drawn their inspiration and support from the Hymns (of the Veda) when they were engaged in developing their Self-culture for the realisation of the ultimate Truth, for conforming their lives to the laws of the Spirit, for the attainment of Brahman-hood while still living on Earth. In their endeavours, in their successes, in their conclusions, they often seek the support of the Vedic seers, though we may not always trace their names or find their hymns in the Samhitas that have come down to us; they make mention of certain verses presumed to be those of the Vedic seers though they are not traceable now; they actually quote the Riks also, but in their own sense and for their purpose though their meanings in the Rig Vedic context may differ or may not be exactly the same. But living in an age far posterior to the Vedic epoch their method of expression is more intellectual and less symbolic and mystical than that of their Vedic forefathers. Even when they use Vedic symbols, they give them often different significances. The results of their explorings in the fields of the inner Life and Spirit, the truths of their intuitive perceptions, the means at their disposal and the lines they proceed along, the fruits of their labour in the occult and spiritual realms, are often

---

[1] Sri Kapali Sastry : *Lights on the Upanishads* (P. 23).

implicitly, but in authentic tones, expressed in a language that is more intelligible to the mentality of our age and fairly far removed from that of the Rig Vedic hymns."[1]

The imagery of the Upanishads is largely taken over from the older symbolism of the Vedas. The Chhandogya Upanishad, for instance, freely and naturally uses the terms and symbols of the Vedic religion. So does the Brihadaranyaka.[2] And, Sri Aurobindo observes : "It is to a great extent this element no longer seizable by our way of thinking that has baffled certain scholars and made them cry out that these scriptures are a mixture of the sublimest philosophical speculations with the first awakened stammerings of the child mind of the humanity."[3] Undoubtedly, in keeping with the changing spirit of the age, the Upanishads extend, or even vary at times, the significance of the earlier imagery and symbolism and also bring out more explicitly the inner sense implicit in them. They make these symbols starting-points

---

[1] Sri Kapali Sastry : *Lights on the Upanishads* (Pp. 74-75).

[2] In a Note on the figure of the Horse of the Ashwamedha with which the Brihadaranyaka opens, Sri Aurobindo subjects the symbolism of the Upanishadic seers to a thorough scrutiny from the modern stand-point and unveils a wealth of meaning and significance lying hidden beneath the figure which has become totally opaque to latter thought.

"The Ashwamedha or Horse-Sacrifice is, taken as the symbol of a great spiritual advance, an evolutionary movement, almost, from out of the dominion of apparently material forces into a higher spiritual freedom. The Horse of the Ashwamedha is, to the author, a physical figure representing like some algebraical symbol, an unknown quantity of force and speed. From the imagery it is evident that this force, this speed is something world-wide, something universal ; it fills the regions with its being, it occupies Time, it gallops through Space, it bears on in its speed men and gods and the Titans. It is the Horse the Worlds,—and yet the Horse sacrificial."

The Vedic-Upanishadic symbolism of the Ashwa, Horse, the Dawn, the Sun, the Wind, the Fire, the Oceans—Eastern and Western, the Heaven and Earth, Day and Night—have received at his hands a most illuminating exposition which awes us into the littleness of our modern minds before the towering magnificence of conception and vastness of vision of these ancient seers. (Vide *Sri Aurobindo Mandir Annual* No. 12 : The Great Aranyaka).

[3] *Foundations of Indian Culture* (P. 314)

for their own statements of experience and realisation
and go on to 'pass beyond them to another magnificently
open and sublime imagery and diction which at once
reveals the spiritual truth in all its splendour'.   Sri
Aurobindo illustrates this development with one or two
examples from the texts and we shall have occasion to
speak of them later while dealing with the respective
Upanishads.

The Gods of the Veda—Surya, Agni, Indra, Vayu—
continue to shine in the firmament of the Upanishads.
But there is a difference.   While in the Veda, each of
them was supreme in his own right and power, holding
as it were the entire Godhead behind him, in the
Upanishads the Gods occupy a subordinate position, the
constant stress being on the Supreme One of whom the
Gods are derivations and on whom they depend for the
discharge of their double function, as Powers of Nature,
adhidaivatam, and as Psychological Powers governing the
faculties of man, *adhyātmam*. It should be noted, however,
that this conception of the One Supreme God is not a
new idea found in the Upanishads.   It is not correct to
say that when 'the half-gods of the Veda die, the true
God arrives'.[1]   There are a number of Riks in the Rig
Veda—not merely in the tenth Mandala which modern
scholars are fond of eulogising as containing the seeds of
'advanced thought', but in the other Mandalas as well—
extolling the One Godhead as the Source and Origin of
all the Gods, the Deity of deities.[2]

---

[1] Dr. Radhakrishnan.
[2] For instance :

एकं सद् विप्रा बहुधा वदन्ति ।

The One Existent, the illumined ones call variously. (Rv. I.164.46)

एकं वा इदं विबभूव सर्वम् ।

The One has become All this. (Rv. VIII.58.2)

The Upanishads, we must note, are not philosophical treatises or systematised manuals of religious discipline. "They are a great store of observations and spiritual experiences with conclusions and generalisations from those observations and experiences, set down without any thought of controversial caution or any anxiety to avoid logical contradiction."[1] To an alien mind not familiar with the peculiar climate of Indian scriptures and religio-philosophical writings these texts may appear to be a mass of inconsistencies.   For instance, it is declared that the Absolute Brahman is unknowable : mind cannot reach it and words return baffled.   And yet passages abound in which Brahman is declared to be the sole object of knowledge, this is Brahman, that is Brahman, everything is Brahman and so on. The Reality is sometimes spoken of as the One Absolute, elsewhere it is stated that there are Two Purushas unborn.

एजद् ध्रुवं पत्यते विश्वमेकं चरत् पतद्रि विषुणुं विजातम् ।

The Universal One that rules over the mobile and the fixed (is) what walks, what flies, what is this manifold birth. (Rv. III.54.8)

महत् देवानाम् असुरत्वमेकम् ।

The powerful Might of the Gods is the Great One. (Rv. III.55.1)

विश्वे देवा: समनस: सकेता एकं क्रतुमभि वि यन्ति साधु……

All the Gods with a single mind, a common Intuition, move aright in their divergent paths towards the One Will. (Rv. VI.9.5.)

यो देवानां नामधा एक एव……

One who alone is the holder of the Names of all the Gods. (Rv. X.82.3)

सुपर्णं विप्रा: कवयो वयोभि: एकं सन्तं बहुधा कल्पयन्ति ।

The One Existent, beautiful of plumage, the illumined seers by their words formulate in many ways (or forms). (Rv. X.114.5)

Vide also :

एको विभुर् अतिथिर्जनानाम्……तं वर्तनिर् अनुवावृत एकम् इत् पुरु ।

The One Lord, Guest of the people……to Him the One Alone, the many paths are turned. (Atharva Veda VII.21.1)

In him all Deities become one Alone. (Atharva XIII.4.1)

[1] Sri Aurobindo : *Philosophy of the Upanishads II (The Advent* Vol. IX. No. 1)

But the seers of these utterances do not care to refute or reconcile these contradictory statements ; they are aware that each is authentic from its own standpoint and the standpoints from which the Reality can be viewed or approached and realised are as many and as diverse as the varied aspects of the Reality in manifestation.   They approach the Truth from varying positions and status, converge upon It from different directions and give expression to the knowledge so obtained in appropriate terms, regardless of their coherence or consistency with the statements of others or of their own under different conditions. As we shall see later, even this contrariety or conflict of statements is more apparent than real.

Again, the texts of the Upanishads may appear to be punctuated with abrupt stops and disconnected beginnings and give the impression of a pronounced lack of sequence.   But it must be remembered that the Upanishads are not verbatim reproductions of the instructions given by the Teacher to the initiates.   The texts are more in the nature of notes and graphs of leading ideas and truths, fundamental starting-points and important conclusions of their exposition.   Again, verbal expositions did not constitute the whole of their instruction even as the external instructions did not form the whole of the method by which the student was initiated and led by the teacher in the mystic or inner Path.   This also accounts for the lack of details or even summary procedures of the inner disciplines which are merely announced in the Upanishads with only a few hints to provide the clues for their working.

The Upanishads thus are a class apart from every other kind of literature. In the words of Sri Aurobindo :

"These works are not philosophical speculations of the intellectual kind…these seers saw Truth rather than merely thought it, clothed it indeed with a strong body of intuitive idea and disclosing image, but a body of ideal transparency through which we look into the illimitable…

"The Upanishads are epic hymns of self-knowledge and world-knowledge and God-knowledge. The great formulations of philosophic truth with which they abound are not abstract intellectual generalisations, things that may shine and enlighten the mind, but do not move the soul to ascension, but are ardours as well as lights of an intuitive and revelatory illumination, reachings as well as seeings of the One Existence, the transcendent Godhead, the divine and universal Self and discoveries of his relation with things and creatures in this great cosmic manifestation…

"The largest metaphysical truths and the subtlest subtleties of psychological experience are taken up into the inspired movement and made at once precise to the seeing mind and loaded with unending suggestion to the discovering spirit. There are separate phrases, single couplets, brief passages which contain each in itself the substance of a vast philosophy and yet each is only thrown out as a side, an aspect, a portion of the infinite self-knowledge. All here is a packed and yet perfectly lucid and luminous brevity and an immeasurable completeness. A thought of this kind cannot follow the tardy, careful and diffuse development of the logical intelligence. The passage, the sentence, the couplet, the line, even the half-line follows the one that precedes with a certain interval full of an unexpressed thought, an echoing silence between them, a thought which is carried in the total suggestion and

implied in the step itself, but which the mind is left to
work out for its own profit, and these intervals of pregnant
silence are large, the steps of this thought are like the
paces of a Titan striding from rock to distant rock across
the infinite waters. There is a perfect totality, a
comprehensive connection of harmonious parts in the
structure of each Upanishad ; but it is done in the way
of a mind that sees masses of truth at a time and stops
to bring only the needed word out of a filled silence.
The rhythm in verse or cadenced prose corresponds to
the sculpture of the thought and the phrase···It is a kind
of poetry—word of vision, rhythm of the spirit—that
has not been written before or after."[1]

[1] *Foundations of Indian Culture* (Pp. 310-313).

CHAPTER III

THE PHILOSOPHY OF THE UPANISHADS

One in many births, a single ocean holder of all streams of movement, sees our hearts. (Rig Veda)[1]

The Unseen, incommunicable, unseizable, featureless, unthinkable, undesignable by Name, self-evident in its one selfhood....that is the Self, this is That which has to be known. (Mandukya Upanishad)[2]

The one Godhead secret in all beings, all-pervading, the inner Self of all. (Shvetashvatara Upanishad)[3]

Thou art That, O Shvetaketu. (Chhandogya Upanishad)[4]

The Spirit who is here in man and the Spirit who is there in the Sun, lo, it is One Spirit and there is no other. (Taittiriya Upanishad)[5]

Two are joined together, powers of Truth, powers of Maya,—they have built the Child and given him birth and they nourish his growth. (Rig Veda)[6]

ALTHOUGH there is no single system of philosophy as such in the Upanishads, we do find in them certain broad lines of spiritual experience rendered as much as possible in terms of the conceptual language of the Intellect. In the course of the inner disciplines which they developed in their endeavour to exceed the normal bounds of the body, life and mind, to push the farthest frontiers of knowledge accessible to the human spirit and

---

[1] Or: the one, the ocean holding the wealths, within our heart of multiple births, widely does he see.

एते अस्मिन् देवा एकवृतो भवन्ति ।

एक: समुद्रो धरुणो रयीणामसद्धृदो भूरिजन्मा विचष्टे । (X.5.1)

[2] अदृष्टमव्यवहार्यमग्राह्यमलक्षणमचिन्त्यं मव्यपपदेश्यमेकात्मप्रत्ययसारं...
स आत्मा स विज्ञेय: । (7)

[3] एको देव: सर्वभूतेषु गूढ: सर्वव्यापी सर्वभूतान्तरात्मा । (VI.II)

[4] तत्त्वमसि श्वेतकेतो । (VI.8.7)

[5] स यश्चायं पुरुषे यश्चासावादित्ये । स एक: । (III.10.4)

[6] ऋतायिनी मायिनी संदधाते मित्वा शिशुं जज्ञतुवर्धयन्ती । (X.5.3)

attain to the realisation of utmost identity with Truth at the fount and core of things, these sages of ancient India had come upon certain fundamental truths of the Universe, both the outer and the inner, and perceived that within their large ambiance there were an infinite number of variations, parallel or even contradictory movements. In a series of Essays (unfortunately left incomplete) under the title *Philosophy of the Upanishads*[1] Sri Aurobindo deals at considerable length with this discovery and its results—the discovery which, he observes, " in its importance to the future of human knowledge dwarfs the divinations of Newton and Galileo; even the discovery of the inductive and experimental method in Science was not more momentous; for they (the ancient seers) discovered down to its ultimate processes the method of Yoga and by the method of Yoga they rose to three crowning realisations."[2]

Behind all the multiplicity and fluidity of things they beheld a Unity and Stability of which all phenomena are seemings and appearances. This Reality, they realised, is something Absolute, transcendent of all, transcendent even of Time and Space. This One, they declared, is the *nityo'-nityānām*, the One Eternal in the many transient.

Secondly, they found that this transcendent Self of things is also the self of all living beings ; the eye of the Yogins perceived that this is the One Intelligence working behind all the myriad forms of the intelligences (and non-intelligences), *cetanaścetanānām,* One Consciousness in many consciousnesses.

---

[1]Written by Sri Aurobindo when he was in Baroda, these manuscripts were recovered recently after over forty years, in an unexpected manner, and were published serially in *The Advent* (Vol. VIII. No. 4—Vol. X. No. 1).

[2]*Philosophy of the Upanishads (The Advent*, Vol. VIII. No. 4).

Third : they attained a realisation of the most momentous consequence to man, viz., they realised that there is an identity between the true Self in the individual man and the Self in the Universe or the universal Self. One who knows his whole Self knows the whole Universe.[1] And since the universal Self is again the same as the Transcendent, the individual Self finds its identity with the It, the Absolute, the Brahman. This truth is enshrined in the two famous formulas *so 'ham* and *aham brahmāsmi*, He am I and I am Brahman the Eternal.

The Supreme Reality, the Brahman of the Upanishads is Absolute and Transcendent. Featureless and incommunicable, it is beyond pragmatic relations. It cannot be known and it cannot be described. Itself Infinite, it cannot be the subject of knowledge by the mind and senses which are but finite ; similarly, finite speech cannot cover the Infinite.[2] However, this is true only of Brahman in its ultimate reality, not in its aspects or manifestations. Even the Ultimate Reality, the Upanishads assert, though it cannot be known by the

---

[1] आत्मनि खल्वरे दृष्टे श्रुते मते विज्ञात इदं सर्वं विदितम् ।   When the Self is seen, listened to, thought upon and perfectly known, then indeed all this is perfectly known. (Brihadaranyaka Up. IV.5.6)

[2] न तत्र चक्षुर्गच्छति न वाग् गच्छति नो मनः । न विद्मो न विजानीमो यथैतदनुशिष्यात् ॥

There light attains not nor space attains, nor the mind. We know not nor can we discover how one should teach of That. (Kena Up. 1.3)

यतो वाचो निवर्तन्ते अप्राप्य मनसा सह, from which words turn away without attaining and the mind also retires baffled. (Taittiriya Up. 11.4)

विज्ञानाद्बद्धरिष्ठं प्रजानाम् , beyond the knowledge of creatures (Mundaka Up. II. 2, 1).

Vide an interesting dialogue in the Brihadaranyaka, driving home the sheer inability of mental understanding to grasp the nature of Brahman :

"Then Gargi Vacaknavi questioned him.

Yajnavalkya, (said she), since all this world is woven, warp and woof, on water, on what, pray, is the water woven, warp and woof ?

On Wind, O Gargi.

mind, can be realised and attained. One can realise it
by one's own self, in one's own being and this realisation
includes as a part of it or as a result of it, a *kind* of
knowledge also, the knowledge of Brahman by identity.
But the way of getting into this awareness is not through
intellect and its normal aids. Acharya Shankara recalls
a telling story in this connection which can well bear
repetition here.

King Vashkalin questioned Bahva the Sage about
Brahman. "Learn Brahman, O friend," said Bahva and
remained silent. The king asked a second time and then
the third time whereupon he replied : "I am, indeed,
telling you but you do not understand. Silent is that
Self."[1]

The intellect is not the only means of knowing.
There are other faculties latent in man which have larger

On what then, pray, is the wind woven, warp and woof?
On the atmosphere-worlds, O Gargi.
On what then, pray, are the atmosphere-worlds woven, warp and woof?
On the worlds of the Gandharvas, O Gargi.
On what then, pray, are the worlds of the Gandharvas woven, warp and
woof?
On the worlds of the sun, O Gargi.
On what then, pray, are the worlds of the sun woven, warp and woof?
On the worlds of the moon, O Gargi.
On what then, pray, are the worlds of the moon woven, warp and woof?
On the worlds of the stars, O Gargi.
On what then, pray, are the worlds of the stars woven, warp and woof?
On the worlds of the gods, O Gargi.
On what then, pray, are the worlds of the gods woven, warp and woof?
On the worlds of Indra, O Gargi.
On what then, pray, are the worlds of Indra woven, warp and woof?
On the worlds of Prajapati, O Gargi.
On what then, pray, are the worlds of Prajapati woven, warp and woof?
On the worlds of Brahma, O Gargi.
On what then, pray, are the worlds of Brahma woven, warp and woof?
Yajnavalkya said : Gargi, *do not question too much, lest your head fall
off*. In truth, you are questioning too much about a divinity about which
further questions cannot be asked. Gargi, do not over-question." (III. 6
Tr. R. E. Hume)
[1] Brahmasutra Bhashya (III. 217)

give higher and still higher knowledge.[1] With means such as these, centred in the self, the Brahman is to be sought, known and realised[2] progressively on any or each of the successive levels of His manifestation. For, this phenomenal universe that we see is not the immediate creation of Brahman. There are other universal extensions between this universe of gross matter and the Brahman in his first poise of manifestation. Thus, surrounding this universe of gross matter where the Brahman is manifest as the *Virāt*, the Mighty One, Ruler, Self, is the universe of subtle matter where He is the *Hiraṇya Garbha*, the Golden Embryo of life and form, Creator, Self; surrounding both is another universe— that of causal matter where Brahman is manifest as the Cause, Self and Inspirer, *Prājna*, the Wise One. Beyond the universe of causal matter is the fourth state regarding which we cannot do better than quote Sri Aurobindo himself:

" The truth then seems to be that there are even in this last or fourth state of the Self, stages and degrees, as to the number of which experience varies ; but for all practical purposes we may speak of three, the first when we stand at the entrance of the porch and look within ; the second when we stand at the inner extremity of the porch and are really face to face with the Eternal ; the third when we enter into the Holy of Holies. Be it remembered that the language I am using is the language

---

[1] दृश्यते त्वग्र्यया सूक्ष्मया सूक्ष्मदर्शिभि :   Yet is He seen by the seers of the subtle by a *subtle and perfect understanding*. (Katha Up. I.3.12)

[2] सत्येन लभ्यस्तयसा...समयग् ज्ञानेन ब्रह्मचर्येण निस्यम् ....
won by truth, by self-discipline, by *integral knowledge, by a life of purity*. (Mundaka Up. III.1.5)

विद्यया तपसा चिन्तया चोपलभ्यते ब्रह्म । By vidya, by austerity, by meditation Brahma is apprehended. (Maitri Up. IV.4)

of metaphor and must not be pressed with a savage literalness. Well then, the first state is well within the possible experience of man and from it man returns to be a Jivanmukta, one who lives and is yet released in his inner self from the bondage of phenomenal existence ; the second stage once reached, man does not ordinarily return, unless he is a supreme Buddha—or perhaps as a world Avatar ; from the third stage none returns, nor is it attainable in the body. Brahman as realised by the Jivanmukta, seen from the entrance of the porch, is that which we usually term Parabrahman, the Supreme Eternal and the subject of the most exalted descriptions of the Vedanta. There are therefore five conditions of Brahman. Brahman Virat, Master of the Waking Universe ; Brahman Hiranya Garbha, of the Dream Universe ; Brahman Prajna or Avyakta of the Trance Universe of Unmanifestation ; Parabrahman, the Highest ; and that which is higher than the highest, the Unknowable."[1] (See figure on p. 32).

---

[1] *Philosophy of the Upanishads.* (*The Advent*, Vol. IX. No. 1)
Cf. Sri Aurobindo's graphic description (in his epic *Savitri*) of the successive manifestations of the Supreme Creative Spirit that greet the soaring Soul in humanity in its highest adventure :

"....the architect of the visible world,
At once the art and artist of his works,
Spirit and seer and thinker of things seen,
Virat, who lights his camp-fires in the suns
And the star-entangled ether is his hold,
Expressed himself with Matter for his speech :
Objects are his letters, forces are his words,
Events are the crowded history of his life,
And sea and land are the pages of his tale,
Matter is his means and his spiritual sign ;
He hangs the thought upon a lash's lift,
In the current of the blood makes flow the soul.
His is the dumb will of atom and of clod ;
A Will that without sense or motive acts,
An Intelligence needing not to think or plan,
The world creates itself invincibly ;

For its body is the body of the Lord
And in its heart stands Virat, King of kings.
In him shadows his form the Golden Child
Who in the Sun-capped Vast cradles his birth :
Hiranyagarbha, author of thoughts and dream,
Who sees the invisible and hears the sounds
That never visited a mortal ear,
Discoverer of unthought realities,
Truer to Truth than all we have ever known,
He is the leader on the inner roads ;
A seer, he has entered the forbidden realms ;
A magician with the omnipotent wand of thought,
He builds the secret uncreated worlds.
Armed with the golden speech, the diamond eye,
His is the vision and the prophecy :
Imagist casting the formless into shape,
Traveller and hewer of the unseen paths,
He is the carrier of the hidden fire,
He is the voice of the Ineffable,
He is the invisible hunter of the light,
The Angel of myterious ecstasies,
The conqueror of the kingdoms of the soul.
A third spirit stood behind, their hidden cause,
A mass of superconscience closed in light,
Creator of things in his all-knowing sleep,
All from his stillness came as grows a tree ;
He is our seed and core, our head and base.
All light is but a flash from his closed eyes :
An all-wise Truth is mystic in his heart,
The omniscient Ray is shut behind his lids :
He is the Wisdom that comes not by thought,
His wordless silence brings the immortal word.
He sleeps in the atom and the burning star,
He sleeps in man and god and beast and stone :
Because he is there the Inconscient does its work,
Because he is there the world forgets to die,
He is the centre of the circle of God,
He is the circumference of Nature's sun.
His slumber is an Almightiness in things,
Awake, he is the Eternal and Supreme.
Above was the brooding bliss of the Infinite,
Its omniscient and omnipotent repose,
Its immobile silence absolute and alone.

(Book Eleven, Canto I)

If we view the same Reality from the other end, i.e. from where creation starts, the sequence we get is naturally in the inverse order. There is, first, the Absolute which is beyond the terms of human understanding. We can only begin conveniently with the Parabrahman who is the front of the Transcendent Supreme turned and poised for manifestation. This Parabrahman is called variously God, the Eternal, the Creator, the Ancient of Days. The seers of Vedanta speak of Him in a double trilogy: subjectively, He is the *Sat-Cit-Ananda*, Existence, Consciousness, Bliss; objectively, *Satyam, Jnānam, Anantam*, Truth, Knowledge, Infinity.

He is the supreme, the absolute Existence, because there is nothing else that is outside of Him. He exists by Himself, subject to nothing. Space, Time, Causality are created by Him, out of Himself as conditions of manifestation; they do not contain Him, they are contained in Him.[1] He is the Absolute Existence. He is also Absolute Consciousness; consciousness is not an attribute, but the very nature of his Existence. The Sat

---

[1] एतस्मिन्नु खल्वक्षरे.....आकाश ओतम्थ प्रोतम्थ :

Across this Immutable, verily, is space woven, warp and woof. (Brihat. Up. III. 8. 11)

यस्मिन् आकाशश्च प्रतिष्ठित: in whom Space is established (Brihat. Up. IV. 4. 17)

ईशानं भूतभव्यस्य.... Lord of what has been and of what is to be. (Brihat. Up. IV. 4. 15)

अन्यत्र भूताच्च भव्याच्च, otherwhere than in that which has been and that which shall be. (Katha Up. I. 2. 14)

यस्मादर्वाक् संवत्सरोऽहोभि: परिवर्तते । That before (below) which rolls the year with its days. (Brihat. Up. IV. 4. 16)

एतस्य वा अक्षरस्य प्रशासने गार्गि निमेषा मुहूर्ता अहोरात्रण्यर्धमासा संवत्सरा विधृतास्तिष्ठन्ति । Verily, O Gargi, under the mighty rule of the Immutable do the moments, the hours, the days, the nights, the fortnights, the months, the seasons stand in their position. (Brihat. Up. III. 8. 9)

and the Chit are in fact the same. Wherever Sat is, in whatever form, there is the inalienable Chit, whatever the appearance. Like Sat, Chit also exists by itself and depends upon nothing for its existence as Pure Awareness. Finally, this Supreme is Pure Bliss. Like Consciousness which is inalienable from Existence, Bliss is inherent in Conscious Existence. The very expression of the acme of Conscious-Existence is Delight.

This Trinity of the Upanishads which is "Absolute Existence ; which is therefore Absolute Consciousness ; which is therefore Absolute Bliss," is paralleled by a second trinity which is really its objective expression.

Brahman is Satyam, Truth or Reality. Satyam is the Idea of Existence viewed objectively. That which exists solely by itself is alone real : Brahman is absolute existence and therefore absolute Truth and Reality.[1]

Similarly, Brahman is Jnanam, Knowledge ; Jnanam is the idea of consciousness viewed objectively. Jnanam is a direct knowledge and Brahman is Jnana absolute.

Brahman is Anantam, Endless, Infinity. This Infinity arises from his Absolute Bliss. There can be no bliss where there is any limitation. The idea of Bliss viewed objectively is Infinity which can be described as Freedom or Immortality. " Regarded from the point of view of Time, Brahman is Eternity or Immortality ; regarded from the point of view of Space He is Infinity or Universality ; regarded from the point of view of Causality He is absolute Freedom."[2]

*   *   *

Parabrahman moves into three different habitations, three successive states of Being as His manifestation

---

[1] सत्यस्य सत्यम् , , Real of the real. (Brihat Up. II. 1. 20)

[2] Sri Aurobindo: *Philosophy of the Upanishads* III. (*The Advent,* Vol. IX. No. 2)

proceeds. First into the *avyakta* or the causal state where all that is to manifest is in its seed-state and He is the *Prājna*, the Master of *Prājna*, Eternal Wisdom ; next comes the subtle state where he shines as the *Hiranya Garbha*, the Golden Embryo of Life and Form, and then the condition of the gross state where he is the *Virāt*, the Cosmic Soul. This process of manifestation, of bringing out of Himself what was in Himself[1] for expression in what is really His own extension,[2] is executed by a Power which is inherent in His Being. It is His own Consciousness *as* Power[3] that works out his intention. " It is the might of the Godhead in the world that turns the wheel of Brahman."[4]......the One becomes the Many by His own Power.[5] The older Vedantic seers called it *Māyā* because of its function of measuring out, *mimite*, the Immeasurable, its skill and cunning in shaping names and forms out of the Nameless and Formless.[6] " Supreme too is his Shakti and manifold the natural working of her knowledge and her force."[7] They found it difficult to spot it amidst the myriad forms in which and through which it executes the Purpose. To realise its nature, says the Upanishad, " they followed after concentration of Yoga and saw the Might of the Spirit of the Lord

---

[1] यथोर्णनाभि: सृजते गृह्णे च...तथाक्षरात् संभवतीह विश्वम् । As the spider puts out and gathers in......so here all is born from the Immutable. (Mund. Up. I. 1. 7)

[2] तस्यावयवभूतैस्तु व्याप्रमिदं जगत् । this whole world is filled with beings who are His members (Shvet. Up. IV. 10)

विश्वस्यैकं परिवेष्टितारं....देवं The One God who encompasses the whole world. (Shvet. Up. IV. 16)

[3] चित् विद्या

[4] देवस्यैष महिमा तु लोके येनेदं भ्राम्यते ब्रह्मचक्रम् । (Shvet. Up. VI. 1)

[5] इन्द्रो मायाभि: पुरुरूप ईयते । Indra by his Maya powers (creative conscious powers) moves on endowed with many forms. (Brihat. Up. II. 5. 19, *cited from* Rig Veda VI. 47. 18)

[6] It is this element of cunning in designing that predominated in the minds of the later thinkers and led them to call it the power of Illusion.

[7] परास्य शक्तिर्विविधैव श्रूयते स्वाभाविकी ज्ञानबलक्रिया च । (Shvet. Up. VI. 8)

hidden deep in the modes of workings of its own nature."[1]
She is the *devātma-śakti*, the Energy of the Divine Self.
Her relation with the Lord, Purusha as the Brahman
self-conditioned in Manifestation is called, is spoken of
in the Upanishads in terms of the Female and the Male,
the executive and the creative aspects of Manifestation.
" The Primal Existence turned towards manifestation
has a double aspect, Male and Female, positive and
negative.   He is the origin of the birth of things and He
is the receptacle of the birth and it is to the Male aspect
of Himself that the word Purusha predominantly applies.
The image often applied to these relations is that of the
man casting his seed into the woman ;[2] his duty is merely
to originate the seed and deposit it, but it is the woman's
duty to cherish the seed, develop it, bring it forth and
start it on its career of manifested life.   The seed, says
the Upanishad, is the self of the Male, it is spirit, and
being cast into the Female, Prakriti, it becomes one with
her and therefore does her no hurt ; spirit takes the
shaping appearance of matter and does not break up the
appearances of matter, but develops under their law.
The Man and the Woman, universal Adam and Eve, are
really one and each is incomplete without the other,
barren without the other, inactive without the other.
Purusha the Male, God, is that side of the One which
gives the impulse towards phenomenal existence ;
Prakriti the Female, Nature, is that side which is and
evolves the material of phenomenal existence ; both of
them are therefore unborn and eternal.   The Male is
Purusha, he who lurks in the Wide ; the Female is
Prakriti, the working of the Male; and sometimes called
Rayi, the universal movement emanating from the
quiescent Male.[3] Purusha is therefore imaged as the

---

[1] ते ध्यानयोगानुगता अपश्यन् देवात्माशक्तिं स्वगुणैर्निगूढाम् । (Shvet. Up. I 3)
[2] Aitareya Up. II. 1. 2. 3
[3] Prashna Up. I.

Enjoyer, Prakriti as the enjoyed ;[1] Purusha as the witness, Prakriti as the phenomena he witnesses ; Purusha as the *getter* or father of things, Prakriti as their *bearer* or mother.[2]   And there are many other images the Upanishad employs, Purusha, for instance, symbolising Himself in the Sun,[3] the father of life, and Prakriti in the Earth, the bearer of life." (Sri Aurobindo)[4]

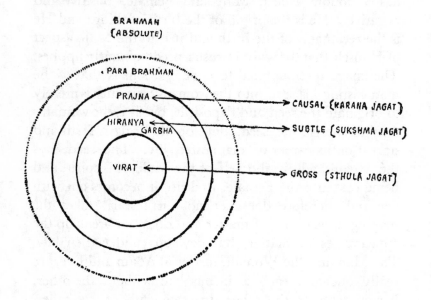

ASPECTS OF BRAHMAN

---

[1]Maitri Up. VI. 10.   Shvet. Up. I. 12
[2]Shvet. Up. I. 9. 10
[3]Brihat. Up. II. 3 ;   V. 15. 1 ; Chhand. Up. I. 6. 6 ;   Maitri Up. VI. 1, VI. 35 ; Isha Up. 16.
[4]*Philosophy of Upanishads* VI. (*The Advent,* Vol. X, No. 1)

CHAPTER IV

THE SADHANA

He should be searched out, Him one should desire to
understand.   Chhand. Up.[1]

This is the Soul of mine within the heart, this is Brahman.
                                                   Chhand. Up.[2]

Faith at dawn, Faith at noon do we invoke ;
Faith at the setting of the sun. O Faith, endow us with Faith.
                                                   Rig Veda[3]

Arise, awake, find out the great ones and learn of them.
                                                   Katha Up.[4]

By askesis do thou seek to know the Eternal.
                                                   Taitti. Up.[5]

Accepted by him the soul attains its goal of immortality.
                                                   Shvet. Up.[6]

With soul serene, stayed in the Soul,
Delight eternal one enjoys.   Maitri Up.[7]

He moves through these worlds at will.   Taitti. Up.[8]

KING Janaka and Yajnavalkya the preceptor, it would
appear, once had a discussion on *Agnihotra* and the sage
was so much captivated by the erudition of the monarch
that he offered him a boon ; the boon was eagerly
accepted, but in an unexpected form.   Janaka asked for
no earthly advancement ; he assured for himself greater
depths of Knowledge than he could fathom on his own.

---

[1] सोऽन्वेष्टव्यः स विजिज्ञासितव्यः ।   (VII.7.1)

[2] एष म आत्मान्तर्हृदय एतद्ब्रह्म ।   (III-14;4)

[3] श्रद्धां प्रातर्हवामहे श्रद्धां मध्यन्दिनं परि ।
     श्रद्धां सूर्यस्य निम्रजि श्रद्धे श्रद्धापयेह नः ॥   (X.151.5)

[4] उत्तिष्ठत जाग्रत प्राप्य वरान्निबोधत   (1.3.14)

[5] तपसा ब्रह्म विजिज्ञासस्व ।   (III.2)

[6] जुष्टस्तनस्तेनामृतत्वमेति ।   (I.6)

[7] प्रसन्नात्मात्मनि स्थित्वा सुखमव्ययमश्नुता ।   (VI.20)

[8] इमांल्लोकान्...अनुसञ्चरन् ।   (III 10)

5

Great riches of Knowledge he had, he was avid for still more; he chose a promise from the wise one to answer whatever question he might ask at any time. And, the legend records, he drew upon this boon on an occasion when the sage,—apparently in the fullness of his soul— was not disposed to talk. And what is the question he asked?

'Yajnavalkya', he said, 'what is the light of man?'

Yajnavalkya replied: "The sun, O King; for, having the sun alone for his light, man sits, moves about, does his work, and returns.'

Janaka Vaideha said: 'So indeed it is, O Yajnavalkya'.

Janaka Vaideha said: 'When the sun has set, O Yajnavalkya, what is then the light of man?'

Yajnavalkya replied: 'The moon indeed is his light; for, having the moon alone for his light, man sits, moves about, does his work, and returns.'

Janaka Vaideha said: 'So indeed it is, O Yajnavalkya.'

Janaka Vaideha said: 'When the sun has set, O Yajnavalkya, and the moon has set, what is then the light of man?'

Yajnavalkya replied: 'Fire indeed is his light; for, having fire alone for his light, man sits, moves about, does his work, and returns.'

Janaka Vaideha said: 'So indeed it is, O Yajnavalkya.'

Janaka Vaideha said: 'When the sun has set, O Yajnavalkya, and the moon has set, and the fire is gone out, what is then the light of man?'

Yajnavalkya replied: 'Speech indeed is his light; for, having speech alone for his light, man sits, moves about, does his work, and returns. Therefore, O King, when one cannot see clear even one's own hand, yet when a voice is raised, one goes towards it.'

Janaka Vaideha said : ' So indeed it is, O Yajnavalkya.'

Janaka Vaideha said : ' When the sun has set, O Yajnavalkya, and the moon has set, and the fire is gone out, and the speech hushed, what is then the light of man ?'

Yajnavalkya replied : ' *The Self indeed is his light* . . '[1]

It is this Self, the Self which is one with the Sole Reality, the Brahman, that is the central objective to which all the roads of the Upanishads lead. To acquire knowledge of the Truth of the Self, to realise one's identity with the utter Self is the one constant preoccupation. The bases from which the seekers commence their voyage are many ; the means and ways by which they proceed are several ; the forms in which the realisations are received are more than one, but the Truth that is attained is the same—the One Reality of All.

This is the Ideal placed before man by the Rishis of the Upanishads. There is a Reality from which all derive their existence and significance ; all are self-expressions or becomings of Something which is their Source and End. They call It Brahman, they call It the Self ; and they declare that it is possible for man to arrive at a realisation of his oneness with this Reality. All life is a preparation, conscious or unconscious, for this endeavour which is indeed the highest and noblest purpose to which one's life could be yoked. The world of the Upanishads hums with the stir of this mighty

---

[1] Brihat. Up. (IV. 3) Adapted from Max Muller's translation.

movement of awakening and aspiration, this eager advance towards the Goal of higher life, not only in the forests and hermitages of sages and disciples but in the courts and assemblies of kings and scholars as well. Questions are raised, discussed and pursued to the farthest limit possible for the human mind ; and once grasped, these truths of Knowledge are faithfully sought to be vertified and made living in one's own experience. The zeal with which these men and women betake themselves to the task is matched only by the enviable perseverance with which they hold to their objective regardless of any consideration of time and effort.

Every achievement has its price and the demands of the higher Path, the sages declare, are severe. No one shall embark on this lofty enterprise whose course is as perilous as the edge of the razor,[1] unless he is sure of himself, sure of the *call*. In the first place he must have been convinced of the futility of the life man normally leads and the necessity of a higher life with a purpose and direction worthy of his status as the most prized in God's creation.[2] He must have the *faith* that there is something other that is greater and truer than himself—the surface personality of which alone he is usually conscious—and that it is possible for him to acquire the nature and character of this Reality in the measure in which he draws close and attains to identity with it. This faith is indispensable to every seeker. "We must believe in God before we know him." (Sri Aurobindo) Knowledge comes only after a long period of travail and till then it is well nigh impossible for man to make headway without this fulcrum

---

[1] क्षुरस्य धारा निशिता दुरत्यया दुर्गं पथस्तत्...(Katha Up. I.3.14)

[2] सुकृतम् बत ... पुरुषो वाव सुकृतम् ।   "O well fashioned truly! Man indeed is well and beautifully made."   (Ait. Up. I.2.3)

of faith. The Katha Upanishad pointedly asks : " Unless
one says *He is* how can one become sensible of Him ?"[1]
One must believe in the existence of God before one can
hope to gain knowledge of the truth of His Existence,
what he is in his essentiality.   One must have faith in
His existence in oneself and around in the world before
one can think of Him Beyond[2].   And this faith is the
sense of certitude of something to which his normal
faculties do not yet testify.   Usually it is the reflection
of a perception of the soul deep within or of an Intelligence above and it is a power that helps to effectuate the
truth of Idea which is so perceived.   " This faith is a
support from above ; it is brilliant shadow thrown by a
secret light that exceeds the intellect and its data ; it is
the heart of a hidden knowledge that is not at the mercy
of immediate appearances." (Sri Aurobindo)

It is to be noted that on the eve of his immortal
adventure, Nachiketas was *seized by Faith*[3]. And it was this
strength of faith, faith in the truth of his seeking that gave
him the voice to tell Yama that he had the competence
to receive the wisdom from Him : "Teach me, I have
faith."[4] Not merely in the beginning, but in the course
and the term also of the Self-Discipline, faith is essential.
Those that are engaged in the Rite of the Soul are men
who are *śraddhayantaḥ*, who are active with faith.   It is
significant that in its description of the Vijnanamaya
Purusha, the Taittiriya describes Faith as the very head
of the Knowledge-Self.[5]   We may note in passing that

---

[1] अस्तीति ब्रुवतोऽन्यत्र कथं तदुपलभ्यते ।   (II.3.12)

[2] अस्तीत्येवोपलब्धस्य तत्त्वभाव: प्रसीदति ।   when he has grasped Him
as the Is, then the essential of God dawns upon a man. (Katha Up. II.3.13)

[3] तं...श्रद्धाऽऽविवेश ।   (Ibid. I. 1. 12)

[4] प्रब्रूहि त्वं श्रद्धानाय मह्यम् ।   (Ibid. I. 1. 13)

[5] आत्मा विज्ञानमय:...तस्य श्रद्धैव शिर: । the Knowledge-Self..Faith is
the head of him. (II. 4)

this emphasis, in the Upanishads, on Faith has been consistently maintained all along in the Indian tradition, the seal of confirmation being given by the Gita in unforgettable words : "This Purusha (soul in man) is made of Faith and whatever is that Faith he is that and that is he."[1]

To have faith is not enough. It should be acted upon. Conditions must be rendered favourable for the faith to grow and express itself. Otherwise it will remain a dormant, ineffective belief. One must subject oneself to a thorough discipline of purification and rectification. "The doors of the body", says the Upanishad,[2] are set "face outwards, therefore the soul of man gazes outward and not at the Self within." A resolute attempt must be made to change the direction of the senses and the energies behind them ; the body must be trained to become more and more conscious inward than outward, the life-energy discouraged from its unchecked flow to outgoing activities and the mind and emotions freed from their mechanical preoccupations and turned and centred round the soul. The Eye must be turned inward[3] and only those movements which help this orientation of consciousness must be cultivated, the others being gradually eliminated. Weakness, negligence, sloth, error, falsehood, indulgence of the senses are to be purged in the course of the puri-fying discipline to equip the being to enter the Gates of

---

[1] श्रद्धामयोऽयं पुरुषो यो यच्छ्रद्धः स एव सः ।   (XVII. 3)

"The Lord says : It is the faith of man that is behind all that he does. It adjusts itself according to one's nature. The very Purusha is filled with faith ; of whatever faith one is, that he becomes. For faith is a power of the spirit, a will in the reason that transcends it and yet possesses and guides it." (Sri Kapali Sastry : *Gospel of the Gita*)

[2] पराञ्चि खानि व्यतृणत् तस्मात् पराइ पश्यति नान्तरात्मन् ।

(Katha Up, II.1.1)

[3] आवृत्तचक्षुः   (Ibid)

the Higher Knowledge.[1] In the place of the fascination and pull with which the objects of the senses hold one captive, there should grow a distaste, a spontaneous shrinking from the ordinary life of ignorance[2] and a consequent, natural turn towards the Higher. This cleansing and upgrading of oneself involves a difficult effort—difficult particularly because old, settled and inherited tendencies, *samskāras*, and habitual movements have to be held in control and gradually replaced by new ones, frequently their opposites—but who ever won the Knowledge of the Soul without austerity?[3]

With this preliminary preparation by way of rejection and purification there comes the need for a right understanding, an authentic knowledge of the Truth of Truths to be realised, the ways and methods to be adopted therefor. The ancients always looked up to the Word of the forefathers, the Word that was handed down by them in the progression of the tapasya, *śruti*. The Sruti contains the essence of the experience and the Realisation of those who have trodden the Path before; it sums up the course and crown of their seekings and embodies in the imperishable form of the Word the truths they found and thus contains in itself the drive of the Power that liberates, the light of the Knowledge that guides. The seeker in the Upanishads takes to a

---

[1] सत्येन लभ्यस्तपसा ह्येष आत्मा सम्यग्ज्ञानेन ब्रह्मचर्येण नित्यम् ।

The Self can always be won by truth, by self-discipline, by integral knowledge, by a life of purity. (Mundaka Up. III. 1. 5)

नायमात्मा बलहीनेन लभ्यो न च प्रमादात्...

This Self cannot be won by any who is without strength, nor with error in the seeking. (Ibid. III. 2. 4)

[2] निर्वेदमायात् (Mundaka Up. I. 2. 12)

[3] नातपस्कस्याऽऽत्मज्ञानेऽधिगमः कर्मसिद्धिर्वा... (Maitri Up. IV. 3)

For him without austerity there is no attainment of the knowledge of the Soul nor perfection of works.

reverent study of these Scriptures that have come of old, pores over their luminous utterances epitomising the wisdom gained and vouchsafed to those who had come and striven as Pioneers in the field. And in so doing, he not only acquires a mental clarity in facing and meeting the various issues that challenge his understanding but also opens himself, in the depths of his being, to the inflow of the dynamic spiritual Power with which the World of the Tapasvin is instinct. The Upanishads themselves being such records of revelation received by the Rishis in their high-strung askesis are invaluable to the earnest aspirant. For, in the words of Sri Auro-bindo : " The business of the Sruti and especially of the Upanishads is to seize the mind and draw it into a magic circle, to accustom it to the thoughts and aspira-tions of God (after the Supreme), to bathe it in certain ideas, surround it with a certain spiritual atmosphere ; for this purpose it plunges and rolls the mind over and over in an ocean of marvellous sound through which a certain train of associations goes ever rolling. In other words it appeals through the intellect, the ear and the imagination to the soul."[1]

The reading and study of the Sruti enlighten the seeker on the highway of Knowledge. But one cannot be sure of grasping the import correctly ; there may be —and usually there is—much more behind the overt expression than what strikes the eye. No one can tap the hidden treasure unaided. Besides, whatever one may have learnt by assiduous study rests as a mental acquisition ; it requires the touch of a live wire to set it aglow and operating in a dynamic manner. This need is fulfilled by the *Teacher*. " When all is said, the fact

---

[1] *Eight Upanishads.* P. XVI.

remains that definite entry into the *sādhanā*, the awakening into the Spirit within, the actual building of the
inner life, usually begins only when one has a Satyakama, the teacher, to transmit the tangible secret and
light the life within of the seeker or one happens to
be a Satyakama, the disciple, whom the Gods looked
upon with favour opening his eye of vision to the
Supreme Truth." (Sri Kapali Sastry)[1] The Upanishads
stress repeatedly that there can be no spiritual life without the Teacher. He is verily the Father[2] who gives
the inner birth. The Teacher is one who has already
realised the Ideal which the seeker is striving for, or
holds in himself the dynamis of that Truth and is capable of communicating the power and fruit of his
realisations to those who seek it from him.[3] He implants
the seed of realisation in the disciple and tends its growth
in him by his constant influence and inner direction.
The power he instils, the knowledge he imparts are
charged with the vibrations of the living Truth housed
in him. That is why it is said that only he who has a
teacher really knows, *ācāryavān puruṣo veda*. For, the
Knowledge of Brahman is the most difficult to acquire
and beyond the reach of the ordinary human intelligence. Only one who is not inferior, *avara*, but superior
in the ways of the Truth and Knowledge can reach it to
the seeking mind. "Unless told of Him by another
thou canst not find the way to Him : for He is subtler
than subtlety and that which logic cannot reach. This

---

[1] *Lights on the Upanishads*. P. 39

[2] त्वं हि न: पिता (Prashna U. P. VI. 8)

[3]*Vide* Ashwapati's declaration to his pupils, Aruni and others:

अभिसम्पादयिष्यामि "I shall make you realise." (Shatapatha
Brahmana. X. 6. 10) *Vide* also *Lights on the Upanishads*, P. 70.

wisdom is not to be had by reasoning...only when told thee by another it brings real Knowledge."[1]

"For the knowledge of That, let him approach, fuel in hand, a Guru."[2]

Knowledge, says the Chhandogya, is most fruitful only if it is learned from the Teacher.[3] He not only gives the knowledge, but shows the way in which it is to be translated into practice. The same Upanishad records how student Upakosala tended the Fires for twelve years and was blessed by them with high knowledge but even they—the divine personages—told him that for the *way*, for the Path, he must go to a Teacher.[4] The Acharya, the Guru, not only shows the way, but, says the *Maitri*, is himself the way. For, those who take refuge in him are lifted up in his protective hands from the depths of ignorance and darkness in which they are submerged and, in his compassion, redeemed. Thus does the aspirant pray to the Teacher : "Be pleased to deliver me. In this cycle of existence I am like a frog in a waterless well : sir, you are our way of escape, yea, you are our way of escape."[5]

---

[1] अनन्यप्रोक्ते गतिरत्र नास्त्यणीयान् ह्यतर्क्यमणुप्रमाणात् ।
नैषा तर्केण मतिरापनेया प्रोक्तान्येनैव सुज्ञानाय प्रेष्ठ ।   (Katha Up.
                                                        I. 2. 8-9)

[2] तद्विज्ञानार्थं स गुरुमेवाभिगच्छेत् समित्पाणिः:... (Mundaka Up. 1. 2. 12)

[3] आचार्याद्ध्येव विद्या विदिता साधिष्ठं प्रापयति ...   (IV. 9. 3)

[4] आचार्यस्तु ते गतिं वक्ता ...   (IV. 14)
    Vide Rig Veda. X. 32. 7:
    अक्षेत्रवित् क्षेत्रविदं ह्यप्राट् स प्रैति क्षेत्रविदानुशिष्टः ।
    एतद्वै भद्रमनुशासनस्योत स्रुतिं विन्दत्यञ्जसीनाम् ॥

    The Stranger asks the way of him who knows it: taught by him who knows he travels onward. This is, in truth, the blessing of Instruction: he finds the path that leads directly forward.

[5] उद्धर्तुमर्हसि ॥ अन्धोदपानस्थो भेक इवाहमस्मिन्संसारे
    भगवंस्त्वं नो गतिस्त्वं गतिः ।   (Maitri Up. I. 4)

The seeker receives the knowledge from the Master; he receives the initial push which sets him on the Path. It is now for him to apply and work out in life what he has learnt ; no doubt the help, guidance and lead of the Guru are always at hand for the sincere disciple ; yet it is he who is to strive and battle to grow in the altitudes of the spirit. He enters into this inner life with the determination *now or never*. The seers of the Upanishads warn him that if he does not reach the Goal *here* itself, in this very life, then vain will have been his birth. " If here one comes not to the knowledge, then great is the perdition."[1] He will have lived truly and greatly, made a success of himself, only if he gets to the Truth during his life-time.[2] The status one attains after the termination of this bodily life depends upon the stage of progress arrived at here, while in body. It is only if one has succeeded in reaching God in this life that one can hope to realise the Truths of the God Beyond. "If in this world of men and before thy body fall from thee, thou wert able to apprehend it, then thou availest for embodiment in the worlds that He creates."[3]

Note that this emphasis on the need of realisation during one's life-time and on earth[4] is a continuation of the Vedic stress on the attainment here, *iha*, and now, today, *adya, idānim*.[5]

---

[1] न चेदिहावेदीन्महती विनिष्टि: ।   (Kena Up. II. 5)

[2] इह चेदवेदीदथ सत्यमस्ति ।   (Ibid)
   If here one comes to that knowledge then one truly is.

[3] इह चेदशकद्बोद्धुं प्राक् शरीरस्य विसस: ।
   तत: सर्गेषु लोकेषु शरीरत्वाय कल्पते ॥   (Katha Up. II. 3. 4)

[4] इहैव सन्तोऽथ विद्मस्तद् वयम् ,   May we know It while we are here
   itself, (Brihad. UP. VI. 4. 14)

[5] कृधी नो अद्य वरिव: स्वस्तिमत् ...   (Rv. IX. 184. 1)
   उतेदानीं भगवन्त: स्याम   (Rv. VII. 41, 4)

And what is the practical discipline, the *sādhanā*, that is commended in the Upanishads for reaching the Goal of Brahman, getting to the core of the Truth of Existence? We find that there is not any one set course of discipline, but many lines of development, Sadhanas or Vidyas, corresponding to the many possible points of approach to the Reality and also to the varying temperament and fitness of the aspirants. We do not find any detailed procedure laid down in the manner of the later systematising treatises. "The Upanishads always give general instructions, but they do not give the actual methods of the *sādhanā;* even when it is possible to find out the method from oral or recorded teachings, the actual and definite working out of the *sādhanā* takes place only when the would-be-sadhaka receives the help, the influence, the power from some source human or Divine or more truly from the Divine in the human.[1]

"The teacher who was always a seer admitted the disciple for initiation on being convinced of his fitness for receiving the Vidya. He trained him for the life, put into him the necessary seed of realisation, allowed it to grow and bear fruit in the right season. Thus these Brahma-Vidyas were communicated in silence through the influence and example of the Guru, rather than through precept which occupied a brief and formal place in the scheme of the spiritual culture of these ancients."[2] "These *sādhanās*, these methods of approach were transmitted by the Master to the disciple and verbal instruction when necessary at all to accompany the initiation given was either not recorded or only briefly

[1]Sri Kapali Sastry : *Lights on the Upanishads*. P. 71.
[2]*Lights on the Upanishads*. Pp. 3-4.

hinted at in these Scriptures. And this is so because the real *sādhanā*, begins with initiation and not with oral instruction though the latter may be in some cases helpful giving just a sort of mental satisfaction."[1]

These Vidyas were so many ways of attaining to the Brahman and were naturally different depending upon what aspect of that Supreme Reality they sought to realise and dwelt upon — Brahman with Qualities, *saguṇa*, or without them, *nirguṇa*, Brahman as the Self, Purusha, Atman or as Consciousness in its diverse manifestations or as Bliss. The Vidyas were known either by terms expressive of their central features[2] or after the Teacher who expounded them[3] or even after the disciple who first pursued the Vidya with notable results.[4] Sri Kapali Sastry has given a luminous exposition of some of the more important of these Vidyas[5] and we reproduce here a few of the relevant passages from his summing up :

"Let us then put in a nutshell the salient features of each of these spiritual disciplines, the Sadhanas of these Scriptures. The Narada-Sanatkumara episode concerns itself with what is called Bhuma Vidya. The discipline aims at the realisation of the Infinite Self beyond the ignorance. Satyakama's forte is Prana Vidya, the discipline that leads to the conscious union with the creative Energy, Prana, the Tapas of Ishwara, and is, as we have noticed, the most dynamic of all the Vidyas of the Upanishads. The *Agnirahasya* gives us the Vidya of Shandilya and here the soul is envisaged as

---

[1]Lights on the Upanishads. P. 158.
[2]E.g. Prana Vidya, Udgitha, Dahara, Vaishvanara etc.
[3]Shandilya Vidya, Satyakama Vidya etc.
[4]Bhargavi Varuni Vidya, Upakosala Vidya, Balaki Vidya etc.
[5]Vide *Lights on the Upanishads*.

Spirit in its relation to its embodiment in life, to its
encasement in mind as well as to its Source, Support,
Power and Light in the all-pervading Purusha. It is
the most comprehensive of all the Sadhanas and begins
with the centre of the Spirit as soul, the seat of God —
the heart ; it takes a survey of and aims at the realisation
of the All Spirit becoming the soul in each.   The Rishis
seek from Ashvapati Kaikeya for a knowledge of the
Universal Fire which is the Self in each and the all.
This discipline called Vaishvanara Vidya aims at the
realisation of the Cosmic Self active in each being and
starts, as usual with most of the Upanishadic Sadhanas,
with the heart...From the Brihadaranyaka we took up
for clarification the Doctrine of the Mystic Honey and
showed that it reconciles the relative Reality of World-
Existence with the Absolute Monism to which the
Brihadaranyaka tends in some of its sections — notably
the Maitreyi Brahmana which precedes the section on
the Mystic Honey, called the Madhu Brahmana. Even
this Upanishad which in some important parts is the
stronghold for the 'Lofty Illusionism' of the later
Vedantins is not wholly in favour of the negation of
world-existence but looks upon it as a Creation of
Delight, an Existence which subsists by interdependence
of the whole and the part, a Manifestation which
subsists because of the Honey, the Madhu in it.....

   " The Bhuma Vidya starts with a strong and
constant remembrance, *dhruvā smṛti*, an intuition — not
the same as realisation — earned by purification of the
stuff of the nstrumental being, *sattva śuddhi*, which is
the same as *dhātuprasāda*, crystalline purity of the
temperament.   It aims at the realisation of Bhuma, the
Plenum, the Infinite Self.   The Prana Vidya starts

with the Life-principle arriving at its source in the
Creative Spirit, the Tapas or the active consciousness of
the Lord. The Shandilya discipline starts with the soul
as related to the instruments of life and mind in the
bodily existence on the one hand and on the other, to
the Light, Power and Will of the Universal Self — a
most comprehensive vision that takes in a sweep all the
complexities of the soul in its various aspects. The
Universal Spirit, the Fire in each being and the all, the
feeling and realisation in each of its oneness with the
Cosmic Self and the Cosmic Life is the theme of
Ashvapati in the Vaishvanara Sadhana. The doubt about
the survival of something of man that afflicts Nachiketas
is just a surface appearance of the hunger of the soul with
which Nachiketas starts and receives the initiation from
Yama into the secrets of the Immortal existence, Manifest and Unmanifest, to be realised in this life before
the body falls."

    This is not all. The seeker, in the Upanishad, starts
with an initial faith, undergoes a preliminary self-training
to purify and equip himself, resorts to the study of the
collective Wisdom of those who have already trod the
Godly Path, finds the Master who launches and leads
him on the career of the Spirit which he pursues with
unflinching courage and perseverance along the lines
chosen for him by the Guide. All these means carry him
far, but not far enough. There are in this mystic path
certain barriers to be crossed, crucial steps to be taken,
disentanglements[1] to be effected which it is not possible
for human effort alone to do. The Upanishads declare

---

[1]Disentanglement from the various knots of involvement in the psycho-
nervous-physical mechanism, the most difficult of which is the knot of
Ignorance, avidyāgranthi (Mundaka Up. II. 1. 10). "When the Upanishad
speaks of the knots, the knots are not a product of poetic fancy or a philosophic

unequivocally that it is only the Divine *Grace*, the Sanction of the Supreme that can effect these decisive realisations in the initiate and give him the final release. When Narada has mastered all the known Sciences of Men, of Gods and of Demons, he still finds it beyond him to cross to the other shore of Ignorance and it is Skanda Sanatkumara, the Divine Deliverer, who has to help him over.[1] Indeed.

Heaven is too high for outstretched hands to seize.
This Light comes not by struggle or by thought ;

(Sri Aurobindo : *Savitri*)

There are bounds over which it is vain for mortal strength to exert; when such limits are reached it is only an intervening Factor that can meet the situation and by its intrinsic action consummate the life-labour of the striving individual. And, as Sri Kapali Sastry points out, "that something is the final means, the supreme help which is either plainly stated or hinted at or implict in the instructions recorded in the Upanishads. Each Upanishad has its own way, the Isha may call for the

concept in the spher of Metaphysics. They are entanglements of subtle nerve-force lodged in a frame of psycho-physical structure which acts on and reacts to the functionings of the nervous system that links the subtler levels and conditions of being to the grosser material body." (Sri Kapali Sastry)

The Katha and the Mundaka expressly speak of the knots to be loosened or strings of the heart which are to be cut asunder before the consummation can take place :

यदा सर्वे प्रभिद्यन्ते हृदयस्येह ग्रन्थयः । अथ मर्त्योऽमृतो भवति....

Yea, when all the strings of the heart are rent asunder, even here, in this human birth, then the mortal becomes immortal... (Katha U. II 3. 15)

गुहाग्रन्थिभ्यो विमुक्तोऽमृतो भवति ।

He is delivered from the knotted cord of the secret heart and becomes immortal. (Mundaka Up. III 2. 9)

भिद्यते हृदयग्रन्थिः:

The knot of the heart strings is rent... (Ibid. II 2. 9)

[1]Chhandogya Up. VII

help of the Gods Agni[1], Vayu[2], Surya[3], the Kena may
point to the supreme guidance of Uma[4], the Katha and
the Mundaka may refer to the Self's gracious revealing
of the body of Itself."[5]

Thus delivered out of the hold of *samsāra*, the web
of Ignorance and Desire, the seeker attains a new state
of being—a Release into a condition of knowledge, freedom and bliss. He has attained to a complete identity
with his true self; he has realised that the self which is
himself is none other than the Greater Self which upholds
the universe. No more for him is grief or sorrow. He
is no more lost in the blinding ignorance of his true
nature and denied the joy of self-possession and enjoyment.[6] He has no fear. For what fear can he have who
has known the Delight of the Eternal? "When the
Spirit that is within us finds the Invisible Bodiless
Undefinable and Unhoused Eternal his refuge and firm

---

[1]It is Agni who is called upon by the Rishi to 'remove the devious attraction of sin' :

अग्ने....युयोध्यस्मज्जुहुराणमेनो ;   (18)

[2]Vayu who is to manifest immortal Life to the seeker of whose body ashes
are the end :

वायुरनिलममृतम् अथेदं भस्मान्तं शरीरम्   (17)

[3]It is the favour of Surya that is sought to remove the lid that stands
between the Rishi and the Truth Supreme:

हिरण्मयेन पात्रेण सत्यस्यपिहितं मुखम् । तत् त्वं पूषन्नपावृणु...   (15)

[4]IV. 1

[5] यमेवैष वृणुते तेन लभ्यस्तस्यैष आत्मा विवृणुते तनूं खाम् ।

Only by him whom It chooses can it be won; to him this Self unveils
its own body. (Katha Up. I. 2. 23) ; (Mundaka Up. III. 2. 3)

[6] समान वृक्षे पुरुषो निमग्नोऽनीशया शोचति मुह्यमान : ॥
जुष्टं यदा पश्यत्यन्यमीशमस्य महिमानमिति वीतशोक: ॥

The soul is the bird that sits immersed on the one common tree; but
because he is not the lord he is bewildered and has sorrow. But when he sees
that other who is the Lord and beloved, he knows that all is his greatness and
his sorrow passes away from him. (Mundaka Up. III. 1. 2)

foundation, then he has passed beyond the reach of Fear."[1] From such a man, liberated while yet living, *jivan-mukta*, all desire falls away. For, as the Sages of the Brihadaranyaka ask, "What shall we do with off-spring, we whose is this Soul, this Home?"[2] "When in the embrace of the Wisdom-Self, he knows nothing without or within... he is without desire, without sorrow."[3] He has nothing to bind him; he lives and moves in the autonomy of his soul.[4] He is free, not only in this world but in all other worlds as well.[5]

In his consciousness the Jivanmukta realises his unity not only with the All, the Self that is manifest in this universe but comes also to find his identity with That which transcends, what is beyond Space and Time. His is the Hymn of Self-Knowledge voiced by sage Trishanku :

> "I am He that moves the Tree of the Universe and my glory is like the shoulders of a high-mountain. I am lofty and pure like sweet nectar in the strong, I am the shining riches of the world, I am the deep thinker, the deathless One who decays not from the beginning."[6]

---

[1]Taittiriya Up. II. 7

यदा ह्येवैष एतस्मिन्नदृश्येऽनात्म्येऽनिलयनेऽभयं प्रतिष्ठां विन्दते । अथ सोऽभयं गतो भवति ॥ आनन्दं ब्रह्मणो विद्वान् । न बिभेति कदाचन । Also, Who knows the delight of the Eternal He shall fear nought now or hereafter. (Ibid. II. 4)

[2] किं प्रजया करिष्यामो येषां नोऽयमात्माऽयं लोक: (Brihad. Up. IV. 4. 22)

[3] प्राज्ञेनात्मना सम्परिष्वक्तो न बाह्यं किञ्चन वेद नान्तरं....अकामं....शोकान्तरम् । (Ibid. IV. 3. 21)

[4]Chhandogya Up. VII. 26. 1

[5] तेषां सर्वेषु लोकेषु कामचारो भवति । (Ibid. VIII. 1. 6)

[6] अहं वृक्षस्य रेरिवा । कीर्ति: पृष्ठं गिरेरिव । ऊर्ध्वपवित्रो वाजिनीव स्वमृतमस्मि । द्रविणं सवर्चसम् । सुमेधा अमृतोक्षित: । (Taitt. Up. I. 10)

This state of full knowledge and uninterrupted bliss, the
Upanishads hint, is still conditioned by the circumstances, the tether of the body in whose dissolution alone
the *liberation*, Mukti, is complete,[1] when, "he goes from
this world having passed to the Self which is of food;
having passed to the Self which is of Prana ; having
passed to the Self which is of Mind ; having passed to
the Self which is of Knowledge ; having passed to the
Self which is of Bliss, lo, he ranges about the worlds, he
eats what he will, and takes what shape he will and ever
he sings the mighty Sama. ' Ho ! ho ! ho ! I am food !
I am food ! I am the eater of food ! I am the eater ! I
am the eater ! I am he who makes Scripture ! I am he
who makes ! I am he who makes ! I am the first born
of the Law ; before the gods were, I am, yea, at the very
heart of immortality. ... I have conquered the whole
world and possessed it, my light is as the sun in its
glory."[2]

---

[1] विमुक्तश्च विमुच्यते (KATHA UP. II 2. 1)

[2] एतमन्नमयमात्मानमुपसङ्क्रम्य । एतं प्राणमयमात्मानमुपसङ्क्रम्य ।
एतं मनोमयमात्मानमुपसङ्क्रम्य । एतं विज्ञानमयमात्मानमुपसङ्क्रम्य ।
एतमानन्दमयमात्मानमुपसङ्क्रम्य । इमांल्लोकान् कामान्नी कामरूप्यनुसञ्चरन् ।
एतत् साम गायन्नास्ते । हा३वु हा३वु हा३वु । अहमन्नमहमन्नमहमन्नम् ।
अहमन्नादो३ऽहमन्नाद: । अहं श्लोककृदहं श्लोककृदहं श्लोककृत् । अहमस्मि
प्रथमजा ऋता३स्य । पूर्वं देवेभ्यो अमृतस्य नाऽभायि ।... अहं विश्वं भुवन-
मभ्यभवाम् । सुवर्णं ज्योती: । (TAITT. UP. III. 10)

CHAPTER V

CONCLUSION

This, then, is the Call of the Upanishads whose notes are heard in the Scriptures of every Religion in the East, and so unexpectedly caught even in some of the soul-strains of the West. Much of their content is couched and preserved in symbols, images, figures and terms which do not have today the same meaning and significance they originally had when the Rishis chose them as living bodies within which to cast their highest thoughts and deepest realisations. It is not every one who is able to enter into the spirit of these writings, get behind their veil of archaic language and ancient imagery, and stand face to face with the living Truth of Knowledge in the penetralia. Sri Aurobindo calls attention, repeatedly, to this aspect of the subject and asks for a scrupulous sincerity of scholarship in one's study of these hallowed texts. Of his own approach, what he records is memorable : "To enter passively into the thoughts of the old Rishis, allow their words to sink into our souls, mould them and create their own reverberations in a sympathetic and responsive material— submissiveness, in short, to the Sruti—was the theory the ancients themselves had of the method of Vedic knowledge—*girām upaśrutim cara, stomam abhi svara, abhi gṛṇīhi ā ruva*. To listen in soul to the old voices and allow the Sruti in the soul to respond, to vibrate, first obscurely, in answer to the Vedantic hymn of knowledge, to give the response, the echo and last to let that response gain in clarity, intensity and fullness—this is the principle of interpretation that I have followed."[1]

---

[1] Sri Aurobindo Mandir Annual No. 12 : *The Great Aranyaka.*

ISHA UPANISHAD

ISHA UPANISHAD

THE Upanishads, Sri Aurobindo points out, are "vehicles of illumination and not of instruction". They are not intended to present ideas or arguments in the ordered sequence of reasoning. They deliver rather certain key truths and hints to seekers who were expected to be familiar with the broad lines of the Vedic and Vedantic thought and spiritual experience; only they could receive the teachings of the Upanishads in their true value, understand the implied thought behind the verbal expression and follow up the suggestions thrown out by each utterance. To an age like ours, separated by vast gulfs of time, mode of thought and life, the full significance of the texts is sure to be missed unless what is stated is studied in its proper background, with an intuitive readiness to grasp and correlate the apparently diverse suggestions shooting from their condensed conclusions. And this is precisely the object behind Sri Aurobindo's commentaries on the Upanishads. He has written only on two or three texts—the Isha, the Kena and partly the Taittiriya. But what he has given goes far to equip the serious student to delve into the other texts as well, since the bases, the lines and goal of all the Upanishads are largely identical. Besides, his translations of the other texts are themselves effective as short commentaries. His is no word-for-word translation; it is 'literary rather than literal', presenting as much as possible, in a modern, occidental language, the thought and spirit of these ancient scriptures. He writes: "I do not say that this translation is worthy of them, for in no other human tongue than Sanskrit is such grandeur and beauty possible."[1]   But in truth, his translations read like living originals and have the same breath and ring.   At times the renderings might appear somewhat paraphrased but they are so done on purpose.   They aim at bringing out the complete sense of the passage, the full import of the terms used—which would otherwise escape attention—rather than at scholastic exactitude[2] and are thus of inestimable value for our understanding of these ancient texts.

---

[1] *Eight Upanishads*, P. XIII.

[2] It is interesting to know what Sri Aurobindo has to say about the translations by western scholars like the well-known Indologist Prof. Max Muller and his own method :

"The series of translations called the Sacred Books of the East, edited by the late Professor Max Muller, was executed in a scholastic and peculiar spirit.   Professor Max Muller, a scholar of wide attainments, great versatility and a refreshingly active, ingenious and irresponsible fancy, has won considerable respect in India by his attachment to Vedic studies, but it must fairly be recognised that he was more of a grammarian and philologist, than a sound Sanscrit scholar.   He could construe Sanscrit well enough, but he could not feel the language or realise the spirit behind the letter.   Accordingly he committed two serious errors of judgment ; he imagined that by sitting in Oxford and evolving new meanings out of his own brilliant fancy he could understand the Upanishads better than Shankaracharya or any other Hindu of parts and learning ; and he also imagined that what was important for Europe to know about the Upanishads was what he and other European scholars considered they ought to mean.   This, however, is a matter of no importance to anybody but the scholars themselves...

"Professor Max Muller in his translation did not make any attempt to render into English the precise shades of Aryan philosophical terms like Atman and Prana which do not correspond to any philosophical conception familiar to the West ; he believed that the very unfamiliarity of the terms he used to translate them could be like a bracing splash of cold water to the mind forcing it to rouse itself and think.   In this I think the Professor was in error ; his proposition may be true of undaunted philosophical intellects   such as Schopenhauer's or of those who are already somewhat familiar with the Sanscrit language, but to the ordinary reader the unfamiliar and unexplained terminology forms a high and thick hedge of brambles   shutting him off from the noble palace and beautiful gardens of the Upanishads.   Moreover, the result of a scholastic faithfulness to the letter has been to make the style of the translation intolerably uncouth and unworthy of these great religious poems. I do not say that this translation is worthy of them, for in no other human

The Upanishads have been listed differently, by various authorities, in the order of their importance. But whatever the enumeration, the Isha or the Ishavasya—so-called after the opening words of the text—has

---

tongue than Sanscrit is such grandeur and beauty possible. But there are ways and their degrees. For instance, *etadvai tat*, the refrain of the Katha Upanishad, has a deep and solemn ring in Sanscrit because *etad* and *tat* so used have in Sanscrit a profound and grandiose philosophical signification which everybody at once feels ; but in English "This truly is that" can be nothing but a juggling with demonstrative pronouns ; it renders more nearly both rhythm and meaning to translate. "This is the God of your seeking", however inadequate such a translation may be.

It may, however, fairly be said that a version managed on these lines cannot give a precise and accurate idea of the meaning. It is misleading to translate Prana sometimes by life, sometimes by breath, sometimes by life-breath or breath of life, because breath and life are merely subordinate aspects of the Prana. Atman again rendered indifferently by soul, spirit and self, must mislead, because what the West calls the soul is really the Atman yoked with mind and intelligence, and spirit is a word of variable connotation often synonymous with soul ; even self cannot be used precisely in that way in English. Again the Hindu idea of 'immortality' is different from the European ; it implies not life after death, but freedom from both life and death ; for what we call life is after all impossible without death. Similarly Being does not render *Puruṣa*, nor 'matter' *rayi*, nor askesis the whole idea of *tapas*. To a certain extent all this may be admitted, but at the same time I do not think that any reader who can think and feel will be seriously misled, and at any rate he will catch more of the meaning from imperfect English substitutes than from Sanscrit terms which will be a blank to his intelligence. The mind of man demands, and the demand is legitimate, that new ideas shall be presented to him in words which convey to him some associations with which he will not feel like a foreigner in a strange country where no one knows his language, nor he theirs. The new must be presented to him in the terms of the old ; new wine must be put to some extent in old bottles. What is the use of avoiding the word "God" and speaking always of the Supreme as "It" simply because the Sanscrit usually,—but not, be it observed, invariably, —employs the neuter gender ? The neuter in Sanscrit applies not only to what is inanimate, not only to what is below gender but to what is above gender. In English this is not the case. The use of "It" may therefore lead to far more serious misconceptions than to use the term "God" and the pronoun "He"...if the new ideas were presented with force and power, a reader of intelligence will soom come to understand that something different is meant by "God" from what ideas he attaches to that word. And in the meanwhile we gain this distinct advantage that he has not been repelled at the outset by what would naturally seem to him bizarre, repulsive or irreverent." (*Eight Upanishads*, Pp. VII—XV)

always occupied the pride of place at the head. This is mainly because it is the only Upanishad to form an integral part of a Samhita while the others belong to the Brahmanas or the Aranyakas. It is the 40th and final chapter of the Shukla Yajur Veda. From the point of view of subject-matter also, the Isha Upanishad is unique. It addresses itself to the question of world-existence, the problem of harmonising human life and activity with the Reality of Immutable Brahman. The solution it finds is one of the most remarkable found by the ancient Indian mind. Its teaching is "the reconciliation, by the perception of essential Unity, of the apparently incompatible opposites, God and the World, Renunciation and Enjoyment, Action and internal Freedom, the One and the Many, Being and its Becoming, the passive divine Impersonality and the active divine Personality, the Knowledge and the Ignorance, the Becoming and the Not-Becoming, Life on earth and beyond and the supreme Immortality.[1]"

The very first lines announce the setting in which the key to the whole problem is found naturally:

[2]*All this is for habitation*[3] *by the Lord, whatsoever is individual universe of movement in the universal motion. By*

---

[1]Sri Aurobindo: *Eight Upanishads*, P. 3

[2] ईशावास्यमिदं सर्वं यत् किञ्च जगत्यां जगत् ।

तेन त्यक्तेन भुञ्जीथा मा गृधः कस्य स्विद्धनम् ॥ १ ॥

(Unless otherwise mentioned, all the English renderings in these studies are by Sri Aurobindo.)

[3]*Vāsyam* is here rendered in the sense of 'to be inhabited', 'dwelt in'—root *vas* to dwell. Acharya Shankara explains it to mean 'to be clothed', 'to be enveloped' *ācchādanīyam* : Look not at this unreal world but at the reality of the pure Brahman by which it shall be covered : our sense of the world must disappear into the perception of the enveloping Reality. While this may suit the adwaitic standpoint, Sri Aurobindo points out, it goes counter to the general spirit of the Upanishad which at every step reconciles the apparent opposites in manifestation.

that renounced thou shouldst enjoy, lust not after any man's possession.

The universe is a movement of the Spirit. It is a continuous unrolling of the Spirit in myriad forms which are so many currents of the Great Movement. Each form is a front, a shaping of the general stream in an individualised unit. Each one has the Whole behind, sustaining it, and thus constitutes a universe in itself. Wherefore this movement? It is meant, says the Upanishad, for the dwelling of the Spirit who has originated and cast out this extension. All is to provide a fitting abode for the Lord of All. This world is a manifestation of God for his enjoyment. He has created it out of himself in joy and takes up his dwelling in it for a yet fuller joy. And this enjoyment implies, necessarily, enjoyment by all, by the many who constitute His manifestation. Yet, joy and happiness are not the normal feature of the world. In fact, the opposite seems to be the rule. Why? It is because the many, the individuals move and act in complete ignorance of their true nature, their identity with the One Spirit informing and basing them, and through It with all the rest. Each looks upon himself as distinct and different from the other and his outlook is governed by this sense of separativity, the ego which gives birth to Desire to affirm himself against others, snatch enjoyment for himself at the cost of others. This effort leads to friction, conflict and suffering. Man is lost in activity in this vain pursuit of happiness. True enjoyment comes naturally with the renunciation of this vitiating desire, the desire for separate self-affirmation and self-aggrandisement and an inner recognition and realisation of the truth of the identity of oneself with the soul within who is always the Lord and its unity with the Soul of All who is same in each.

Thus, we learn that the world is a movement of God; it has a purpose which is to provide a habitation for God for His enjoyment. The individual is a living term and front of this manifestation and should share in this enjoyment; but his ignorance of his true nature shuts him from this happiness and gives rise to the ego-sense of a separate self-living and its consequent struggle and strife. This principle of Desire should be put behind if one is to participate in the Lord's enjoyment. The individual must become aware of his soul, the true source of enjoyment and identify himself with this Lord of his individualised universe.

But to realise this identity with the soul within does not mean that he should withdraw from the life without, the activity of the body and mind. On the contrary:

[1]*Doing verily, works in this world one should wish to live a hundred years. Thus it is in thee and not otherwise than this; action cleaves not to a man.*

He must, indeed, *eva*, do works[2]. He cannot but do that. No man can desist from activity; even what is called inactivity is a kind of action and has its own results. Even as the Lord has projected this world as the means of a certain fulfilment, the individual too has

---

[1] कुर्वन्नेवेह कर्माणि जिजीविषेत् शतं समा: ।
एवं त्वयि नान्यथेतोऽस्ति न कर्म लिप्यते नरे ॥ २ ॥

[2] Sri Aurobindo notes how unnatural is the interpretation by Shankara of the word *karmāṇi* in two different ways in the same verse. In the first line *karmāṇi* is taken to mean sacrifices and other religious acts which are expected to be performed by the ignorant for reaping fruits from good actions and averting the results of the evil; in the second line the word is taken as the opposite, evil deeds. The Acharya says that for those who do not aim at the realisation of *ātman* and are content with the normal human life, *naramātrabhimāni*, doing the rituals is the only way of escaping the taint of evil deeds.

a self-fulfilment to achieve and he is to participate in this
activity to that end.   One should live the full span of
life, says the text, doing one's part ; the previous verse
has laid down the right mode of action and life, viz., to
renounce desire and participate in this Manifestation
which is meant for the enjoyment of the one Lord of
All, in All. Thus done, no action can bind the doer
with the motivating desire, the executing energies or
with the ensuing chain of consequences. That is the
true law of living. For those who follow this Law there
is joy and felicity. But for those who in their ignorance
and egoism choose to ignore the truth and persist in
their own false and egocentred way of life the future is
different :

¹ *Sunless are those worlds and enveloped in blind gloom*
whereto all they in their passing hence resort who are slayers of
their souls.

There are other worlds besides this material one in
which we live. And when the physical body dies, the
being of man goes to and through these other worlds of
varying substances, of different kinds, obscure and illumined. The kind of world to which one is drawn depends
upon the tendencies formed and the equipment wrought
during life in body on the earth.   They who have risen
above the life of the senses, of preoccupation with bodily
wants and pleasures, and have strived and achieved a
progressive synthesis in themselves of higher knowledge,
purity and luminous dynamism and peace—in a word,
developed a soul-life—are naturally gravitated to like
worlds of light and joy.   But those who have refused to
listen to the call of the soul and have forced it to slog

---

¹ असूर्या नाम ते लोका अन्धेन तमसावृताः ।
तांस्ते प्रेत्याभिगच्छन्ति ये के चात्महनो जनाः ॥ ३ ॥

in the quagmires of inertia and falsehood or hover round and round in the blind circle of desire and passion, pleasure and pain—these, says the Upanishad, have to pass to worlds which are sunless,[1] bereft of the light of the Sun of spiritual truth, worlds of Darkness.

If so, is movement, eternal movement the sole truth ? Is it not rather that the Truth in the final sense lies in Stability, an Immutability ? The Upanishad affirms both as truths of the Brahman, the Supreme Reality ; both are poises of IT ; each is relative to the other.

[2]*One unmoving that is swifter than Mind, That the Gods reach not, for It progresses ever in front. That, standing, passes beyond others as they run. In That the Master of Life establishes the Waters.*

That moves and That moves not ; That is far and the same is near ; That is within all this and That also is outside all this.

Brahman is beyond Space, Time and Causality. Movement and quiescence, duration and eternity, action and inaction, are not terms in which It can be described

---

[1]Of the two readings *asoorya*, sunless, and *asurya*, titanic, undivine, Sri Aurobindo chooses the former in the light of the last four verses of the text. The prayer to the Sun in those verses "refers back in thought to the sunless worlds and their blind gloom, which are recalled in the ninth and twelfth verses. The sun and his rays are intimately connected in other Upanishads also with the worlds of Light and their natural opposite is the dark and sunless, not the Titanic worlds." (Sri Aurobindo)

Vide Rig Veda, V. 32. 6, where Vritra the Enemy is referred as thriving in *sunless darkness*.

[2] अनेजदेकं मनसो जवीयो नैनद्देवा आप्नुवन् पूर्वमर्षत् ।

तद्धावतोऽन्यानत्योति तिष्ठत्तस्मिन्नपो मातरिश्वा दधाति ॥ ४ ॥

तदेजाति तन्नैजति तद् दूरे तद्वन्तिके ।

तदन्तस्य सर्वस्य तदु सर्वस्यास्य बाह्यतः ॥ ५ ॥

or contained. In itself it is indescribable. But turned
towards manifestation, it is poised in the two statuses,
the stable and the motional ; Space, Time, Causality are
terms of its manifestation, its own self-extension. It
contains all these as their continent and yet transcends
them. Moveless, it contains and holds beyond all
movement. The Gods, the Powers it puts forth to work
out its self-expression cannot, naturally, surpass it ; it is
always vaster than its own emanations.

The Brahman extends itself variously, not singly in
one form, Its consciousness expresses and forms itself in
several gradations, organises itself around several principles, each active in the forefront on its level. These
extensions, Sri Aurobindo points out, are in the ancient
system septuple, known by the *vyāhṛtis* Bhuh, Bhuvah,
Suvah, Mahas, Jana, Tapas and Satya which in modern
language are the principles, and planes based on them,
of Matter, Life, Mind, Idea, Bliss, Consciousness and
Force, and Existence. Thus does the text say that in
His own extension as the Mother of things,—Earth, the
physical matter, He, the Brahman as the Life-Force
wakes and spreads Himself, i.e. enlivening all that He
enters into and sets aflow the Waters which, in the
Vedic system, represent currents of conscious being.
"The Waters, otherwise called the seven streams or the
seven fostering Cows, are the Vedic symbol for the
seven cosmic principles and their activities, three inferior, the physical, vital and mental, four superior, the
divine Truth, the divine Bliss, and divine Will and
Consciousness, and the divine Being. On this conception
also is founded the ancient idea of the seven worlds in
each of which the seven principles are separately active
by their various harmonies."[1]

---

[1] In a note on *apas*, Sri Aurobindo points out : "Apas, as it is accentuated
in the version of the White Yajurveda, can mean only 'waters'. If this

Thus it is He that is the origin, the end and the container of the things ; creating, He indwells the forms of his manifestation, enjoys variously His thousand abodes. He is the One, the same everywhere. And if each individual formation behaves and acts as if it is a separate entity, different from others, it is because it is clouded in its outer consciousness, it has temporarily lost touch with the unifying knowledge and consciousness at its back—that which sustains it as well as it does all the rest in a common extension. The moment one realises this truth effectively and gets aware of the one Self in all and as the All, gets the right perspective of the union of all in the One Self, the sense of separativity loses its validity and with it goes the need to affirm oneself at the cost of others, the sense of opposition from other forms. Thus declares the Upanishad :

[1] *But he who sees everywhere the Self in all existences and all existences in the Self, shrinks not thereafter from aught. He in whom it is the Self-Being that has become all existences that are Becomings, for he has the perfect knowledge, how shall he be deluded, whence shall he have grief who sees everywhere oneness ?*

For such a one there is no Conflict and Sorrow ; for "all grief is born of the shrinking of the ego from the contacts of existence, its sense of fear, weakness, dislike,

accentuation is disregarded, we may take it as the singular *apas*, work, action. Shankara, however, renders it by the plural, works. The difficulty only arises because the true Vedic sense of the word had been forgotten and it came to be taken as referring to the fourth of the five elemental states of Matter, the liquid. Such a reference would be entirely irrelevant in the context."

[1] यस्तु सर्वाणि भूतानि आत्मन्येवानुपश्यति ।
सर्वभूतेषु चात्मानं ततो न विजुगुप्सते ॥ ६ ॥
यस्मिन् सर्वाणि भूतानि आत्मैवाभूद्विजानतः ।
तत्र को मोहः कः शोक एकत्वमनुपश्यतः ॥ ७ ॥

etc., and this is born from the delusion of separate existence, the sense of being my separate ego exposed to all
these contacts of so much that is not myself. Get rid of
this, see oneness everywhere, be the One manifesting
Himself in all creatures ; ego will disappear ; desire born
of the sense of not being this, not having that, will
disappear ; the free inalienable delight of the One in
His own existence will take the place of desire and its
satisfactions and dissatisfactions." (Sri Aurobindo)[1]

That is not all. The truth of Brahman in manifes-
tation is not confined to the subjective projection as the
Self of all things. It is not merely an impersonal Being
in which the becoming takes place. Brahman is also
He, the Person who originates, inhabits and governs the
Universe. For,

[2] *It is He that has gone abroad—That which is bright,
bodiless, without scar of imperfection, without sinews, pure,
unpierced by evil. The Seer, the Thinker, the One who
becomes everywhere, the Self-existence has ordered objects
perfectly according to their nature from years sempiternal.*

In his *going abroad*, i.e. in his self-extension there are,
it should be noted, two aspects : one, an Infinite Immutability and the other, Mutation, a working out of
possibilities in Time, Space and Causality. The Upanishad speaks of the former—the Pure Immutable as the
bright, self-luminous without a shadow, bodiless,
unlimited by form and division, without scar of

---

[1] Isha Up. IX.

[2] स पर्यगाच्छुक्रमकायमव्रणमस्नाविरं शुद्धमपापविद्धम् ।
कविर्मनीषी परिभू: स्वयम्भूर्याथातथ्यतोऽर्थान् व्यदधात
शाश्वतीभ्य: समाभ्य: ॥ ८ ॥

imperfection and sinews, flawless, unaffected by the
play of clashing circumstances and not subject to the
currents and cross currents of diminution and increase,
pure and unpierced by evil, i.e. not contaminated by
Ignorance and its issue, the wrong, the crooked as
opposed to what is normally right and straight.
The same Absolute is spoken of in the other aspect
successively, as the Kavi, the Seer, who before he
proceeds to manifest *sees* in his luminous vision the
Truth, the principles of things that are to manifest, then,
as the Manishi, Thinker, who conceives and thinks out
the processes in the evolution of the possibilities, the
Paribhu, He who eventuates, *becomes everywhere*, in Space
and Time as impelled by the Manishi. It is all, it must
be noted, a one becoming of the Self-existent Purusha
who moves into these three poises, seeing, conceiving and
fixing things in accord with the Truth which is being
expressed, the eternal Truth which forms and governs
the nature of each formation as its innate Law.[1]

Thus the Movement has its truth as much as the
Stability ; multiplicity is as real as unity. Both are twin
ends of the one pole of Reality in manifestation and
should be comprehended as such. To ignore or deny

---

[1] *Vide* Sri Aurobindo's commentary :

"The Lord appears to us in the relative notion of the process of things
first as Kavi, the Wise, the Seer. The Kavi sees the Truth in itself, the truth
in its becoming, in its essence, possibilities, actuality. He contains all that in
the Idea, the Vijnana, called the Truth and Law, *Satyam Ritam*. He contains
it comprehensively, not piecemeal ; the Truth and Law of things is the Brihat,
the Large. Viewed by itself, the realm of Vijnana would seem a realm of
predetermination, of concentration, of compelling seed-state. But it is a
determination not in previous Time, but in perpetual Time ; a Fate compelled
by the Soul, not compelling it, compelling rather the action and result, present
in the expansion of the movement as well as in the concentration of the Idea.
Therefore the truth of the Soul is freedom and mastery, not subjection and

one and accept and pursue only the other is to shut
oneself from the full reality of things. To accept the
truth of both in a large vision and seek to realise it in
one's own life is the path of wisdom.

1 *Into a blind darkness they enter who follow after the
Ignorance, they as if into a greater darkness who devote themselves to the Knowledge alone.*

*Other, verily, it is said, is that which comes by the Know-
ledge, other that which comes by the Ignorance; this is the lore
we have received from the wise who revealed That to our
understanding.*

---

bondage. Purusha commands Prakriti, Prakriti does not compel Purusha. *Na
karma lipyate nare.*

The Manishi takes his stand in the possibilities. He has behind him the
freedom of the Infinite and brings it in as a background for the determination
of the finite. Therefore every action in the world seems to emerge from a
balancing and clashing of various possibilities. None of these, however, are
effective in the determination except by their secret consonance with the Law
of that which has to become. The Kavi is there in the Manishi and upholds
him in his working. But viewed by itself the realm of the Manishi would seem
to be a state of plasticity, of free-will, of the interaction of forces ; but of a
free-will in thought which is met by a fate in things.

For the action of the Manishi is meant to eventuate in the becoming of the
Paribhu. The Paribhu, called also Virat, extends Himself in the realm of
eventualities. He fulfils what is contained in the Truth, what works out in the
possibilities reflected by the mind, what appears to us as the fact objectively
realised. The realm of Virat would seem, if taken separately, to be that of a
Law and Predetermination which compels all things that evolve in that realm,
—the iron chain of Karma, the rule of mechanical necessity, the despotism of
an inexplicable Law." (*Isha Upanishad*, IV)

1 अन्धं तम : प्रविशन्ति येऽविद्यामुपासते ।
ततो भूय इव ते तमो य उ विद्यायां रता: ॥ ९ ॥
अन्यदेवाहुर्विद्ययाऽन्यदाहुरविद्यया ।
इति शुश्रुम धीराणां ये नस्तद्विचचक्षिरे ॥ १० ॥
विद्याञ्चाविद्याञ्च यस्तद्वेदोभयं सह ।
अविद्यया मृत्युं तीर्त्वा विद्ययामृतमश्नुते ॥ ११ ॥

He who knows That as both in one, the Knowledge and the Ignorance, by the Ignorance crosses beyond death and by the Knowledge enjoys Immortality.

Knowledge, *vidyā*, Sri Aurobindo explains, is the consciousness, the effective awareness of the Unity of things, the Oneness of all. Ignorance, *avidyā*, is the consciousness of multiplicity. Those who are aware of only the multiplicity of forms and not their reconciling oneness and live in line with that understanding are closed to the light of true knowledge and sink into obscurity. But those who look only at the Unity of things, the sheer oneness alone, denying the fact of the Many, withdraw themselves gradually from the scene of life-activity and merge into a state of non-being, a state of consciousness where everything is, as if, *iva*,[1] a blank of still greater darkness. In the words of Sri Aurobindo:

"Those who are devoted entirely to the principle of indiscriminate Unity and seek to put away from them the integrality of the Brahman, also put away from them knowledge and completeness and enter as if into a greater darkness. They enter into some special state and accept it for the whole, mistaking exclusion in consciousness for transcendence in consciousness. They ignore by choice of knowledge, as the others are ignorant by compulsion of error. Knowing all to transcend all is the right path of Vidya. Although a higher state than the other, this supreme Night is termed a greater darkness,

---

[1]This sense of *iva* seems to be left out in the commentary of Shankara; there it is explained as *eva*, verily. The point is that this state attained by the pursuit of sheer unity alone is so void, that its emptiness resembles—though, be it noted, it is not the same—in its benumbing blankness, the darkness of Ignorance raised to a degree.

bceause the lower is one of chaos from which reconstitution is always possible, the higher is a conception of Void or Asat, an attachment to non-existence of Self from which it is more difficult to return to fulfilment of Self."[1]

But rightly pursued and realised, the results of Knowledge and Ignorance, says the Upanishad, are different. They are both related to each other. Multiplicity is supported and sustained by the underlying Unity and Unity is realised in its full potential only *vis-a-vis* the multiplicity. The Many, the manifestation in diversity provides the field for the soul to live and grow in the experience of a multitudinous becoming —in all its richness—and arrive progressively at a point where the impact of multiplicity begins to be informed and regulated by the consciousness of the governing Unity—Vidya. When one realises this Knowledge, not only in the mind but in other parts of the being, specially related to life-activity, the knot of Ignorance, the sense of separativity is lost and the range of one's consciousness begins to transcend the barriers of the normal human existence—physical and other,—in a word, it partakes of immortality. This is the truth seen by the ancients, the *dhiras* who saw 'steadfast in the gaze of their thought' and revealed widely, comprehensively, to the seers of the Upanishad, *vicacakśire*.

So also, birth and non-birth, acceptance of manifestation and withdrawal from manifestation, are truths which yield their full value only when taken together and lead to disastrous results if followed exclusively.

---

[1] *Isha Upanishad*, V.

[1]*Into a blind darkness they enter who follow after the Non-Birth, they as if into a greater darkness who devote themselves to the Birth alone.*

Other, verily, it is said, is that which comes by the Birth, other that which comes by the Non-Birth; this is the lore we have received from the wise who revealed That to our understanding.

He who knows That as both in one, the Birth and the dissolution of Birth, by the dissolution crosses beyond death and by the Birth enjoys Immortality.

Sambhuti and *Asambhuti*, Birth and Non-Birth, Sri Aurobindo clarifies, are not so much conditions of the body as states of the soul. One who chooses the state of Non-Birth rejects Birth and the line of manifestation and prepares himself to withdraw into a non-being, goes to a Nihil, a Void where all is blank. But he who is content to remain in the Birth alone, in the field of multiplicity and movement, without realising the saving truth of freedom and transcendence from Birth, goes under in an abysm of darkness. Both Birth and Non-Birth are facts of Existence, and both are to be integrated in oneself.

The lynch-pin that holds together the continually changing movements and experiences in the normal life of the individual is the ego-sense. When that is dissolved the main prop of the life in ignorance is destroyed, *vināśa*.

---

1 अन्धं तम: प्रविशन्ति येऽसम्भूतिमुपासते ।
ततो भूय इव ते तमो य उ सम्भूत्यां रता: ॥ १२ ॥
अन्यदेवाहु: सम्भवादन्यदाहुरसम्भवात् ।
इति शुश्रुम धीराणां ये नस्तद्विचचक्षिरे ॥ १३ ॥
सम्भूतिं च विनाशं च यस्तद्वेदोभयं सह ।
विनाशेन मृत्युं सम्भूत्यामृतमश्नुते ॥ १४ ॥

It does not mean the end of the body; the physical frame can very well continue after the death of the ego. The seeker breaks the bonds imposed by the self-limiting ego, the subjection to incapacity, limitation and desire which are the agents of death. And once he realises this freedom, the seeker after the integral truth of manifestation accepts the Birth : the soul chooses to participate in the general manifestation in order to more fully enjoy its freedom. As Sri Aurobindo says, " it is enjoyed by a free and divine becoming in the universe and not outside the universe ; for there it is always possessed, but here in the material it is to be worked out and enjoyed by the divine Inhabitant under circumstances that are in appearance the most opposite to its terms, in the life of the individual and in the multiple life of the universe."[1]

Thus, "Through Avidya, the Multiplicity, lies our path out of the transitional egoistic self-expression in which death and suffering predominate ; through Vidya consenting with Avidya by the perfect sense of oneness even in that multiplicity, we enjoy integrally the immortality and the beatitude. By attaining to the Unborn beyond all becoming we are liberated from this lower birth and death ; by accepting the Becoming freely as the Divine, we invade mortality with the immortal beatitude and become luminous centres of its conscious self-expression in humanity." (Sri Aurobindo)[2]

This is the thought-movement in the Upanishad so far. The opening lines lay it down that this universe of movement is governed by the One inhabiting Spirit. The object of this manifestation is enjoyment and right living consisting in one's full participation in this enjoyment

---

[1]*Isha Upanishad*, VI.

[2]*The Life Divine* (Vol. I, Chap. V).

which is truly possible only when there is an inner renunciation of Desire. This done, activity ceases to bind the doer who is one in soul with the Lord of All. Those who do not follow this rightful course of life not only miss enjoyment here on earth, but go to worlds of darkness after death. The multiple Movement and the One Stability, are the same Brahman in different poises. Brahman the Reality is both and beyond both. Man realises his unity with the rest of his fellow-beings only in proportion as he gains his identity with this cosmic and transcendental Self who is extended *as* and *in* all. In this unity are true harmony and happiness achieved displacing the elements of friction, grief, and illusion which are the results of a false sense of separativity born of ego. Life is a manifestation of God. The universe is really an unfoldment of the Spirit; it is the Supreme who has gone abroad and " has unrolled the universe in His three modes as All-Seer of the Truth of things, Thinker-out of their possibilities, Realiser of their actualities. He has determined all things sovereignly in their own nature, development and goal from years sempiternal."[1] Vidya and Avidya, consciousness of the inherent unity and the consciousness of the phenomenal multiplicity, are twin powers of this Manifestation, each complementary—and not contradictory—to the other and when a right use is made of both, they carry the individual on their wings towards a supreme fulfilment. So also are Birth and Non-Birth; they are not opposite and irreconcilable; they are two states of the being, each necessary to the completeness of the other and a realisation of both the states is indispensable if the object of Manifestation, Immortality, is to be achieved.

---

[1] *Isha Upanishad*, VI.

To fulfil this aim, to arrive at this Goal of Beatitude with all the opulence of Knowledge, Power and Joy that go with it, the Upanishad invokes the aid of the Gods, the famed guardians of Immortality. It proceeds to call Surya, the God of Illumination and Agni, the Lord of divine Will and Action.

[1] *The face of Truth is covered with a brilliant golden lid; that do thou remove, O Fosterer, for the law of the Truth, for sight.*

O Fosterer, O sole Seer, O Ordainer, O illumining Sun, O power of the Father of creatures, marshal thy rays, draw together thy light; the Lustre which is thy most blessed form of all, that in Thee I behold. The Purusha there and there, He am I.

"In the inner sense of the Veda, Surya, the Sun-God, represents the divine Illumination of the Kavi which exceeds mind and forms the pure self-luminous Truth of things. His principal power is self-revelatory knowledge, termed in the Veda 'Sight'. His realm is described as the Truth, the Law, the Vast. He is the Fosterer or Increaser, for he enlarges and opens man's dark and limited being into a luminous and infinite consciousness. He is the sole Seer, Seer of Oneness and Knower of the Self, and leads him to the highest Sight. He is Yama, Controller or Ordainer, for he governs man's action and manifested being by the direct Law of the Truth, *satyadharma*, and therefore by the right

---

[1] हिरण्मयेन पात्रेण सत्यस्यापिहितं मुखम् ।
तत्त्वं पूषन्नपावृणु सत्यधर्माय दृष्टये ॥ १५ ॥
पूषन्नेकर्षे यम सूर्यं प्राजापत्य व्यूह रश्मीन् समूह ।
तेजो यत्ते रूपं कल्याणतमं तत्ते पश्यामि
योऽसावसौ पुरुषः सोऽहमस्मि ॥ १६ ॥

principle of our nature, *yāthātathyatah*, a luminous power
proceeding from the Father of all existence, he reveals in
himself the divine Purusha of whom all beings are the
manifestations. His rays are the thoughts that proceed
luminously from the Truth, the Vast, but become
deflected and distorted, broken up and disordered in the
reflecting and dividing principle, Mind. They form
there the golden lid which covers the face of the Truth.
The Seer prays to Surya to cast them into right order
and relation and then draw them together into the
unity of revealed truth. The result of this inner process
is the perception of the oneness of all beings in the divine
Soul of this Universe." " This is Surya's goodliest form
of all. For it is the supreme Light, the supreme Will, the
supreme Delight of existence. This is the Lord, the
Purusha, the self-conscient Being. When we have this
vision, there is the integral self-knowledge, the perfect
seeing, expressed in the great cry of the Upanishad,
so'ham. The Purusha there and there, He am I."[1]

---

[1]*Sri Aurobindo :* Isha Upanishad, Verse 15 and Section VII. This verse is
one of the most typical in the Upanishadic literature bringing out the close
relation that exists between the Upanishads and the Veda. As noted earlier,
the sages of the Upanishads always quote from the more ancient scripture in
support, justification or in clinching a line of thought they develop. The
present verse is not only an instance to the point but much more valuable for
the transparency with which it enables one to see how the thought development
has taken place, how the Upanishads make explicit what was implicit in the
Veda. The original Rik reads :

ऋतेन ऋतमपिहितं ध्रुवं वा सूर्यस्य यत्र विमुचन्ति अश्वान् ।
दश शता सह तस्थु: तदेकं देवानां श्रेष्ठं वपुषामपश्यम् । (RV. V. 62. 1)

"There is a Truth covered by a Truth where they unyoke the horses of the
Sun ; the ten hundreds stood together, there was That One ; I saw the greatest
(best, most glorious) of the embodied gods."

Compare this with the two verses of the Isha, under discussion. Drawing
attention to this, Sri Aurobindo writes : "....mark how the seer of the
Upanishad translates this thought or this mystic experience into his own later

¹*The Breath of things is an immortal Life, but of this body ashes are the end. OM! O Will, remember, that which was done, remember! O Will, remember, that which was done, remember.*

O God Agni, knowing all things that are manifested, lead us by the good path to the felicity; remove from us the devious attraction of sin. To thee completest speech of sub-mission we would dispose.

Through the grace and the intervention of Surya the mind of man grows into illumination. But Knowledge is not all. There has to be a corresponding

style, keeping the central symbol of the Sun but without any secrecy in the sense..The golden lid (of the Upanishad) is meant to be the same as the inferior covering truth, *rtam*, spoken of in the Vedic verse ; the 'best of the bodies of the Gods' is equivalent to the 'fairest form of the Sun', it is the supreme Light which is other and greater than all outer light ; the great formula of the Upanishad, 'He am I' corresponds to That One, *tad ekam*, of the Rig Vedic verse ; the 'standing together of the ten hundreds' (the rays of the Sun, says Sayana, and that is evidently the meaning) is reproduced in the prayer to the Sun 'to marshal and mass his rays' so that the supreme form may be seen. The Sun in both the passages as constantly in the Veda and frequently in the Upanishad, is the Godhead of the supreme Truth and Knowledge and his rays are the light emanating from that supreme Truth and Knowledge. It is clear from this instance—and there are others—that the seer of the Upanishad had a truer sense of the meaning of the ancient Veda than the mediaeval ritualistic commentator with his gigantic learning, much truer than the modern and very different mind of the European scholars." (*Hymns to the Mystic Fire*, Pp. XVIII-XIX)

In his Commentary on the Rig Veda, Sri Kapali Sastriar has gone into this interesting parallel in greater detail and has shown how close is the thought of the Upanishad to the spirit of the Vedic Mantra. He also points out other instances, e.g., Rv. J. 25. 3 in the Samhita which contain the seeds of the perception that found its full unveiled expression in this verse of the Isha Upanishad.

1 वायुरनिलममृतमथेदं भस्मान्तं शरीरम् ।
    ओम् क्रतो स्मर कृतं स्मर क्रतो स्मर कृतं स्मर ॥ १७ ॥
    अग्ने नय सुयथा राये अस्मान् विश्वानि देव वयुनानि विद्वान् ।
    युयोध्यस्मज्जुहुराणमेनो भूयिष्ठां ते नमउक्तिं विधेम ॥ १८ ॥

upliftment and enlargement of the faculties of action. They too should be liberated from the limitations under which they labour. But the body, the physical frame of man is circumscribed on all sides and subject to the conditions of birth and death over which he has little control. However, there is, says the seer, a power active in the body, the dynamism of life-energy which is the effective source and executor of all action and that in its true nature—which is revealed in the light of the Surya, the Lord of illumination,—is immortal. To manifest this this Life-principle more and more and enable it to speed into its own untrammelled course of conquest and progress, the God of Life, Vayu (Matarishwan in an earlier verse) is remembered in prayer.

Normal human activity, however, proceeds under the drive and impulsion of Prakriti, Nature, which is shot through and through with Ignorance and revolves round the fulcrum of the ego. Man is a slave of this activity, he is rushed into it and becomes the creature instead of its master he is meant to be. It is only in proportion as he awakens to the liberating knowledge and releases himself from the hold of the lower ignorant nature that he is in a position to dis-engage himself from this thraldom and assume his rightful place. He begins to see that behind all action there is a secret Will leading things to a destined goal. Whatever may be the apparent motives and circumstances which govern activities there is at their base a secret Will and Power whose origin is deeper than the surface nature. This is the *Kratu*, the Divine Will which is called Agni in the Veda —the Will which motivates and executes, with its dynamic power, in the universe as well as in the individual. "He is the divine force which manifests first in matter as heat and light and material energy and then, taking different forms in the other principles of man's consciousness, leads him by a progressive manifestation upwards to the Truth and Bliss."[1] One has to realise this truth in one's own being; gain oneness with this secret spring of Movement if one hopes to acquire control and direction over all one's activities. The seer calls upon this God Agni to come into his own, retain the thread of continuity in the actions put forth in this life-time and before, and relate them in the walking consciousness also in the right sequence, so that the control ensuing from a conscious coordination of doings may perfect itself. This the Agni can do, because being at the fount of manifestation on earth, he *knows;* he knows the truth of all that is born, *jātavedas*, the Intention governing all activities; and knowing, he also sees the direct way in which things lead to their fulfilment. Amidst the maze of ways and byways with which the course of man's life is strewn, he knows which is the straight Path. Caught up in the web of ignorance and false-hood, impelled by the goad of conflicting desires and passions, man turns and deflects, loses sight of the good and the obvious direction. This is pull of *sin* which man suffers and which keeps him away from the natural, the straight course. As Sri Aurobindo states: " Sin, in the conception of the Veda, from which this verse is taken bodily, is that which excites and hurries the faculties into deviation from the good path. There is a straight road or road of naturally increasing light and truth, *rjuh panthā, rtasya panthā*, leading over infinite levels and towards infinite vistas, *vitāni, prsthāni*, by which the law of our nature should normally take us towards our

---

[1] *Isha Upanishad*, Verse 17.

fulfilment.   Sin compels it instead to travel with stumbl-
ings amid uneven and limited tracts and along crooked
windings (*duritāni, vṛjināni*)."[1]

The seer invokes the aid of Agni to pass beyond the
range of this sin and to that end offers " completest sub-
mission and the self-surrender of all the faculties of the
lower egoistic human nature to the divine Will-force,
Agni, so that, free from internal opposition, it may lead
the soul of man through the truth towards a felicity full
of the spiritual riches, *raye*." (Sri Aurobindo)[2]

It hardly needs to be pointed out that these four
crowning verses are not the last prayer of a dying man[3]
as taken by some, but powerful invocations from the
seeker who has by dint of lifelong effort arrived at a
crucial stage when the intervention from the very Gods
alone can enable him to surmount the last barriers, uplift
him and open still higher vistas of Light and Power
leading to the final goal of Immortality while still living
on earth for a full span of life, for a hundred years,
śatam samāḥ.

---

[1] *Isha Upanishad*, Verse 18.
[2] Ibid.
[3] Who is preparing to shed the body to dissolve into the material elements,
and to merge the breath in the primary Prana, summoning up the accumulated
puṇya of rituals performed during his life, and with speech—which is all that
is left to him at that moment as means of worship—pleads to God Agni to lead
him by the bright path—the *devayāna*—to his destination in the Brahmaloka.

KENA UPANISHAD

KENA UPANISHAD

The Upanishad alone of extant scriptures gives us without veil of stinting, with plenitude and a noble catholicity the truth of the Brahman; its aid to humanity is therefore indispensable.

Sri Aurobindo

Like the Isha, the Kena Upanishad is one of the twelve great texts recognised by tradition as scriptures. Like the other, this Upanishad derives its name from the first word of its first verse—*kena*[1]. Its subject is the same —Brahma Vidya, Knowledge of Brahman. The relation of Brahman to the cosmos and the individual human consciousness, the mastery of the Superconscient over all that is manifest and the winning of the highest state of Knowledge and Immortality are discussed in both. Even the concluding notes are the same, viz. the Isha closes with an invocation to the Supreme Felicity for the human; the Kena ends with an injunction to him to seek and worship the Brahman as That Delight, *tad vanam*. But there is a difference of approach and of detail. While the Isha Upanishad addresses itself to the fundamental problems of existence, the Supreme Self and its becomings, the Lord and His workings, the Way of works and life in the world, the Kena concerns a more limited and precise enquiry : the relation of mind and

---

[1] Also known as *Tālavakāra Upanishad*, this text forms the ninth chapter of the Talavakara Brahmana or the Jaiminiya Brahmana, of the Sama Vedins. (*Tālavakāra*-musician). This text is also found, with a few alterations, in the Atharva collection. It is the Talavakara text which is in four parts—unlike the Atharva text without divisions—that Acharya Shankara has chosen for his *Bhāṣya*. He has commented upon it twice, once word by word and again sentence by sentence.

11

other subtle human faculties to Brahman. The Isha assumes that the hearer is an awakened seeker and goes on to lay down grand truths for him to work out and realise. The Kena on the other hand seeks to awaken the individual to the truth of existence, point out to him the poverty and dependent nature of his means of knowledge and action and the necessity of getting at the springs of all life and activity if he is to grow into his fullness and attain to the Goal of all Life—Immortality.

The world is to us essentially what our mind and senses find it to be and declare to us; we know it only in so far and as much as the impressions of our different senses governed by mind transcribe it for us. So also, the life-force, our main instrument for dealing with the outside world, does as it is directed by the mentality determining its course. Now the Upanishad asks, what are the mind and its instruments? Are mind and the senses the last truth? Are they the final powers? or are they also dependent on something else just as the material world depends upon life for its movement, and the life on mind for its direction? Does the mind function on its own? Do the faculties of mind act and move on their own volition or is there something above or behind them which gives them this impulsion? Does the life-force which is such a dynamic element in creation move and activate by itself or is there something that drives it? And what is the secret of speech—that powerful agency by which human thought and will relate and effectuate themselves in the world? Is it a creative cause by itself or is it itself a result of a greater Cause behind? And so also what about the senses like the hearing and the sight? What is it that has set them at work? Is there anything behind or above, governing all these or are they by themselves the ultimate powers?

By whom missioned falls the mind shot to its mark? By whom yoked moves the first life-breath forward on its paths ? By whom impelled is this word that men speak ? What god set eye and ear to their workings ?[1]

The Upanishad answers this question in the affirmative. There is, it says, a greater hearing behind our normal hearing ; it is that which makes the later possible. Similarly there is a Sight behind sight, a Word behind speech and a Life that is the origin of our life-breath, a Mind that is the Cause of our mind—in a word, a Master-Consciousness of which our life-force, mentality, and derived faculties are subsidiary terms. This is the " Brahman consciousness, Mind of our mind, Sense of our senses, Speech of our speech, Life of our life. Arriving at that, we arrive at Self; we can draw back from mind the image into Brahman the Reality."

" Obviously, Brahman is not a thing subject to our mind, senses, speech or life-force ; it is no object seen, heard, expressed, sensed, formed by thought, nor any state of body or mind that we become in the changing movement of the life.... not only is it not an object of mind, or a formation of life, but it is not even dependent on our mind, life and senses for the exercise of its lordship and activity. It is that which does not think by the mind, does not live by the life, does not sense by the senses, does not find expression in the speech, but rather makes these things themselves the object of its superior, all-comprehending, all-knowing consciousness." (Sri Aurobindo)[2]

_____

[1] I. 1

केनेषितं पतति प्रेषितं मनः ।   केन प्राणः प्रथमः प्रैति युक्तः ।
केनेषितां वाचमिमां वदन्ति ।   चक्षुः श्रोत्रं क उ देवो युनक्ति ।

[2] *Kena Upanishad,* IV

The Upanishad has described this Brahman as the Mind of the mind, Sense of our senses etc. It now goes on to explain more elaborately the truth it sought to convey, but even these explanations are terse and fully packed with meaning. And it is here that Sri Aurobindo's commentary is specially invaluable for its explanations of the pregnant phrases, its systematic development and modern exposition of the thought underlying these ancient declarations which are so deceptively simple in their bare, almost austere form.

But before proceeding to explain its description of Brahman, it warns that Brahman cannot be known, much less taught as an object of knowledge.

There sight travels not, nor speech, nor the mind. We know It not nor can distinguish how one should teach of It; for It is other than the known; It is there above the unknown. It is so we have heard from men of old who declared That to our understanding."[1]

The Upanishad gives a warning " that neither the description nor the explanation must be pushed beyond their proper limits or understood as more than guide-posts pointing us towards our goal. For neither Mind, nor Speech, nor Sense can travel to Brahman; therefore Brahman must be beyond all these things in its very nature, otherwise it would be attainable by them in their function. The Upanishad although it is about to teach of the Brahman, yet affirms, 'we know It not, we cannot distinguish how one should teach of It'. The two

------

[1] I. 3

न तत्र चक्षुर्गच्छति न वाग् गच्छति नो मनो ।
न विद्मो न विजानीमो यथैतदनुशिष्यात् ।
अन्यदेव तद्विदितादथो अविदितादधि ।
इति शुश्रुम पूर्वेषां ये नस्तद्व्याचचक्षिरे ।

Sanskrit words that are here used *vidmah* and *vijānimah*, seem to indicate, the one a general grasp and possession in knowledge, the other a total and exact comprehension in whole and detail, by synthesis and analysis. The reason of this entire inability is next given, 'for It is other than the known and It is there over the unknown', possessing it and, as it were, presiding over it. The known is all that we grasp and possess by our present mentality; it is all that is not the supreme Brahman but form and phenomenon of it to our sense and mental cognition. The unknown is that which is beyond the known and though unknown, is not unknowable if we can enlarge our faculties or attain to others that we do not yet possess." (Sri Aurobindo)[1]

Brahman is the Speech of our speech, declared the Upanishad. Behind this cryptic statement lies a whole philosophy of the Logos.

That which is unexpressed by the word, that by which the word is expressed, know That to be the Brahman and not this which men follow after here.[2]

What is this Speech of our speech, the Word which is equated with Brahman itself? "We must recollect that in the Vedic system the Word was the creatrix; by the Word Brahman creates the forms of the universe. . . All creation is expression by the Word; but the form which is expressed is only a symbol or representation of the thing which is. We see this in human speech which only represents to the mind a mental form of the object; but the object it seeks to express is itself only a form or

---

[1] *Kena Upanishad,* VII
[2] I. 4

यद्वाचानभ्युदितं येन वागभ्युद्यते ।
तदेव ब्रह्म त्वं विद्धि नेदं यदिदमुपसते ॥

presentation of another Reality. That Reality is Brahman. Brahman expresses by the Word a form or presentation of himself in the objects of sense and consciousness which constitute the universe, just as the human word expresses a mental image of those objects. The Word is creative in a deeper and more original sense than human speech and with a power of which the utmost creativeness of human speech can be only a far-off and feeble analogy.

" The word used here for utterance means literally a raising up to confront the mind. Brahman, says the Upanishad, is that which cannot be so raised before the mind by speech... Brahman is not expressed by speech, but speech is itself expressed by Brahman. And that which expresses speech in us, brings it up out of our consciousness with its strivings to raise up the truth of things to our mind, is Brahman himself as the Word, a Thing that is in the supreme superconscience. That Word, Speech of our speech, is in its essence of Power the Eternal himself and in its supreme movements a part of his very form and everlasting spiritual body, *brahmano rūpam*." (Sri Aurobindo)[1]

Just as the Speech is Brahman in its expressive aspect, the Upanishad continues, there is a cognitive aspect of Brahman. Presiding over the faculty of mind, there is a corresponding consciousness in the Brahman-Reality, what the Upanishad calls the Mind of our mind, that which does not need to cognise or conceive with the aid of human mind but which is itself the stuff out of which the mind is fashioned, that which cannot be contained in the conceptual frame of the mind which is its own incomplete emanation. This cognitive principle

---

[1] *Kena Upanishad*, V

is that from which the lower derivative, the human mind is formed and governed. Our mind cognises, thinks and functions as a result—however partial and deformed the result—of the impulsion of this higher consciousness pressing upon it; in itself it is inadequate. Sri Aurobindo points out: " Mind tries to arrive at Truth and succeeds only in touching it imperfectly with a veil between; there must be in the nature of things a faculty or principle which sees the Truth unveiled, an eternal faculty of knowledge which corresponds to the eternal fact of the Truth. There is, says the Veda, such a principle; it is the Truth-Consciousness which sees the truth directly and is in possession of it spontaneously. Mind labours to effect the will in it and succeeds only in accomplishing partially, with difficulty and insecurely the potentiality at which it works; there must be a faculty or principle of conscious effective force which corresponds to the unconscious automatic principle of self-fulfilment in Nature, and this principle must be sought for in the form of consciousness that exceeds Mind."[1] This Mind of mind, says the Upanishad, is the nature or description of Brahman-Consciousness— Brahman as related to our mental existence.

The Upanishad then proceeds to enunciate the same greater truth regarding our senses, specially mentioning the faculties of hearing and seeing, which are the most typical and subtle of the senses. It repeats the same truth about our life-force. They are projections, however much imperfect and incomplete, of their absolutes which are contained in the manifestational status of Brahman. Sri Aurobindo discusses the process of the derivation of these human faculties from their original principles in

---

[1] *Kena Upanishad,* VI

Brahman and the course they are taking towards a culminating fulfilment in their growth and assumption of this their original nature.[1] It is That which is the Absolute of all our relatives, says the Upanishad, which must be sought after—as That is truly Brahman the Master—and not the gods of our mind, senses and life which we are wont to worship in ignorance.

This is the purport of the First Part :

" The life of the mind, senses, vital activities in which we dwell is not the whole or the chief part of our existence, not the highest, not self-existent, not master of itself. It is an outer fringe, a lower result, an inferior working of something beyond ; a superconscient Existence has developed, supports and governs this partial and fragmentary, this incomplete and unsatisfying consciousness and activity of the mind, life and senses. To rise out of this external and surface consciousness towards and into that superconscient is our progress, our goal, our destiny of completeness and satisfaction."[2] (Sri Aurobindo)

The normal human life of an ignorant mind, restricted life, and labouring senses with limited range is besieged with the inevitable dualities of knowledge and ignorance, joy and pain, birth and death, power and incapacity, unity and division. The wise, the ones who have strived and arrived at a certain luminosity in thought-fulness and thought-power, *dhirāh*, put away this lower life from themselves and realising the Truth

---

[1] For Sri Aurobindo's illuminating analysis of the several kinds of the mode of action of the mental consciousness viz *vijnāna*, the comprehensive seizure by the consciousness of its object, *prajnāna*, the apprehending possession, *samjnāna*, the sensible or contactual possession and *ajnāna*, the possession and governance of the object in power, we refer the reader to his Commentary. So too with regard to the Prana of the Upanishads and its fivefold movement as *prāna, apāna, samāna, vyāna* and *udāna.*

[2] *Kena Upanishad,* XI

of Brahman pass beyond into Immortality. What is this Immortality of which the Upanishad speaks? To that we shall turn later on.

II

We have seen in the foregoing section how the Upanishad warns that Brahman cannot be known, that human faculties cannot measure it : even the wise forefathers have cautioned against this delusion of knowing Brahman. And yet, the text proceeds to describe Brahman in several forms and enjoins upon the hearer to know Brahman *as such* and no other. The paradox is resolved in the Second Part.

The Upanishad affirms there are three states of existence—first the human, the mortal status, second a Consciousness which is the absolute of all that is in the universe, its Lord governing,—Brahman the Self and Lord of the cosmos, and third, beyond both the world and its Lord, the utter Reality, the Brahman Unknowable and Incommunicable. This ineffable Reality is naturally beyond the pale of knowing and beyond our grasp. Even the Brahman turned towards manifestation, that real Form of Brahman which is the Absolute of all our relatives—cannot be grasped and contained by the human intelligence; but it is possible to enter into relation with it—this Master-Consciousness, the Self and Lord—for the reason that it is related to the manifestation. It contains and governs it. And through some relation it is possible to acquire a kind of knowledge of this Brahman. One can approach it through the very terms in which it is manifest—through the very relatives of which it is the absolute. Thus can one know *of* it. But if he thinks that in so knowing of it, he has known it well, entirely, then he is mistaken. He knows only a

12

part of it, only such of it as yields itself to his uplooking intelligence. And what is thus capable of being known, is not known in the normal way of human knowledge. The seeker has to get behind the mere forms and phenomena in the universe; he learns to look beyond and behind the multitude of forms around, he feels out for the central core of his being which upholds all his mind, life and body and becomes aware of Something Essential which is supporting them as their Self; he looks deeper into the movements of the senses within himself and the cosmic functionings in the universe—the activities of the gods[1]—and becomes aware of Brahman who is sustaining and governing them as their Lord. This simultaneous awakening to the Brahman as the Self and Brahman as the Lord is the Gateway to Knowledge of Brahman as related to His manifestation. Thus it is not mind which can capture Brahman in the net of its conceptual operation. It is a movement of expanding consciousness in which a plastic and silently responsive movement of the mental faculties plays a helpful, indispensable role, but only a role.

Elucidating the meaning of these difficult verses, Sri Aurobindo writes : " If we fancy that we have grasped

---

[1]Who are the gods? Sri Aurobindo explains : "The gods of the Upanishad have been supposed to be a figure for the senses, but although they act in the senses, they are yet much more than that. They represent the divine power in its great and fundamental cosmic functionings whether in man or in mind and life and Matter in general; they are not the functionings themselves but something of the Divine which is essential to their operation and its immediate possessor and cause. They are, as we see from other Upanishads, positive self-representations of the Brahman leading to good, joy, light, love, immortality as against all that is a dark negation of these things. And it is necessarily in the mind, life, senses and speech of man that the battle here reaches its height and approaches to its full meaning. The gods seek to lead these to good and light ; the Titans, sons of darkness, seek to pierce them with ignorance and evil. Behind the gods is the Master Consciousness of which they are the positive cosmic self-representations." (*Kena Upanishad*, XII)

the Brahman by the mind and in that delusion fix down our knowledge of Him to the terms our mentality has found, then our knowledge is no knowledge; it is the little knowledge that turns to falsehood. So, too, those who try to fix Him into our notion of the fundamental ideas in which we discern Him by the thought that rises above the ordinary mental perception, have no real discernment of the Brahman, since they take certain idea-symbols for the Reality. On the other hand, if we recognise that our mental perceptions are simply so many clues by which we can rise beyond mental perception and if we use these fundamental idea-symbols and the arrangement of them which our uttermost thought makes in order to go beyond the symbol to that reality, then we have rightly used mind and the higher discernment for their supreme purpose. Mind and the higher discernment are satisfied of the Brahman even in being exceeded by Him.

" The mind can only reflect in a sort of supreme understanding and experience the form, the image of the Supreme as He shows Himself to our mentality. Through this reflection we find, we know ; the purpose of know-ledge is accomplished, for we find immortality, we enter into the law, the being, the beatitude of the Brahman-consciousness. By self-realisation of Brahman as our self we find the force, the divine energy which lifts us beyond the limitation, weakness, darkness, sorrow, all-pervading death of our mortal existence; by the knowledge of the one Brahman in all beings and in all the various movements of the cosmos we attain beyond these things to the infinity, the omnipotent being, the omniscient light, the pure beatitude of that divine existence." And further :

" This great achievement must be done here in this mortal world, in the limited body ; for if we do it, we arrive at our true existence and are no longer bound down to our phenomenal becoming. But if here we find it not, great is the loss and perdition;[1] for we remain continually immersed in the phenomenal life of the mind and body and do not rise above it into the true supramental existence. Nor, if we miss it here, will

---

[1] इह चेदवेदीदथ सत्यमस्ति ॥   न चेदिहावेदीन्महती विनष्टि: ॥

If here one comes to that knowledge, then one truly is ;

If here one comes not to the knowledge, then great is the perdition. (II. 5)

We may note in passing that this stress on realisation *here*, while in body and on earth, determining the state of man after-life recurs in other Upanishads also, notably in the Brihadaranyaka :

इहैव सन्तोऽथ विद्मस्तद्वयं न चेदवेदीर्महती विनष्टि: ।

ये तद्विदुरमृतास्ते भवन्त्येतरे दु:खमेवापियन्ति ॥

Verily, while we are here we may know this.
If you have known it not, great is the destruction.
Those who know this become immortal.
But others go only to sorrow. (IV.4.14)

or in the Katha :

इह येदशकद्ब्रोद्धुं प्राक् शरीरस्य विस्रस: ।

तत: सर्गेषु लोकेषु शरीरत्वाय कल्पते ॥

'If in this world of men and before thy body fall from thee, thou wert able to apprehend it, then thou availeth for embodiment in the worlds that He creates.'(VI.4)

What he becomes or attains is determined by what he has been. "It is understood that the physical life is not the sole life and that the human soul does not end with its end, but continues its existence in another state of consciousness, in another plane of being corresponding to the condition and level of being it has risen to in the terrestrial existence. If man is to survive the physical death with a spiritual status, he has to establish in himself in the period of his bodily life on earth points of contact with the higher powers of the Spirit, must have awakened and opened in him the subtle psychic and spiritual centres of knowledge and will communicating with the higher planes of being in other fields of Consciousness, in the supraphysical and still subtler and higher worlds that are the constituents of this Cosmos. For, thus and not otherwise, when the hour comes for the material body to fall or when the physical life has no further use for the Spirit, he can switch on the escalator of the Yoga Force that gives him the lift to those regions of the Spirit with which he has already familiarised himself in a way under conditions obtaining in embodied life on earth." (Sri Kapali Sastry : *Lights on the Upanishads*, P. 45)

death give it to us by our passage to another and less difficult world. Only those who use their awakened self and enlightened powers to distinguish and discover that One and Immortal in all existences, the all-originating self, the all-inhabiting Lord, can make the real passage which transcends life and death, can pass out of this mortal status, can press beyond and rise upward into a world-transcending immortality."[1]

III

So is the Unknowable Brahman known, though only known in a way and in a certain status. The human consciousness can relate itself to it and is meant to grow and pass into it ; that is the culmination of its Knowledge of Brahman. In its Third Part, the Upanishad proceeds to indicate the means of achieving this object, the way in which the human, the subject-consciousness of man can contact, relate itself to and gain knowledge of the Master-consciousness which is Brahman, the Lord and Self of the Cosmos. And this it does through an apologue.

The gods are, as we have noted, powers of Brahman put out from Him for the execution of functions necessary for the purpose of manifestation. They preside over and direct the several principles that are released into manifestation—both on the cosmic and the individual level, in the physical as well as the pyschological and other spheres. They are the Powers that ensure the operation of universal forces in Nature and also the Powers that govern and direct the evolution of the same underlying principles in man.[2] They are the Powers of

---

[1]*Kena Upanishad*, XII

[2]Thus Agni is the Power that embodies the principle of heat and light, Will and Knowledge, Vayu the Power of Life and forward Movement, Indra

the Divine Truth that affirm and build the empire of Truth, Light and Good and Beatitude as opposed to the powers of Ignorance—the Asuras and their brood—that deny and oppose. Now the text begins the parable with the assembly of the gods rejoicing over a victory that has been won. They are happy and content in their greatness. What is this victory they have won? Commentators have sought to connect it with stories related elsewhere in other texts and given different interpretations. Sri Aurobindo explains :[1]

" The gods, the powers that affirm the Good, the Light, the Joy and Beauty, the Strength and Mastery have found themselves victorious in their eternal battle with the powers that deny. It is Brahman that has stood behind the gods and conquered for them ; the Master of all, who guides all, has thrown His deciding will into the balance, put down his darkened children and exalted the children of Light. In this victory of the Master of all, the gods are conscious of a mighty development of themselves, a splendid efflorescence of their greatness in man, their joy, their light, their glory, their power and pleasure. But their vision is as yet sealed to their own deeper truth ; they know of themselves, they know not the eternal ; they know the godheads, they do not know

the Lord of the heavens, the highest attained summits of humanity, the pure mental skies. Sri Aurobindo draws attention to one important difference between the position of the gods in the Vedas and the position they hold in the Upanishads. "The gods of the Upanishad differ in one all-important respect from the gods of the Rig Veda ; for the latter are not only powers of the One, but conscious of their source and true identity ; they know the Brahman, they dwell in the supreme Godhead, their origin, home and proper plane is the superconscient Truth..But in the Upanishads the Brahman idea has grown and cast down the gods from this high pre-eminence so that they appear only in their lesser human and cosmic workings."

[1] *Kena Upanishad*, XIII

God. Therefore they see the victory as their own, the greatness as their own. This opulent efflorescence of the gods and uplifting of their greatness and light is the advance of man to his ordinary ideal of a perfectly enlightened mentality, a strong and sane vitality, a well-ordered body and senses, a harmonious, rich, active and happy life, the Hellenic ideal which the modern world holds to be our ultimate potentiality. When such an efflorescence takes place whether in the individual or the kind, the gods in man grow luminous, strong, happy ; they feel they have conquered the world and they proceed to divide it among themselves and enjoy it."[1]

He proceeds : " But such is not the full intention of Brahman in the universe or in the creature. The greatness of the gods is His own victory and greatness, but it is only given in order that man may grow nearer to the point at which his faculties will be strong enough to go beyond themselves and realise the Transcendent. Therefore Brahman manifests Himself[2] before the exultant gods in their well-ordered world and puts to them by His silence the heart-shaking, the world-shaking question, ' If ye are all, then what am I ? for see, I am and I am here.' Though He manifests, He does not reveal Himself, but is seen and felt by them as a vague and tremendous presence, the Yaksha, the Daemon, the

---

[1] ब्रह्म ह देवेभ्यो विजिग्ये तस्य ह ब्रह्मणो विजये देवा अमहीयन्त।
त ऐक्षन्तास्माकमेवायं विजयोऽस्माकमेवायं महिमेति ॥   (III. 1)

The Eternal conquered for the gods and in the victory of the Eternal the gods attained to greatness. This was what they saw, "Ours the victory, ours the greatness." (III. 1)

[2] तद्वैषां विजज्ञौ तेभ्यो ह प्रादुर्बभूव तन्न व्यजानत किमिदं यक्षमिति (III.2)

The Eternal knew this thought and appeared before them ; and they knew not what was this mighty Daemon. (III. 2)

Spirit, the unknown Power, the Terrible, beyond good
and evil, for good and evil are instruments towards His
final self-expression. Then there is alarm and confusion
in the divine assembly; they feel a demand and a
menace...."

They cannot brook the challenge and are impatient
to know the truth of this Daemon. They must find out
who it is and from where it has appeared. They choose
Agni, the god who presides over the material manifestation, the Earth, and who knows everything that comes
to birth in the cosmos, *jātavedas*, and mission him to
know and report. Agni advances upon That and is
confronted with the challenge :

" *Who art thou ?* "

" *I am Agni,*" he said, " *I am he that knows all things
born.*"

" *Since such thou art, what is the force in thee ?* "

" *Even all this I could burn, all that is upon the earth.*"

*The Eternal set before him a blade of grass; " This
burn;" and he made towards it with all his speed, but he could
not burn it. There he ceased, and turned back; " I could not
know of it, what might be this mighty Daemon.*"[1] " So Agni
is compelled to return, not having discovered. One thing
only is settled that this Daemon is no Birth of the
material cosmos, no transient thing that is subject to the
flame and breath of Time; it is too great for Agni."
(Sri Aurobindo)

---

[1] तमभ्यवदत्कोऽसीत्यग्निर्वा अहमस्मीत्यब्रवीज्जातवेदा वा अहमस्मीति ।
तस्मिंस्त्वयि किं वीर्यमीत्यपीदं सर्वं दहेयं यदिदं पृथिव्यामिति ।
तस्मै तृणं निदधावेतद्दहेति तदुपप्रेयाय सर्वजवेन तन्न शशाक दग्धुं स तत
एव निववृते नैनदशकं विज्ञातुं यदेनद्यक्षमिति ।   (III. 4,5,6,)

Then it is the turn of Vayu, the Lord of the life-world. If That be no phenomenon of earth, the material world, perhaps it is some great product of the life-force in the mid-world, *antarikṣa*, the domain of Vayu. And so he sets out.

He rushed upon That; It said to him, " Who art thou ? "

" I am Vayu," he said, " and I am he that expands in the Mother of things."

" Since such thou art, what is the force in thee ? "

" Even all this I can take for myself, all this that is upon the earth."

That set before him a blade of grass, " This take."

He went towards it with all his speed and he could not take it. Even there he ceased, even thence he returned. I could not discern That, what is this mighty Daemon."[1]

" One thing only is settled that this is no form or force of cosmic Life which operates within the limits of the all-grasping vital impulse; it is too great for Vayu." (Sri Aurobindo)

" Indra next arises, the Puissant, the Opulent. Indra is the power of the Mind ; the senses which the Life uses for enjoyment, are operations of Indra which he conducts for knowledge and all things that Agni has upbuilt and supports and destroys in the universe are Indra's field and the subject of his functioning. If then

---

[1] तदभ्यद्रवत्तमभ्यवदत्। कोऽसीति वायुर्वा अहमस्मीत्यब्रवीन्मातरिश्वा वा अहमस्मीति तस्मिंस्त्वयि किं वीर्यमीत्यपीदं सर्वमाददीयं यदिदं
पृथिव्यामिति।
तस्मै तृणं निदधावेतदादत्स्वेति तदुपप्रेयाय सर्वजवेन तन्न शशाकादातुं स तत एव निववृते नैतदशक विज्ञातुं यदेतद्यक्षामिति।   (III. 8,9,10)

this unknown Existence is something that the senses can grasp or, if it is something that the mind can envisage, Indra shall know it and make a part of his opulent possessions."

Then they said to Indra, " Master of plenitudes, get thou the knowledge, what is this mighty Daemon."

He said, " So be it." He rushed upon That.

That vanished before him.[1]

" But it is nothing that the senses can grasp or the mind envisage, for as soon as Indra approaches it, it vanishes. The mind can only envisage what is limited by Time and Space and this Brahman is that which, as the Rig Veda has said, is neither today nor tomorrow and though it moves and can be approached in the conscious being of all conscious existences, yet when the mind tries to approach it and study it in itself, it vanishes from the view of the mind. The Omnipresent cannot be seized by the senses, the omniscient cannot be known by the mentality." (Sri Aurobindo)

However, Indra, the lord of the Mind, does not return. He advances further in the etherial summits of pure mentality and is met by Uma, the great Goddess of many forms, the Para Shakti. From her he learns that That was the Brahman, the Eternal and that the victory and the greatness which they the gods ascribed to themselves really belonged to That. It is by force of Brahman, their origin and support that Indra, Vayu, and Agni, the gods of mind, life and body conquer and affirm themselves.

Who is Uma that appears before Indra and what is the purport of her revelation?

---

[1] अथेन्द्रमब्रुवन्मघवन्नेतद्विजानीहि किमेतद्यक्षमिति तथेति तदभ्यद्रवत् तस्मात्तिरोदधे ।   (III.11)

" Uma, the Daughter of Snowy Summits is the Para Prakriti, the Supreme Nature, the highest Power of the Ultimate Truth, the Supreme Consciousness of Brahman. It is from her the whole cosmic action takes its birth, from her the gods must learn their own truth, for she has the necessary knowledge and consciousness of the One above the lower nature of mind, life and body ; and, Creatrix of the gods, she mediates between the One above and beyond, and gods and men here in the lower creation. The import, the lesson then, of the story of the gods is that all the life-activities and senses and mind, the functionings of the Cosmic Powers in man must learn to surrender consciously to their One true Master-consciousness leaving behind the wrong and false notion of independence and self-will and self-ordering which is an egoism of life and mind and body." (Sri Kapali Sastry)[1]

The gods must receive and reflect in themselves the truth of the One which She, the Supreme Consciousness holds in Herself. Agni and Vayu are no doubt great gods because they came so near in the proximity of Brahman,[2] Indra still greater because he was the first to know the existence of That. Yet they can know and possess Brahman only when they, i.e. the powers of the physical, vital and mental manifestations, consciously surrender, passively reflect and faithfully reproduce the nature and movement of the Master-

---

[1]*Lights on the Ancients,* Pp. 63-64

[2]Sri Aurobindo draws attention to a textual error in the second verse of the Fourth Part which has been somehow explained away where it has not escaped attention of the commentators. It reads :

तस्माद्वा एते देवता अतितरामिवान्यान्देवान्यदग्निर्वायुरिन्द्रस्ते ह्येनन्नेदिष्ठं पस्पर्शुस्ते ह्येनत्प्रथमो विदञ्चकार ब्रह्मेति ।

Power, the Eternal ; only then "we may hope to know
and through knowledge to rise into that which is superconscient to us ; we shall enter into the Silence that is
master of an eternal, infinite, free and all-blissful
activity."   (Sri Aurobindo)

IV

We are to withdraw our eye and preoccupation
with the outer forms and get to what is essential in the
cosmos—the gods in Nature and the self in ourselves.
And having done that we have to realise That which is
behind both, the gods and self—the One Supreme of
which they are representations. Our entire being—
with the mind, the senses, the life and the body--has to
learn to be passive to That which is larger and looming
over it and to grow into its Nature. The human nature
has to pass into Supernature. How is that done ? What
is the process by which this upliftment and transcendence takes place ?

The Upanishad hints at it in two cryptic verses—as
the Upanishads always do when it comes to practical

Sri Aurobindo translates : "Therefore are these gods as it were beyond all
the other gods, even Agni and Vayu and Indra, because they came nearest to
the touch of That..."   He leaves out the last part, and explains :

"By some mistake of early memorisers or later copyists the rest of the
verse has become hopelessly corrupted. It runs, 'They he first came to know
that it was the Brahman,' which is neither fact nor sense nor grammar. The
close of the third verse has crept into and replaced the original close of the
second."

(The third verse reads :

तस्माद्वा इन्द्रो ऽतितरामिवान्यान्देवान्स ह्येनन्नेदिष्ठं पस्पर्श स ह्येनन्प्रथमो
विदाञ्चकार ब्रह्मेति ।

Therefore is Indra as it were beyond all the other gods because he came
nearest to the touch of That, because he first knew that it was the Bra hman.)

instruction which was left to the Guru to communicate orally and otherwise to the disciple. The process of change of the nature and functionings of the gods is one and that of the upliftment and enlargement of the individual self is another.

Now this is the indication of That, as is this flash of the lightning upon us or as is this falling of the eyelid, so in that which is of the gods.[1]

When the gods i.e. the Powers presiding over the cosmic functionings are aware of their Master and are consciously passive, the Superconscient " comes by flashes, revelations, sudden touches and glimpses ; there is as if a leap of the lightning of revelation flaming out from those heavens for a moment and then returning into its secret source ; as if the lifting of the eyelid of an inner vision and its falling again because the eye cannot look long and steadily on the utter light. The repetition of these touches and visitings from the Beyond fixes the gods in their upward gaze and expectation, constant repetition fixes them in a constant passivity ; not moving out any longer to grasp at the forms of the universe, mind, life and senses will more and more be fixed in the memory, in the understanding, in the joy of the touch and vision of that transcendent glory which they have now resolved to make their sole object ; to that only they will learn to respond and not to the touches of outward things. The silence which has fallen on them and which is now their foundation and status will become their knowledge of the eternal silence which is Brahman." (Sri Aurobindo)[2]

---

[1] IV. 4

तस्मैष आदेशो यदेतद्विद्युतो व्यद्युतदा इतीन्न्यमीमिषदा इत्यधिदैवतम् ।

[2] *Kena Upanishad*, XIV

Then in that which is of the Self,—as the motion of this mind seems to attain to That and by it afterwards the will in the thought continually remembers it.[1]

The self of man must enter into the One Self of all individual existences. This is even more imperative than the transfiguration of the gods; for it is the self in us that supports the action of the gods and the realisation, by this central core of our being, of identity and a resolution into oneness with the Brahman as the One Self is more fundamental in necessity and consequence. And this "the self of man, since it is the essentiality of a mental being, will do through the mind. In the gods the transfiguration is effected by the Superconscient itself visiting their substance and opening their vision with its flashes until it has transformed them; but the mind is capable of another action which is only apparently movement of mind, but really the movement of the self towards its own reality. The mind seems to go to That, to attain to it; it is lifted out of itself into something beyond and although it falls back, still by the mind the will of knowledge in the mental thought continually and at last continuously remembers that into which it has entered. On this the Self through the mind seizes and repeatedly dwells and so doing it is finally caught up into it and at last able to dwell securely in that transcendence. It transcends the mind, it transcends its own mental individualisation of the being, that which it now knows as itself; it ascends and takes foundation in the Self of all. . . " (Sri Aurobindo)[2]

---

[1]IV. 5

अथाध्यात्मं यदेतद् गच्छतीव च मनोऽनेन चैतदुपसरत्यभीक्ष्णं संकल्प: ।

[2]*Kena Upanishad,* XIV

Transcendence, but transcendence in consciousness while yet living and participating in the creation of Brahman the Lord. The Upanishad in calling for the exceeding of the gods and the outgrowing of the limitations of the human self, does not counsel the abandonment of the world in favour of a paradise beyond or a final absorption into the one, pure, indeterminate, immutable Brahman.[1] On the other hand, it emphatically enjoins upon the seeker to worship and realise the Reality, the Brahman, in its nature as That Delight, *tadvanam*, the Bliss that makes all life possible and sustains the manifestation in all its forms. " *Vana* is the Vedic word for delight or delightful, and *tadvanam* means therefore the transcendent Delight, the all-blissful Ananda of which the Taittiriya Upanishad speaks as the highest Brahman from which all existences are born, by which all existences live and increase and into which all existences arrive in their passing out of death and birth. It is as this transcendent Delight that the Brahman must be worshipped and sought. It is this beatitude therefore

---

[1]Neither heaven nor Nirvana. "As the lures of earth have to be conquered, so also have the lures of heaven......The lure of a release from birth and death and withdrawal from the cosmic labour must also be rejected...As the virtues we practise must be done without demand of earthly or heavenly reward, so the salvation we seek must be purely internal and impersonal ; it must be the release from egoism, the union with the Divine, the realisation of our universality as well as our transcendence, and no salvation should be valued which takes us away from the love of God in his manifestation and the help we can give to the world....The connection with the universe is preserved for the one reason which supremely justifies that connection ; it must subsist not from the desire of personal earthly joy as with those who are still bound, but for help to all creatures. Two then are the objects of the high-reaching soul, to attain the Supreme and to be for ever for the good of all the world,—even as Brahman Himself; whether here or elsewhere, does not essentially matter ; still where the struggle is thickest, there should be the hero of the spirit, that is surely the highest choice of the son of Immortality ; the earth calls most. because it has most need of him, to the soul that has become one with the universe." (*Sri Aurobindo: Kena Upanishad*, XV)

which is meant by the immortality of the Upanishads. And what will be the result of knowing and possessing Brahman as the supreme Ananda ? It is that towards the knower and possessor of the Brahman is directed the desire of all creatures. In other words, he becomes a centre of the divine Delight shedding it on all the world and attracting all to it as to a fountain of joy and love and self-fulfilment in the universe." (Sri Aurobindo)[1]

This is the Upanishad, the 'inner knowledge, that which enters into the final Truth and settles in it'—that has been uttered in response to a seeking. It set out with a search for the Lord, the Absolute of our mind, life and speech and senses. It affirmed the existence of a Master-Consciousness, the Brahman who governs and directs all the cosmic operations and enjoined upon the hearer to seek to know and worship this true Brahman and not the eidolon that men run after here. But it warned that Brahman cannot be known in the way of human knowledge and that what can be known is only so much of It as yields itself to us through the forms in which It is manifest. By means of a parable it drove home the dependence of the gods, the powers that govern cosmic functionings, on the Lord who is their Origin and Support and pointed out that their full growth and efflorescence lay in an utterly passive receptivity to His Consciousness and Power. It stressed the indispensable need for the enlargement of the self of our being to embrace the One Great Self of the universe. Only thus, the Upanishad pointed out, is it possible for our subject nature to rise into the Supernature and taste the transcendent bliss of Brahman—the Delight that is unconditioned, transcendent of Time, Space and Causality. And lastly, it called upon him who partakes of this

_____
[1] *Kena Upanishad*, XIV

Beatitude, this Immortality in consciousness, to continue
in the world as a well of joy and bliss from which the
rest of fellow-beings can draw sustenance and happiness.

This is the doctrine of the Knowledge of Brahman
which, the text declares, has *tapas*, austerity, *dama*, self-
mastery, and *karma*, works—egoless activity in dedication,
as its first foundation. The Vedas, the truths that are
enshrined in the soul-stirred utterances of the ancient
seers who first laid the large lines of the Ascent to the
Truth are the several parts that make the body, the limbs
of the Upanishad ; the knowledge and the practice that
comprise the teaching of the Upanishads rests upon and
is formed by the verities and disciplines embedded in the
Veda. Truth is its Home. Satyam, the Right and the
True as expressed in man's aspiration, thought, consciousness and life, is its abode, the only environment in which
it thrives on the progressively complete elimination of the
shade of the falsehood of egoism and ignorance, and leads
in its fullness to the Goal, the vaster world and infinite
heaven, the Svarga-loka which Sri Aurobindo points out,
" is not the lesser Svarga of the Puranas or the lesser
Brahma-loka of the Mundaka Upanishad, its world of
the sun's rays to which the soul arrives by works of virtue
and piety, but falls from them by the exhaustion of
their merit ; it is the higher Svarga or Brahman-world of
the Katha which is beyond the dual symbols of birth and
death, the higher Brahman-worlds of the Mundaka which
the soul enters by knowledge and renunciation. It is
therefore a state not belonging to the Ignorance, but to
Knowledge. It is, in fact, the infinite existence and
beatitude of the soul in the being of the all-blissful
existence ; it is too the higher status, the light of the
Mind beyond the mind, the joy and eternal master of

14

the Life beyond the life, the riches of the Sense beyond the senses. And the soul finds in it not only its own largeness but finds too and possesses the infinity of the One and it has firm foundation in that immortal state because there a supreme Silence and eternal Peace are the secure foundation of eternal Knowledge and absolute Joy."[1]

---

[1] *Kena Upanishad,* XIV

TAITTIRIYA UPANISHAD

TAITTIRIYA UPANISHAD

Sri Aurobindo has not written a commentary on the Taittiriya Upanishad. But in a sense a good deal in his Philosophy and Teaching is a development and an elaboration of the truths that are adumbrated in this ancient text. The comprehensive vision of the Upanishad embracing the entire creation in its several grades of becoming out of the One Being of Brahman, the perception of the divine Principle of Ananda as the origin, motive-force and goal of all manifestation, the all-inclusive nature of the discipline it expounds for the realisation of this truth of Life and God—all these go naturally into the framework of the Master's Teaching which affirms the truth and high purpose of this multi-tiered creation issued out of the One Omnipresent Reality and shows the effective way to arrive at its integral Fulfilment.

The Taittiriya[1] Upanishad forms part of the Aranyaka of the Taittiriya or the Krishna (Black)

---

[1] The Vishnu Purana narrates (III. 5) an interesting story behind the appellation Taittiriya. Vaishampayana, disciple of Vyasa, had to perform an expiatory ceremony for a lapse in absenting himself from a Council of Elders on Mount Meru. He commissioned his disciples to perform the ceremony. Yajnavalkya, one of them, boastfully offered to do what was necessary all by himself and belittled his co-disciples. Vaishampayana was offended and ordered Yajnavalkya to return all that he had received from him. Yajnavalkya gave back all including his most precious gift, the Yajurveda. And this Veda, it is said, he disgorged concretely and it was picked up by the other disciples taking the form of *tittiri* birds, partridges. That is how this Veda came to be known as the Taittiriya Samhita.

The story goes on to narrate how Yajnavalkya, brave spirit that he was, proceeded to do penance and invoked the Sun who appeared to him in the form of a Horse, *vāja*, and gave him the same Veda (though differently constituted) which got the name *vājasaneyji samhitā* ; the one unique feature of this collection being that unlike the Taittiriya, it has no Brahmana attached to the Mantra Samhita but has an Upanishad instead.

Yajurveda. The VII, VIII and IX Prapathakas (chapters) of the Taittiriya constitute the three sections of the Upanishad, the *Sikṣāvalli*, *Ānandavalli* and the *Bhṛguvalli*.[1] This Upanishad, it may be added, is the most popular text for purposes of chanting wherever Vedic recitation is still in vogue. The poetic prose of the Upanishad, with its short crisp sentences, its happy refrains, has a peculiarly sonorous melody which creates an arresting atmosphere.

It is to be noted that unlike the two Upanishads dealt with before, the Taittiriya is not a compact text with a developing sequence. Certain chapters are so abrupt and dis-jointed in their subject-matter that some scholars even doubt whether it is not simply a collection of floating sayings and lessons. In our survey of this Upanishad we shall take note only of its more significant and major topics with a view to present its main teaching—of which, however, there can be no mistaking —in the light of Sri Aurobindo's thought.

SHIKSHA VALLI

The text opens with a Chant of Peace to the Gods, the Cosmic Powers who mould the destinies of men and worlds :

Hari Om. Be peace to us Mitra. Be peace to us Varuna. Be peace to us Aryaman. Be peace to us Indra and Brihaspati. May far-striding Vishnu be peace to us. Adoration to thee, O Vayu. Thou, thou art the visible Eternal and as the visible Eternal I will declare thee. I will declare Righteousness! I will declare Truth! May that protect the speaker! Yea, may it

---

[1] The X, the last Prapathaka of the Aranyaka forms a separate Upanishad, the Mahanarayana Upanishad.

*protect me ! May it protect the speaker ! Om. Peace ! Peace !
Peace !*[1]

This is an invocation taken from a Hymn to the
Vishwadevas (All-Gods) in the Rig-veda.[2] In the Veda,
each of the Gods has a specific purpose to fulfil in the
cosmic scheme of which they are collectively the presiding functionaries. They not only manifest but are
also themselves manifest in the universe to urge and
lead it towards the Beatitude which is its supreme
culmination. They play a decisive part in the journey
of man onwards and upwards, in his outer and inner
life. And for a self-fulfilment *within* the universe—not
outside of it—as taught in this Upanishad, the active
presence and contributory co-operation of these cosmic
deities is indispensable. Thus Mitra is the God who
promotes harmony (as much among the different parts
of man's being as between him and others—men and
gods), Varuna the God of Purity and Vastness, the
keeper of the Law of Truth, Aryaman a leading
Personality manifesting the Consciousness-Force of the
Sun-God who symbolises the Supreme Truth, Brihaspati
the Deity presiding over the Potent Word, the Power of
Creative Speech, Indra the lord of the Divine Mind,
Vishnu the All-pervader—striding across with his

---

[1]   हरि : ओं ॥ शं नो मित्र : शं वरुण : ।
शं नो भवत्वर्यमा । शं न इन्द्रो बृहस्पति : ।
शं नो विष्णुरुरुक्रम : ॥ नमो ब्रह्मणे ।
नमस्ते वायो । त्वमेव प्रत्यक्षं ब्रह्मासि ।
त्वमेव प्रत्यक्षं ब्रह्म वदिष्यामि । ऋतं वदिष्यामि ।
सत्यं वदिष्यामि । तन्मामवतु ।
तद्वक्तारमवतु । अवतु माम् ।
अवतु वक्तारम् ॥ ओं शान्ति : शान्ति : शान्ति : ॥

[2] I. 90-9

celebrated three steps—, sustaining the Creation, and Vayu the God of Life-force which palpably pervades and enlivens all existence. To all of these who have it in their power to build and shape the Realisation,[1] the seer offers his homage and prays for their benediction; he prays thrice—for a threefold protection and blessing, bearing on the welfare of the body, of the soul, of his dealings with the universal powers, *adhibhautika*, *adhyatmika* and *adhidaivika*, as the commentators say, or for the weal and progress of his threefold being, the physical, the life or vital and the mental.

The object of this Upanishad, as indeed of all others, is to lead the aspirant to the Knowledge of Brahman. But before initiation into the mysteries of the High Science, the seeker had to be given a certain preliminary training in cultivating the right modes of thought, articulation and speech. The Wisdom of the ancients was embedded—as far as may be—in their inspired Word. And to evocate its living sense and power, one had to reproduce the exact sound-form in which the Word was manifest to the audience of the Seer who first received it. Each word-content had its natural sound-value or counterpart and the full meaning and power of the word could be realised or brought forth only by an

---

[1] Certainly the Gods do not hinder man in his progress. At any rate not the Gods of the Vedic (or Upanishadic) pantheon. They are his allies, friends. " Children of Light, Sons of the Infinite, they recognise in the soul of man their brother and ally and desire to help and increase him by themselves increasing in him so as to possess his world with their light, strength and beauty. The Gods call man to a divine companionship and alliance; they attract and uplift him to their luminous fraternity, invite his aid and offer theirs against the Sons of Darkness and Division." (Sri Aurobindo : *On the Veda*, P. 433) It is the fallen gods, the Asuras and their brood who bar the way and seek to prevent the human soul from increasing towards Light and Knowledge and it is from their hold that man is to struggle out with the vigilant help of the Gods. The belief that Gods treat man as their rival and are interested in suppressing him in Ignorance is too anthropomorphic to merit scrutiny.

exact reproduction of these sound-vibrations.[1] And hence the seers attached a particular importance to *śikṣā*, " the syllable, the accent, pitch and effort, even tone and continuity "[2], the elements that go to form enunciation.

The mind is to be trained to perceive and conceive newly. Behind the multitudinous variety of forms which people this universe, one must begin to see that there is one underlying Reality which manifests as the many and governs them in an indissoluble unity. Whatever the categories or the terms of the manifestation, they are all interlinked and interdependent. Look at the worlds. The earth below and heaven above are not disparate entities ; they are formations of the same Substance of Being though of different grades. The ether—also another form of Substance--links them both and air, its less subtle condition is the joint of their linking. Look at the Shining Fires. The Fire on the earth, the Sun in the sky are forms of the same Consciousness-Energy ; they are linked by the Waters (of consciousness) and the electricity form of energy is the joint of their linking. Similarly with regard to other categories. There is one Principle, one Term of the Sole Being which manifests in several forms—all mutually forming one connected Whole. One must meditate upon this truth in the creation around and let it naturally govern the inlook and outlook.

---

[1] The Taittiriya Samhita narrates, for instance (II. 4-12), the story of Twashtri the celestial architect, whose son was killed by Indra. He desired to produce an avenger of his son and performed the appropriate austerities. But instead of uttering the word *Indraśatru* with the *udātta* accent on the last syllable he accented the first syllable with the fatal result that there appeared not one who was to slay Indra but he whose slayer was to be Indra !

[2] वर्णः स्वरः । मात्रा बलम् । सन्तानः ॥   (I. 2)

15

To prepare and equip the seeker in these ways of Knowledge, the Teacher should be one who has already realised and holds in himself the truth of what is to be taught. His mind must be illumined by the pure light of the Knowledge he is to radiate, his very body must become a pouring vessel for the riches of Knowledge, Power and Immortality that flow naturally from the heights of God-realisation. Towards this end, to establish and confirm this high state in himself the Guru invokes the Lord of the Gods at the summit of this triple World, Indra the Master of the Divine Mind who presides over the altitudes of the purified mental consciousness and who alone can open up for man the splendours of illumined Knowledge and Power. To him he prays:

He who is the Bull of the Vedas of the universal form, he who was born in the sacred rhythms from the Immortal,—may Indra satisfy me through the intelligence. O God, may I become a vessel of the Immortal. May my body be full of vision and my tongue of sweetness, may I hear the much and vast with my ears. For thou art the sheath of Brahman covered over and hidden by the intelligence.[1]

Brimming with this Illumination vouchsafed by the Lord of the Divine Intelligence, scintillating with this dynamis of Knowledge which he wishes to share with as

---

[1] यः छन्दसाम् ऋषभो विश्वरूप : । छन्दोभ्योऽध्यमृतात्सम्बभूव ।
समेन्द्रो मेधया स्पृणोतु । अमृतस्य देव धारणो भूयासम् ।
शरीरं मे विचर्षणम् । जिह्वा मे मधुमत्तमा ।
कर्णाभ्याम् भूरि विश्रुवम् । ब्रह्मणः कोशोऽसि मेधया पिहितः : ।

This is one of the notable passages cited by Sri Aurobindo to illustrate how the psychological and spiritual character and function of the Gods implicit in the Veda is made explicit in the Upanishads. Here Indra is invoked plainly and unequivocally as the Godhead of the divine Mind, *brahmanah kosyosi medhaya pihitah*—behind the veil of Intelligence stands Indra, form and emanation of Brahman. (I. 4)

large a number of his fellow-beings as possible, the Rishi
calls for worthy seekers from everywhere :

[1]*May the Brahmacharins come unto me. Svāhā!*

*From here and there may the Brahmacharins come unto
me. Svāhā!*

May the Brahmacharins set forth unto me. Svāhā!

And for what immediate purpose?

May the Brahmacharins attain self-mastery. Svāhā!

May the Brahmacharins attain to peace of soul. Svāhā!

He is fully conscious that the Knowledge that he
holds, the Powers of Light with which his being bristles,
are not his own but are the Lord's and he seeks to keep
himself an untrammelled channel of His. He prays :

*O Gracious Lord, into that which is thou may I enter.
Svāhā!*

He knows that by himself he cannot rise high
enough, sustain himself there long enough ; his nature is
clamped with the triple knot of Ignorance and dogged
by the hold of Inertia. The Waters of the purifying and
uplifting Consciousness, the irresistible currents of Grace
have to flow into his being in torrents and cleanse and
release him out of his obstinate imperfections.

*Thou art a river with a hundred branching streams, O
Lord of Grace, in Thee may I wash me clean. Svāhā!*

Do thou also enter into me, O Shining One. Svāhā!

It is the Divine Lord who is to bend and take up
into Himself him who is striving to reach out to Him,
who by dint of *tapasyā* has arrived near his proximity but
cannot go further without His Grace.

---

[1] (I. 5)

O Lord, thou art my neighbour, thou dwellest very near me. Come to me, be my light and sun.

x   x   x

We are familiar with the three worlds of the Earth, the Sky and the Heavens to which the ancients applied the three great well-known terms, *vyāhṛtis, bhūr, bhuvar* and *svar*.[1] There is, says the Upanishad, a fourth with which they are intimately connected. That is the world of Mahas, the world of the Vast,[2] the Light, which we are told, was first announced by the Rishi Maha-chamasya. This is the *vyāhṛti* which is termed the Supermind by Sri Aurobindo, the Gnosis standing at the summit of this lower creation of the worlds of matter, life and mind. The Upanishad declares that this is Brahman itself, the very Self of the Manifesting Reality, of which the other worlds, the Gods presiding over them, are limbs. They live, increase and prosper by the Power of this Mahas which is compared to the Sun—Mahas is the source of Light (and fire) of the worlds. If the Bhur, earth, vibrates with the rhythms of the Riks, Bhuvar with the Saman and Svar with the Yajus, the Mahas pulsates with the vibrations of the Eternal Word which is at the root of all of them. Similarly, the several currents of the life-force that flow in the three worlds derive their sustenance from the world of Mahas which is like food to them. Mahas "is called the fourth world, because it is above the triple world of ours, *bhūh, bhuvah,*

---

[1] There are in all seven *vyāhṛtis* in the ancient conception of the Veda and the Upanishads viz. *bhūr, bhuvar, svar,* constituting this lower creation, *aparārdha* and the *jana, tapas* and *satya* of the higher, *parārdha,* with the world of Mahas in between. But the text before us deals with only the first four of them.

[2] *Mahas* is derived from the root *mah* which means the same as *bṛh,* to grow vast, grow without bounds.

svah. It stands between the two—between the higher triple world of the plenary Sat-Chit-Ananda above on the one hand and the lower triple on the other. It carries within it, above it, and one with it in a sense the higher triple, and it also releases the lower triple world through various agencies for the formation and perfection of the higher half—what is called Parardha—in terms of the lower, the created lower triple. Radically, it is this world of the Mahas that is responsible for the lower triple creation and it is from this world that forces of manifestation of the Many are released and set to play to work out certain possibilities of the Immense Intelligence and power of the Spirit in the finite formations of the world-being and Force-movement. Because its centre is charged with the infinitude of Sat-Chit-Ananda, it is one with it Above ; because its face is turned towards Manifestation, it is one with the Many that represent the self-limiting and self-conditioning attitude and capacity of the Supreme Spirit." (Sri Kapali Sastry)[1]

x   x   x

Brahman is, indeed, the All—these worlds which are his manifestations, himself the several gods Agni, Vayu, Sun etc. who sustain the respective worlds over which they preside[2] ; Speech, Sight, Hearing, Knowledge are but the functionings of his own emanations. The whole etherial Space in which the universe is spread is but one self-extension of Brahman ; Life and Immortality, Truth and Bliss are the very stuff of his being. And man can approach and realise Brahman in any of these forms. But the most direct and, in a manner, the easiest way is

---

[1] *Lights on the Fundamentals,* P. 42.

[2] Thus Agni is the God who presides over the material world, the Earth, Vayu over the Sky-World and Surya over the Heavens.

to find Him in oneself. In him, says the Upanishad, the
Immortal, the Radiant Person, Purusha, is there stationed
in the pure spaces of the heart. *He is there.* There one has
to delve and there gain identity with the Purusha who is
the Self at once of himself and also the Self of All. In
man, the mental being, in whom the awakened and active
consciousness normally centres itself and finds expression
on the mind level, the divine Delegate poises himself in
the characteristic form of the Mental Person, *manomaya
puruṣa*, and governs his becoming. But his essential
station in the individual is in the heart which is not to be
confused with the physical heart, but " the inner or
secret heart, not the outer vital emotional centre ",[1] the
subtler spaces within which defy the norms of material
space and open out into endless vistas as one pursues
their track in the Sadhana.

"This Atman who is too subtle for comprehension
like the Akasha is everywhere present, the universal
Being, the Creator who constitutes the worlds and beings
and directs them and their forces : He is at the same time
awake in the heart of things, seated within in the deepest
depths, in the heart of man, *antar hṛdaye.* Silent and un-
concerned, yet he is the Divine Being within transmitting
this Truth-Will to the luminous soul of the mental person,
manomaya puruṣa, embodied in the *prāṇa*, for its realisation and expression in the outer existence. He is smaller,
aṇīyān, than the smallest we can perceive or conceive of.
He is the Divine in the heart of every creature, the
Divine as the Individual but not a finite Being although
he founds Himself in the limited and the conditioned
existence, and supports the individuality as the Individual. For this self-differentiation, the self-limiting

---

[1] *Sri Aurobindo*

itself is an expression of the all-seeing Power of His
Infinite Being. He is greater, *jyāyān*, than the Earth,
the Sky, the High Heaven and all other worlds, greater
and vaster than the greatest and vastest of our comprehension. Both as subtle or small, *aṇuh* and great or large,
mahān, he transcends our understanding. He is therefore
the Beyond, the Transcendent, the Atman, who is also
the Universal Self and Godhead of all existence and in
all creatures, and is yet the same Self, the Self of my
being, *eṣa me ātmā*, the Divine Master of my individuality whose Truth-Will constitutes the poise and attitude
of the Purusha encased in the Mind with pranic body
for action and expression in the vast field of this created
Existence." (Sri Kapali Sastry)[1]

x   x   x

We said earlier that the mind of the seeker must get
trained to look and think in a clear and direct manner
which goes straight to the root of things. The text harks
back to this imperative need and to facilitate clear
thinking analyses the fivefold categories of the Universe,
world-wise, deity-wise, being (or element)-wise and
breath-wise, and sense-wise and substance-wise, and
points to their co-ordination.

As to the concentration of the mind, for centering
the consciousness progressively upon the Ideal of Brahman, there are many aids, a variety of supports
recommended to the seeker in the Upanishads. But the
most important and celebrated is the repetition of the
sacred syllable OM which is held to be the nearest sound-
approximation to Brahman and whose vibrations go to
open up the heights of the Supreme Self for the aspiring
consciousness of man.

---

[1] *Lights on the Upanishads,* Pp. 56-57.

OM is the Eternal, OM is all this universe. OM is the syllable of assent : saying ' OM ! let us hear,' they begin the citation. With OM they sing the hynms of the Sāma; with OM Shom they pronounce the Sastra. With OM the priest officiating at the sacrifice says the response. With OM Brahma begins creation.[1] With OM one sanctions the burnt offering. With OM the brahmin ere he expounds the Knowledge, cries ' May I attain the Eternal.' The Eternal verily he attains.[2]

The syllable OM has a special significance each, to the seeker, to the Jnanin, to the priest, to the grammarian. Sri Kapali Sastry points out, in the course of a profound discussion on the *Sphota and the Spoken Word :*[3] " ...the Primordial Eternal sensible Sound, which is the Immutable repository of Vibrant Intelligence whence spring the Vedas, all words of Wisdom and Works. . .is signified by the mystic syllable Om, which is as much a symbol as a living word expressive of the ' Immutable, supreme Ether or Akasha ' (*akṣaram paramam vyoma*). Here again, it is not the external aspect of the letter, but the inner sensible sound OM that raises the necessary set of vibrations to manifest the sense of the Supreme Being, Ishwara, in the consciousness of the utterer and the hearer. Apart from the inherent potency as the Sound-substance of all sounds, OM is used in the Sanskrit language as a word of affirmation and sanction. The Chhandogya Upanishad calls it *anujnākṣara*, the word

---

[1] Or, ' with OM the chief priest gives sanction.'

[2] ओमिति ब्रह्म । ओमितीदं सर्वम् । ओमित्येतदनुकृति ह स्म वा अप्योश्रावयेत्याश्रावयन्ति । ओमिति सामानि गायन्ति । ओं शोमिति शस्त्राणि शंसन्ति ओमित्यध्वर्युः प्रतिगरं प्रतिगृणाति । ओमिति । ब्रह्मा प्रसौति । ओमित्यग्निहोत्रमनुजानाति । ओमिति ब्राह्मण : प्रवक्ष्यन्नाह ब्रह्मोपाप्नवानीति । ब्रह्मैवोपप्नोति ॥ (I. 8)

[3] Vide *Sri Aurobindo : Lights on the Teachings,* P. 142.

of sanction or approval.[1] In classical Sanskrit and in conversation, it is a word of agreement or affirmation conveying the sense of ' O yes '....It is called Pranava because it is highly praised, *prakarṣeṇa nūyate iti praṇavah.* Undoubtedly, it is this Pranava, OM that represents the Eternal Word, *nityā vāk,* of the Rig-veda."

In the words of Sri Aurobindo : OM is "the mantra, the expressive sound-symbol of the Brahman Consciousness in its four domains from the Turiya to the external or material plane. The function of a mantra is to create vibrations in the inner consciousness that will prepare it for the realisation of what the mantra symbolises and is supposed indeed to carry within itself. The mantra OM should therefore lead towards the opening of the consciousness to the sight and feeling of the One Consciousness in all material things, in the inner being and in the supraphysical worlds, in the causal plane above now superconscient to us and, finally, the supreme liberated transcendence above all cosmic existence."[2]

Meditation, study and intellectual grasp of the truths in the sacred lore are not enough. There should be, says the Upanishad, a conscientious living out of the Veda. What one learns, one has to translate into practice ; not only make part of one's own life but also impart it to others aspiring for it, both by example and by precept.

Righteousness with the study and teaching of Veda; Truth with the study and teaching of Veda; askesis with the study and teaching of Veda; self-mastery with the study and teaching of Veda.

---

[1] The voice that chants to the creator Fire,
The symboled OM, the great assenting Word,
                    (*Sri Aurobindo* : *SAVITRI.* III. 2)

[2] *Letters*

16

Peace of soul with the study and teaching of Veda. The house-hold fires with the study and teaching of Veda. The burnt offering with the study and teaching of Veda. Progeny with the study and teaching of Veda. Joy of thy child's mother with the study and teaching of Veda. Children of thy children with the study and teaching of Veda—" these duties."

The text narrates how three different sages assevera-ted the primacy of their respective disciplines:

' Truth is first ', said the truth-speaker, the Rishi, son of Rathitara.

' Askesis is first ', said the constant in austerity, the Rishi, son of Purushishta.

' Study and teaching of Veda is first ', said Naka, son of Mudgala.

And it concludes:

For this too is austerity and this too is askesis.[1]

Indeed a study in the sense of enlivening in oneself the Knowledge-content of the Veda and the teaching of it in the sense of communicating to others what is thus made dynamic in one's own person, is a tapasya *par excellence.*

A splendid Hymn[2] voiced by sage Trishanku in the ecstasy of his illumined realisation is then held aloft before the seeker to give a vision of the Goal he is to strive for, of the State Beatific he is to progressively realise in himself. Here is the testament of his glorious arrival at Self-Knowledge:

I am He that moves the Tree of the Universe and my glory is like the shoulders of a high-mountain. I am lofty and pure like sweet nectar in the strong, I am the shining riches of the

----

[1] I. 9.   [2] I. 10.

world, I am the deep thinker, the deathless One who decays not from the beginning.

The Supreme Reality in manifestation, its manifold Creation, is often compared in the ancient traditions—Indian and non-Indian—to a gigantic Tree with innumerable branches and leaves. The Rig-veda speaks of the Tree out of which the Earth and the Heaven have been fashioned,[1] the Shvetashvatara Upanishad compares the One Purusha by whom all this is filled to an Immovable Tree,[2] the Katha refers to the Eternal Ashwattha Tree whose roots are above and branches downward[3] and the Gita repeats the very epithet describing the Cosmic Tree.[4]

Verily, he alone who has attained complete identity with Brahman, the immortal Source, the immanant Sustainer and the transcendent Overlord of Creation,

---

[1] क उ स वृक्ष : आस यतो द्यावापृथिवी निष्टतक्षु :   (X. 31.7)

[2] वृक्ष इव स्तब्धो दिवि तिष्टत्येकत्तेनेदं पुरुषेण सर्वम् ।   (III. 9)

[3] ऊर्ध्वमूलोऽवाक्शाख एशोऽश्वत्थ : सनातन :   (II. 3.1)

[4] ऊर्ध्वमूलमघ : शाखमश्वत्थं प्राहुरव्ययम्   (XV. 1)

Commenting on this passage, Sri Aurobindo writes : " First there comes a description of cosmic existence in the Vedantic image of the Aswattha tree. This tree of cosmic existence has no beginning and no end, *nānto na cādih*, in space or in time ; for it is external and imperishable, *avyaya*. The real form of it cannot be perceived by us in the material world of man's embodiment, nor has it any apparent lasting foundation here ; it is an infinite movement and its foundation is above in the supreme of the Infinite. Its principle is the ancient sempiternal urge to action, *pravṛtti*, which for ever proceeds without beginning or end from the original Soul of existence, *ādyam puruṣam yatah pravṛtti prasṛtā purāni*. Therefore its original source is above beyond Time in the Eternal, but its branches stretch down below and it extends and plunges its other roots, well-fixed and clinging roots of attachment and desire with their consequences of more and more desire and an endlessly developing action, plunges them downward here into the world of men....the branches of this cosmic tree extend both below and above, below in the material, above in the supraphysical planes." (*Essays on the Gita*, Second Series)

could speak in such assured accents as the *Mover of the World-Tree!*

Then follows the famous peroration by the Teacher who has declared the Veda, charging the disciple with injunction to live *fully*, to live a life of high purpose, not only given to the spiritual endeavour of his soul but embracing also his duties and responsibilities to his parents, to his elders, to the society in which he is born and from which he draws means for his progress, to the divinities who protect, aid and lead him to the Goal Supreme towards which he is pointed the way and given the means wherewith to advance. He commands:

Speak truth, walk in the way of thy duty, neglect not the study of Veda. When thou hast brought to thy Master the wealth that he desires, thou shalt not cut short the long thread of thy race. Thou shalt not be negligent of truth; thou shalt not be negligent of thy duty, thou shalt not be negligent of welfare ; thou shalt not be negligent towards thy increase and thy thriving; thou shalt not be negligent of the study and teaching of Veda.

Thou shalt not be negligent of thy works unto the Gods or thy works unto the Fathers. Let thy father be unto thee as thy God and thy mother as thy Goddess whom thou adorest. Serve the Master as a God and as a God the stranger within thy dwelling. The works that are without blame before the people thou shalt do these with diligence and no others. The deeds we have done that are good and righteous thou shalt practise these as a religion and no others.

Whosoever are better and nobler than we among the Brahmins, thou shalt refresh with a seat to honour them. Thou shalt give with faith and reverence; without faith thou shalt not give. Thou shalt give with shame, thou shalt give with fear; thou shalt give with fellow-feeling. Moreover if thou doubt of thy course or of thy action, then whatsoever Brahmins be there who are careful thinkers, devout, not moved by others, lovers of virtue, not severe or cruel, even as they do in that thing, so do thou. Then as to men accused and arraigned by their fellows, whatsoever Brahmins be there who are careful thinkers, devout, not moved by others, lovers of virtue, not severe or cruel, even as they are towards these, so be thou.

This is the law and the teaching. These are the Commandments. In such wise shalt thou practise religion, yea, verily, in such wise do ever religiously.[1]

The Section concludes with a chant of thanksgiving to the Gods who were fervently invoked at the outset. The disciple has been enabled by their Grace to receive the preliminary knowledge from the Preceptor, to perceive the lines on which his inner life is to be oriented and the corresponding mould in which even his outer life is to be shaped. He hymns his gratitude with a full heart:

Be peace to us Mitra. Be peace to us Varuna. Be peace to us Aryaman. Be peace to us Indra and Brihaspati. May far-striding Vishnu be peace to us. Adoration to the Eternal. Adoration to thee, O Vāyu. Thou, thou art the visible Eternal I have declared thee. I have declared Righteousness; I have declared Truth. That has protected me. That has protected the speaker. Yea, it protected me; it protected the speaker. OM! Peace! Peace! Peace![2]

And what is the High Knowledge, the Brahma Vidya, for whose reception the whole being of the aspirant is so meticulously processed? The succeeding Section, *Brahmānanda Valli,* provides the answer.

---

[1] I. 11
[2] I. 12

BRAHMANANDA VALLI

THE Brahmananda Valli commences with a solemn prayer to the Divine laying emphasis on the joint nature of the endeavour upon which the Teacher and the disciple are to presently embark. Between the Teacher who gives the knowledge and the seeker who receives it, there should be a complete harmony of understanding, an identity of seeking, even a union of being for the study to be fully fruitful in its result. Only thus can it be ensured that there is no diminution of the light and power, of the knowledge imparted, no misprision in the course of the communication. No disharmony of any kind shall depress the even course of their communion. With this purpose the prayer is hymned :

Hari OM. Together may He protect us, together may He possess us, together may we make unto us strength and virility. May our study be full to us of light and power. May we never hate. OM! Peace! Peace! Peace![1]

The text straightway plunges into the very heart of the subject.

The knower of Brahman, it declares, *reaches that which is supreme.*[2] And in anticipation of the natural query, ' But what is Brahman ? ' it proceeds to answer in the words of the more ancient seers :

Brahman is Truth, Brahman is Knowledge, Brahman is the Infinite.[3] Brahman is That which exists fundamentally, the Sole Truth from which all existences derive their

---

[1] हरि ओं । सह नाववतु । सह वीर्यं करवावहै । तेजस्विनावधीतमस्तु ।
मा विद्विषावहै । ओं शान्ति : शान्ति : ॥

[2] ब्रह्मविदाप्नोति परम् ।

[3] सत्यं ज्ञानमनन्तं ब्रह्म ।

ultimate significance. " Whatever reality is in existence by which all the rest subsists, that is Brahman. An Eternal behind all instabilities, a Truth of things which is implied, if it is hidden in all appearances, a Constant which supports all mutations, but is not increased, diminished, abnegated ", that is Brahman. But not that alone. Brahman is not merely the stubstratum of Truth that underlies all existence. It is also Knowledge, the Truth-awareness, the Consciousness that is inherent in the Truth-Being, and is spontaneously in possession of the truth of all things—absolute and supreme Knowledge. It is Knowledge one with its content, and its content embraces All since there is nothing outside this Self-aware Existence. And It is the Infinite. Brahman is *ananta*,[1] endless. Its endlessness includes, as Sri Aurobindo points out, all kinds of infinity. It is limited neither by Time nor Space both of which are only terms of Its manifestation. And more. " For by the Infinite we do not mean solely an illimitable self-extension in Space and Time, but something that is also spaceless and timeless, a self-existent Indefinable and Illimitable which can express

[1] It was not necessary for the German scholar Deussen to suggest that *ananta* may be an error handed down the generations and that the original word must have been *ānanda*—an idea which evidently occurred to him by the conception and repeated mention of *sat-cit-ānanda* in Vedantic literature. It is not a mistake. On the other hand there is a significance in the use of the term *ananta*. *Ananta* is the condition, *ānanda* is the consequence. For without *ananta*, endlessness, absence of limitation, no real *ānanda* is possible—*bhūmaiva sukham*, Immensity that is Felicity (Chhandogya Up. VII. 23). "Absoluteness of conscious existence is illimitable bliss of conscious existence ; the two are only different phrases for the same thing. All illimitableness, all infinity, all absoluteness is pure delight. Even our relative humanity has this experience that all dissatisfaction means a limit, an obstacle,—satisfaction comes by realisation of something withheld, by the surpassing of the limit, the overcoming of the obstacle. This is because our original being is the absolute in full possession of its infinite and illimitable self-consciousness and self-power ; a self-possession whose other name is self-delight. And in proportion as the relative touches upon that self-possession, it moves towards satisfaction, touches delight." (*Sri Aurobindo* : The Life Divine, Vol. I, Chap. XI)

itself in the infinitesimal as well as the vast, in a second of time, in a point of space, in a passing circumstance." It is not bound or limited either by the laws of Causality to which all phenomena are subject; there is absolute freedom in the immutability of Brahman.

This is the Brahman, the Eternal, to be *known*. Where is He to be found and known? He is not patent to the human eye amidst the myriad forms of the physical universe which crowd upon it.   He is to be sought behind the veil of forms and the search must proceed and be pursued from the more dense to the less dense layers of existence, from the less dense to the subtle and yet more subtle regions until one arrives at the sheer core of things where *hidden in the secrecy in the supreme ether*[1] Brahman awaits to be cognised and realised.[2]   This is the "hidden head of the Infinite and the secret heart of the Eternal.   It is the highest and this highest is the all; there is none beyond and there is none other than it. To know it is to know the highest and by knowing the highest to know all. For as it is the beginning and source of all things, so everything else is its consequence; as it is the support and constituent of all things, so the secret of everything else is explained by its secret; as it is the sum and end of all things, so everything else amounts to it and by throwing itself into it achieves the sense of its own existence.   This is the Brahman." (Sri Aurobindo)[3]

---

[1] निहितं गुहायां परमे व्योमन् ।

[2] O human copy and disguise of God
Who seekest the deity thou keepest hid
And livest by the Truth thou hast not known,
Follow the world's winding highway to its source.
There in the silence few have ever reached,
Thou shalt see the Fire burning on the bare stone
And the deep cavern of thy secret soul.
(*Savitri*, Book VII, Canto 3)

[3] *Readings in the Taittiriya Upanishad* (Arya, Vol. V, No. 4)

And it is possible to *know* this Eternal Brahman. The Reality determines itself, defines and reveals itself in certain Truths of its Being seizable by our consciousness and thus renders itself to be known. And Knowledge of Brahman is knowledge with a consequence. To know Brahman, the Upanishad has declared, is to attain to the highest. He who knows Brahman, it continues:

Enjoyeth all desires along with the wise-thinking Brahman.[1]

In the words of Sri Aurobindo: " The knowledge of Brahman is not a thing luminous but otiose, informing to the intellectual view of things but without consequence to the soul of the individual or his living; it is a knowledge that is a power and divine compulsion to change; by it his existence gains something that now he does not possess in consciousness. What is this gain? it is this that he is conscious now in a lower state only of his being, but by knowledge he gains his highest being.

" The highest state of our being is not a denial, contradiction and annihilation of all that we now are; it is a supreme accomplishment of all things that our present existence means and aims at, but in their highest sense and in the eternal values.

" The true knowledge is that of the highest, the inmost, the infinite. The knower of the Brahman sees all these lower things in the light of the Highest, the external and superficial as a translation of the internal and essential, the finite from the view of the Infinite. He begins to see and know existence no longer as the thinking animal, but as the Eternal sees and knows it. Therefore he is glad and rich in being, luminous in joy, satisfied of existence.

---

[1] यो वेद...सोऽश्नुते सर्वान् कामान् सह ब्रह्मणा विपश्चितेति ।

" Knowledge does not end with knowing, nor is it pursued and found for the sake of knowing alone. It has its full value only when it leads to some greater gain than itself, some gain of being. Simply to know the eternal and to remain in the pain, struggle and inferiority of our present way of being, would be a poor and lame advantage.

" A greater knowledge opens the possibility and, if really possessed, brings the actuality of a greater being. To be is the first verb which contains all the others ; knowledge, action, creation, enjoyment are only a fulfilment of being. Since we are incomplete in being, to grow is our aim, and that knowledge, action, creation, enjoyment are the best which most help us to expand, grow, feel our existence.

" Mere existence is not fullness of being. Being knows itself as power, consciousness, delight ; a greater being means a greater power, consciousness and delight. If by greater being we incurred only a greater pain and suffering, this good would not be worth having. Those who say that it is, mean simply that we get by it a greater sense of fulfilment which brings of itself a greater joy of the power of existence, and an extension of suffering or a loss of other enjoyment is worth having as a price for this greater sense of wideness, height and power. But this could not be the perfection of being or the highest height of its fulfilment ; suffering is the seal of a lower status. The highest consciousness is integrally fulfilled in wideness and power of its existence, but also it is integrally fulfilled in delight.

" The knower of Brahman has not only the joy of light, but gains something immense as the result of his knowledge, *brahmavid āpnoti.*

"What he gains is that highest, that which is supreme; he gains the highest being, the highest consciousness, the highest wideness and power of being, the highest delight; *brahmavid āpnoti param.*

"The Supreme is not something aloof and shut up in itself. It is not a mere indefinable, prisoner of its own featureless absoluteness, impotent to define, create, know itself variously, eternally buried in a sleep or a swoon of self-absorption. The Highest is the Infinite and the Infinite contains the All. Whoever attains the highest consciousness, becomes infinite in being and embraces the all.

"To make this clear the Upanishad has defined the Brahman as the Truth, Knowledge, Infinity and has defined result of the knowledge of Him in the secrecy, in the cave of being, in the supreme ether as the enjoyment of all its desires by the soul of the individual in the attainment of its highest self-existence.

"Our highest state of being is indeed a becoming one with Brahman in his eternity and infinity, but it is also an association with him in delight of self-fulfilment, *aśnute saha brahmaṇā.* And that principle of the Eternal by which this association is possible, is the principle of his knowledge, his self-discernment and all-discernment, the wisdom by which he knows himself perfectly in all the worlds and all beings, *brahmaṇā vipaścitā.*

"Delight of being is the continent of all the fulfilled values of existence which we now seek after in the forms of desire. To know its conditions and possess it purely and perfectly is the infinite privilege of the eternal Wisdom."[1]

---
[1] *Readings in the Taittiriya Upanishad* (Arya, Vol. V, No. 4)

This Supreme Reality is no absolute self-Being that exists only in transcendence of the universe. Brahman is not the Beyond alone. It is here, says the Upanishad, the Self of all existence and around this Self is the whole creation centred. Brahman is Atman—the Self. From the Brahman-Atman have issued all the existences in this Creation.

This is the Self, the Spirit, and from the Spirit ether was born; and from the ether, air; and from the air, fire; and from the fire, the waters; and from the waters, earth.[1]

From the most subtle to the utmost gross state of existence all are the modifications of this Self. The Manifestation of Brahman proceeds through an extension in graded self-modifications of its Being. Describing this process in regard to the creation of the physical universe, as viewed by the old Indian seers, Sri Aurobindo writes:

" The elementary state... is a condition of pure material extension in Space of which the peculiar pro- perty is vibration typified to us by the phenomenon of sound. But vibration in this state of ether is not sufficient to create forms. There must first be some obstruction in the flow of the Force Ocean, some contraction and expansion, some interplays of vibrations, some impinging of force upon force so as to create a beginning of fixed relations and mutual effects. Material Force modifying its first ethereal status assumes a second, called in the old language the aerial, of which the special property is contact between force and force, contact that is the basis of all material relations. Still we have not as yet real forms but only varying forces. A sustaining principle is

---

[1] II. 1

needed. This is provided by a third self-modification of the primitive Force of which the principle of light, electricity, fire and heat is for us the characteristic manifestation. Even then, we can have forms of force preserving their own character and peculiar action, but not stable forms of Matter. A fourth state characterised by diffusion and a first medium of permanent attractions and repulsions, termed picturesquely water or the liquid state, a fifth of cohesion, termed earth or the solid state, complete the necessary elements."[1]

And from Earth, physical Matter, issue the rest:

From the earth, herbs and plants; and from the herbs and plants food; and from food man was born.

Even man, the highest evolved creature that walks the earth, is a product of the physical substance of matter, what the text calls Food.

---

[1] *The Life Divine* (Vol. I, Chap. X)
Vide also *Savitri* (Book II, Canto V) :

> At first was only an etheric Space :
> Its huge vibrations circled round and round
> Housing some unconvinced initiative :
> Upheld by a supreme original Breath
> Expansion and contraction's mystic act
> Created touch and friction in the void,
> Into abstract emptiness brought clash and clasp :
> Parent of an expanding universe
> In a matrix of disintegrating force,
> By spending it conserved an endless sum.
> On the hearth of Space it kindled a viewless Fire
> That, scattering worlds as one might scatter seeds,
> Whirled out the luminous order of the stars.
> An ocean of electric Energy
> Formlessly formed its strange wave-particles
> Constructing by their dance this solid scheme,
> Its mightiness in the atom shut to rest ;
> Masses were forged or feigned and visible shapes ;
> Light flung the photon's swift revealing spark
> And showed, in the minuteness of its flash
> Imaged, this cosmos of apparent things.

Verily, man, this human being, is made of the essential substance of food.

Man comes into being with the birth of his body which is constituted of the essence and the modifications of Matter and he dies with the disintegration of that body of Matter. Whatever the other principles active in him like mind, life etc. they depend for their existence and functioning on the physical body and are, normally, wholly conditioned by it. Whichever way one looks at this human being in creation, horizontally or vertically, he is an evolute of Matter—Food. " Here in the material world everything is founded upon the formula of material substance. Sense, Life, Thought found themselves upon what the ancients called the Earth-Power, start from it, obey its laws, accommodate their workings to this fundamental principle, limit themselves by its possibilities and, if they would develop others, have even in that development to take account of the original formula, its purpose and its demand upon the divine evolution. The sense works through physical instruments, the life through a physical nerve-system and vital organs, the mind has to build its operations upon a corporeal basis and use a material instrumentation, even its pure mental workings have to take the data so derived as a field and as the stuff upon which it works." (Sri Aurobindo)[1]

Not only man but all creatures upon earth—we do not speak at the moment of worlds or planes other than earth where things can well be and are organised on a different basis—are visibly products issued out of Matter.

Food is the eldest of created things and therefore they name it the Green Stuff of the universe.

---

[1] *The Life Divine* (Vol. I, Chap. XXVI)

They come into being from Matter; they keep themselves in existence and increase by taking in more and more of the essence of Matter. And in the process of this 'eating' there comes an invasion; in the very process of the increasing there is a subtle decrease : something of the eater is automatically absorbed by the universal Matter through the portion that has entered into him. And when they thus decline and cease they dissolve again into the vast sea of Matter :[1]

Verily, all sorts and races of creatures that have their refuge upon earth, are begotten from food; thereafter they live also by food and it is to food again that they return at the end and last...

From food all creatures are born and being born they grow[2] by food. Lo, it is eaten and it eats ; yea, it devours the creatures that feed upon it, therefore it is called food from the eating.[3]

---

[1] *Vide*

> Matter on the firm earth sits strong and sure.
> It is the first-born of created things,
> It stands the last when mind and life are slain,
> And if it ended all would cease to be....
> A careful steward of Truth's limited means,
> Treasuring her founded facts from the squandering Power,
> It tethers mind to the tent-posts of sense,
> To a leaden grey routine clamps Life's caprice
> And ties all creatures with the cords of Law.
> A vessel of transmuting alchemies,
> A glue that sticks together mind and life,
> If Matter fails, all crumbling cracks and falls.
> All upon Matter stands as on a rock.
>
> (*Savitri*, Book X, Conto II)

[2] or, ' increase '

[3] II. 2

Matter is the one reality that strikes the eye and the seeker, says the Upanishad, must look upon this Matter as Brahman itself; Brahman has taken the form of Matter. "Brahman is not only the cause and supporting power and indwelling principle of the universe, he is also its material and its sole material. Matter also is Brahman and it is nothing other than or different from Brahman. If indeed Matter were cut off from Spirit, this would not be so; but it is...only a final form and objective aspect of the divine Existence with all of God ever-present in it and behind it." (Sri Aurobindo)[1]

And one who realises this truth of Brahman as Matter necessarily arrives at the secret of this material manifestation of the Spirit.

Verily, they who worship the Eternal as food, attain the mastery of food to the uttermost.

Now the Brahman-Being or Self which is related to and presides over this manifestation of the Physical principle in the Reality—*annam* of the Upanishads—is called the Annamaya Purusha. "Poised in the principle of Matter it (Spirit, Self or Being) becomes the physical self of a physical universe in the reign of a physical Nature; Spirit is then absorbed in its experience of Matter; it is dominated by the ignorance and inertia of the tamasic Power proper to physical existence. In the individual it becomes a materialised soul, *annamaya puruṣa*, whose life and mind have developed out of the ignorance and inertia of the material principle and are subject to their fundamental limitations. For life in Matter works in dependence on the body; mind in Matter works in dependence on the body and on the

---

[1] *The Life Divine* (Vol. I, Chap. XXV)

vital or nervous being ; spirit itself in Matter is limited
and divided in its self-relation and its power by the
limitations and divisions of this matter-governed and
life-driven mind.   This materialised soul lives bound to
the physical body and its narrow superficial external
consciousness, and it takes normally the experiences of
its physical organs, its senses, its matter-bound life and
mind, with at most some limited spiritual glimpses as the
whole truth of existence." (Sri Aurobindo)[1]

This, however, is not the whole truth of the matter.

Physical substance, Matter, provides indeed the
base, the hard rock of existence. But it needs something
else to vivify it, to enliven it. And that is done by
Prana, the Life-force. Without this life-element in it,
Matter is dead matter. Enlivening the physical form of
all entities in the universe there flows a life-energy,
'a constant act or play of the Force which builds up
forms, energises them by a continual stream of stimula-
tion and maintains them by an unceasing process of
disintegration and renewal of their substance.'[2]   It
envelops, it enters and constitutes the life-stuff of All :

*The Gods live and breathe under the dominion of Prana
and men and all these that are beasts; for Prana is the life of
created things and therefore they name it the Life-Stuff of the
All.*[3]

"...there is one all-pervading Life or dynamic energy—
the material aspect being only its outermost movement—
that creates all these forms of the physical universe, Life
imperishable and eternal which, even if the whole figure

---

[1] *On Yoga.* P. 531
[2] *The Life Divine* (Vol. I, Chap. XIX)
[3] II. 3

of the universe were quite abolished, would itself still go on existing and be capable of producing a new universe in its place, must indeed, unless it be held back in a state of rest by some higher Power or hold itself back, inevitably go on creating. In that case Life is nothing else than the Force that builds and maintains and destroys forms in the world ; it is Life that manifests itself in the form of the earth as much as in the plant that grows upon the earth and the animals that support their existence by devouring the life-force of the plant or of each other. All existence here is a universal Life that takes form of Matter." (Sri Aurobindo)[1]

Even as on the physical plane man has a physical nature governed by the physical *purusa*, soul, so also on this life level, there is a life-soul governing his life-nature. Brahman or Atman stations himself as the *prāṇamaya puruṣà* supporting and filling from within the outer *annamaya puruṣa*.

Now there is a second and inner Self which is other than this that is of the substance of food; and it is made of the vital stuff called Prana.   And the Self of Prana fills the Self of food . . . .

And this Self of Prana is the soul in the body of the former one which was of food.[2]

Of this Pranamaya Purusha the Upanishad says that *Prāṇa* 'the breath of life which brings the universal life-force into the physical system and gives it there to be distributed ', is the head ; *Vyāna* the breath that distributes and *Apāna* ' the breath of death which gives away the vital force out of the body ' are the twin sides ; earth, physical matter, is its base and foundation ; and ether is the very soul of its being, *ākāśa ātmā.*

---

[1] *The Life Divine* (Vol. I, Chap. XIX)
[2] II. 2, 3.

To quote Sri Aurobindo on the subject :

"....the spirit can be poised in the principle of Life, not in Matter. The Spirit so founded becomes the vital self of a vital world, the Life-soul of a Life-energy in the reign of a dynamic Nature. Absorbed in the experiences of the power and play of a conscious Life, it is dominated by the desire, activity and passion of the rajasic principle proper to vital existence. In the individual this spirit becomes a vital soul, *prāṇamaya puruṣa*, in whose nature the life-energies tyrannise over the mental and physical principle. The physical element in a vital world readily shapes its activities and formations in response to desire and its imaginations, it serves and obeys the passion and power of life and their formations and does not thwart or limit them as it does here on earth where life is a precarious incident in inanimate Matter. The mental element too is moulded and limited by the life-power, obeys it and helps only to enrich and fulfil the urge of its desires and the energy of its impulses. This vital soul lives in a vital body composed of a substance much subtler than physical matter, it is a substance surcharged with conscious energy, capable of much more powerful perceptions, capacities, sense-activities than any that the gross atomic elements of earth-matter can offer. Man, too, has in himself behind his physical being, subliminal to it, unseen and unknown but very close to it and forming with it the most naturally active part of his existence, this vital soul, this vital nature and this vital body; a whole vital plane connected with the life-world or desire-world is hidden in us, a secret consciousness in which life and desire find their untrammelled play and their easy self-expression

and from there throw their influences and formations on
our outer life.''[1]

And this too is Brahman. Prana is to be experienced and realised as Brahman itself, as a manifestation of
Brahman as Power, for its fullest potency to be dynami-
sed in oneself.

Verily, they who worship the Eternal as Prana, reach[2]
Life to the uttermost.[3]

Prana, the life-force which vitalises the physical body
does not, however, operate all by itself. It is not a blind,
mechanically active Force. It is informed, guided and
led by the operation of a principle of Consciousness.
Wherever there is life, there is behind it an operating
consciousness which in its awakened form is termed
Mind, *manas*. And the Atman as the Self of this Mind-
plane of existence is called the *manomaya puruṣa*. This
Mind-being is the leader of the life and body, *prāṇa śarira
netā*, as another Upanishad puts it.

*Now there is yet a second and inner Self which is other than
this that is of Prana, and it is made of Mind....And the Self
of Mind fills the Self of Prana...And this Self of Mind is
the soul in the body to the former one which was of Prana.*[4]

This Purusha of the Mind, says the Upanishad, is
constituted of the stuff of the Eternal Word in expression
in Creation—*Veda-ātman* (Shankara). The Word of
Illumination and the Word of Harmonies are its twin
sides and the Word of Execution is its head. The *vidhi*,
an imperative Directive to ever sacrifice and progress is
its centre and a settled, fixed flame of Aspiration is its
urging base.

---

[1] *On Yoga*, Pp. 533-34
[2] Or, ' attain mastery of '
[3] II. 3.
[4] II. 3, 4.

" Above matter and life stands the principle of mind, nearer to the secret Origin of things. The Spirit poised in mind becomes the mental self of a mental world and dwells there in the reign of its own pure and luminous mental Nature. There it acts in the intense freedom of the cosmic Intelligence supported by the combined workings of a psycho-mental and a higher emotional mind-force, subtilised and enlightened by the clarity and happiness of the sattwic principle proper to the mental existence. In the individual the spirit so poised becomes a mental soul, *manomaya puruṣa*, in whose nature the clarity and luminous power of the mind acts in its own right independent of any limitation or oppression by the vital or corporeal instruments; it rather rules and determines entirely the forms of its body and the powers of its life. For mind in its own plane is not limited by life and obstructed by matter as it is here in the earth-process. This mental soul lives in a mental or subtle body which enjoys capacities of knowledge, perception, sympathy and interpenetration with other beings hardly imaginable by us and a free, delicate and extensive mentalised sense-faculty not limited by the grosser conditions of the life-nature or the physical nature.

" Man too has in himself, subliminal, unknown and unseen concealed behind his waking consciousness and visible organism this mental soul, mental nature, mental body and a mental plane, not materialised, in which the principle of Mind is at home and not as here at strife with a world which is alien to it, obstructive to its freedom and corruptive of its purity and clearness. All the higher faculties of man, his intellectual and psychological being and powers, his higher emotional life awaken and increase in proportion as this mental plane in him presses upon him. For the more it manifests, the more it influences the physical parts, the more it enriches and elevates the corresponding mental plane of the embodied nature. At a certain pitch of its increasing sovereignty it can make man truly man and not merely a reasoning animal; for it gives then its characteristic force to the mental being within us which our humanity is in the inwardly governing but still too hampered essence of its psychological structure.

It is possible for man to awaken to this higher mental consciousness, to become this mental being, put on this mental nature and live not only in the vital and physical sheaths, but in this mental body." (Sri Aurobindo)[1]

The Mental Self is not the last word either. For in the very nature of things Mind is imperfect, incomplete and patently too limited in its field and power to be the ultimate Purusha of the manifestation, individual or universal. Mind is dependent. It cannot know or act by itself. It depends upon the senses and other faculties for its function. And what knowledge it thus acquires or forms is naturally circumscribed by the limitations of those instrumental agencies. That apart, by its own constitution, the human mind proceeds by a separative, analytic process of thought and can hence arrive at only partial truth of things. It is only a greater Faculty with a larger and other sweep of Vision and Power that can possess the Knowledge and the Secret of the Manifestation. And there is, says the Upanishad, such an active Principle, *Vijñāna*, and the Supreme Being expressing and governing it is the *Vijñānamaya Puruṣa*.

---

[1] *On Yoga*, P. 536.

Now there is yet a second and inner self which is other than this which is of Mind and it is made of Knowledge. And the Self of Knowledge fills the Self of Mind...And this Self of Knowledge is the soul in the body to the former which was of Mind.[1]

It is to be noted that the word *vijñāna* in the Upanishads does not signify what it has come to mean in the later day literature—*buddhi* or intellect. For the faculty of Intellect is included in the Mind of the Upanishadic conception. The Vijnana is the term for a yet higher principle in the cosmic manifestation; not even mind at its highest, it is above mind. This is what is called the Mahas in the ancient literature and the Supermind by Sri Aurobindo. The Mind is only a derivation of the *Vijñāna* which is a principle of Truth-Knowledge. "Vijnana, the principle of the world of Mahas, is neither the intellect, *buddhi*, nor knowledge of the intellectual kind, the mind. It is Knowledge indeed, but Knowledge proper to a higher grade of the Spirit's Being in its Self-extension in the supernal altitudes of Self-projection, a Knowledge immense with Power, or it is something that is at once Knowledge and Power or Knowledge that is Power. This is the Purusha, Vijnanamaya, the Supramental Person." (Sri Kapali Sastry)[2]

---

[1] II. 4, 5.

[2] *Lights on the Fundamentals*, P. 48.
    Vide also :

" One error of intellect-bounded thinkers takes *vijñāna* as synonymous with the other Indian term *buddhi* and the *buddhi* as synonymous with the reason, the discerning intellect, the logical intelligence. The systems that accept this significance, pass at once from a plane of pure intellect to a plane of pure spirit. No intermediate power is recognised, no diviner action of knowledge than the pure reason is admitted; the limited human means for facing truth is taken for the highest possible

And the Mental Self, the *manomaya puruṣa*, is filled in and supported by this Self of Knowledge. Of this Self, the Upanishad says in a shining image, Satya, Truth of Being, is one side and Rita, Truth of Action, the other; Faith, an invincible Truth-certitude[1] is the head and the Mahas, the Vast Light, its base. Yoga, union, a constant and spontaneous union with the heart of things is the spirit of its being. This is the *vijñānamaya puruṣa* which the Upanishad goes on to describe as He whose Knowledge-Power renders all activity, all sacrifice most widely effective and to whom,

All the gods offer adoration to him as to Brahman and the Elder of the Universe. For if one worship Brahman as the knowledge and if one swerve not from it, neither falter, then he casts sin from him in body and tastes all desire.[2]

To realise the Truth of this Knowledge-being, the Vijnanamaya Purusha, in oneself is to transcend the

dynamics of consciousness, its topmost force and original movement. An opposite error, a misconception of the mystics identifies *vijñāna* with the consciousness of the Infinite free from all ideation or else ideation packed into one essence of thought, lost to other dynamic action in the single and invariable idea of the One. This is the *caitanyaghana* of the Upanishad and is one movement or rather one thread of the many-aspected movement of the gnosis. The gnosis, the Vijnana is not only this concentrated consciousness of the infinite Essence ; it is also and at the same time an infinite knowledge of the myriad play of the Infinite. It contains all ideation (not mental but supramental), but it is not limited by ideation, for it far exceeds all ideative movement. Nor is the gnostic ideation in its character an intellectual thinking; it is not what we call the reason, not a concentrated intelligence. For the reason is mental in its methods, mental in its acquisitions, mental in its basis, but the ideative method of the gnosis is self-luminous, supramental, its yield of thought-light spontaneous, not proceeding by acquisition, its thought-basis a rendering of conscious identities, not a translation of the impressions born of indirect contacts." (*Sri Aurobindo* : On Yoga, P, 544)

[1] The Faith which the Vedic seers described as attainable by the yearnings of the heart : *sraddhām hṛdayyayā ākutyā vindate* and that which the Gods adore and draw upon. Rv. X. 151.

[2] II. 5

limitations and falsehood of the mortal nature in the Ignorance. In the words of Sri Aurobindo :

" In our perfect self-transcendence we pass out and up from the ignorance or half-enlightenment of our mental conscious-being into a greater wisdom-self and truth-power above it, there to dwell in the unwalled light of a divine knowledge. The mental man that we are is changed into the gnostic soul, the truth-conscious godhead, the *vijñānamaya puruṣa*. Seated on that level of the hill of our ascension we are in a quite different plane from this material, this vital, this mental poise of the universal spirit, and with this change changes too all our view and experience of our soul-life and of the world around us. We are born into a new soul-status and put on a new nature ; for according to the status of the soul is the status of the Prakriti. At each transition of the world-ascent, from matter to life, from life to mind, from mind bound to free intelligence, as the latent, half-manifested or already manifest soul rises to a higher and higher level of being, the nature also is elevated into a superior working, a wider consciousness, a vaster force and an intenser or larger range and joy of existence. But the transition from the mind-self to the knowledge-self is the great and the decisive transition in the Yoga. It is the shaking off of the last hold on us of the cosmic ignorance and our firm foundation in the Truth of things, in a consciousness infinite and eternal and inviolable by obscurity, falsehood, suffering or error."[1]

But even the self of Knowledge-Power is not the inner-most self. There is behind it, says the Upanishad, yet another Self which constitutes the soul of the

---

[1] *On Yoga,* P. 542

Vijnanamaya Purusha, in fact the ultimate core of all other Purushas, of all the tiers of manifestation.

Now there is yet a second and inner self which is other than this which is of Knowledge and it is fashioned out of Bliss. And the Self of Bliss fills the Self of Knowledge....And this Self of Bliss is the soul in the body to the former one which was of Knowledge.[1]

It is this Bliss or Anandamaya Purusha who makes possible the existence of all the other Purushas. Ananda, bliss, is the very nature of Brahman from whom all is derived; and it is from the fountain-spring of Ananda in its supreme ebullience that all creation issues forth, is motivated and maintained. The Self of Ananda is not supported by any other Self like the previous selves, but it is based, indeed arises directly out of Brahman of which it is the very nature. " Ananda, a supreme Bliss eternal, far other and higher in its character than the highest human joy or pleasure is the essential and original nature of the spirit. In Ananda our spirit will find its true self, in Ananda its essential consciousness, in Ananda the absolute power of its existence. The embodied soul's entry into this highest absolute, unlimited, unconditional bliss of the spirit is the infinite liberation and the infinite perfection." (Sri Aurobindo)[2]

Of this Self, a spontaneous Joy and Happiness are the twin sides; Love is its head, *priyameva śirah*—Love the culmination of Delight. It is this self-existent Bliss which flows out and over others and envelops them as Love.[3] Brahman itself is its direct base and Ananda—the Supreme Bliss, is the core.

---

[1] II. 5, 6

[2] *On Yoga*, P. 568

[3] *Vide*

" The Vedic Seers looked at Love from above, from its source and root and saw it and received it in their humanity as an outflowing of the divine

This is the well-known doctrine of the Five Koshas, the five sheaths of the five Purushas constituting the Personality in manifestation, individual and universal. These are the Five Persons, the Annamaya Purusha, Pranamaya Pursha, Manomaya Purusha, Vijnanamaya Purusha and Anandamaya Purusha, each ensouling the previous one, governing their respective Kshetras, fields of Matter, Life, Mind, Vijnana and Bliss, closely corresponding to the Five Peoples, *panca janāh*, of the Five Earths, *panca ksitīh*, in the ancient Veda.

Such are the gradations of the Reality in manifestation. Brahman, the Eternal, presents Himself on these several tiers of His Becoming. It is possible to realise Brahman on any of these levels of one's being. It is also possible to realise Him successively on all these planes and embrace Brahman in the full glory of His manifestation. Yet another realisation is also possible. Behind and basing this aspect of the Reality which we may conveniently call the Active Brahman, there is another— the Static Brahman, the Silent, the Immutable. When one seeks this Brahman, He is experienced as the Immobile, Ineffable and beyond all manifestation. The human mind when it approaches this status of Brahman is overpowered by its sense of Silence and Immutability and a strong, almost compelling sense of the unreality of everything else seizes upon it; it comes to take non-manifestation, non-existence as the ultimate Truth. The

Delight. The Taittiriya Upanishad expounding the spiritual and cosmic bliss of the godhead, Vedantic Ananda, Vedic Mayas, says of it, 'Love is its head.' But the word it chooses for Love, *priyam*, means properly the delightfulness of the objects of the soul's inner pleasure and satisfaction. The Vedic singers used the same psychology. They couple *mayas* and *prayas*,—*mayas*, the principle of inner felicity independent of all objects, *prayas*, its outflowing as the delight and pleasure of the soul in objects and beings." (*Sri Aurobindo* : On the Veda, P 568)

individual begins to look upon the world as unreal, or
at best as something inferior to the Immutable and
Ineffable Brahman and all his effort is turned to a
gradual withdrawal from this lesser truth of life activity
to the pure white heights of the Silence Beyond. Thus it
is that

*If one knows Him as Brahman the Non-Being, he becomes
merely the non-existent.*[1]

But as we have seen, that is only one side of the
truth. The Truth of Non-Being is not the whole of
Brahman. Brahman is equally and more patently the
Absolute Being, Absolute Consciousness and Absolute
Bliss. He is here manifest as and in the Universe which
presses upon our consciousness at every moment in a
thousand ways, constantly asserting the reality of its
Being. One who sees and recognises this fact, has
perceived the Truth, the real foundation of all existence.
And as he realises it and organises his life around this
perception, his life begins to acquire a new significance;
he becomes a centre of new values, one who radiates
and instils something of the positive Truth he is in
possession of and all creatures look to him as an
exemplar, as a Pillar to hold to amidst the bewildering
vicissitudes of the life of Ignorance to which they are
subject. Thus declares the Upanishad :

*If one knows that Brahman Is, then is he known as the
real in existence.*[2]

One becomes what he conceives. The aspirant who
seeks and strives to become one with Reality in its status

---

[1] असन्नेव स भवति ।   असद्ब्रह्मेति वेद चेत् । (II. 6)

[2] अस्ति ब्रह्मेति चेद्वेद ।   सन्तमेनं ततो विदुरिनि । (II. 6)

of Becoming, manifests and renders in his own being that Truth of Brahman in the measure of his realisation.[1] Even so, he who approaches It as the Immutable, the Silent, the Inactive, loses his being in that Immutability, Silence and Inactivity—the Nirvana, and cancels himself from the fact of manifestation around.

Be that as it may, be the faith and knowledge of man whatever it is during his life-time, does it make any difference after he dies? Is it not that both he who knows and he who does not know, the wise and the ignorant, are equal in death and both are overtaken by the same fate? The Upanishad takes note of this doubt likely to arise in the common mind. Does the man who has not the knowledge go to the world of Brahman when he passes? or does he fail to do so? Does the man of knowledge, when he sheds the body, go on to taste and share the riches of Brahman the Immortal,—the Knowledge, the Power, the Bliss?

When one who has not the Knowledge, passes over to that other world, do any such travel farther? Or when one who

---

[1] " Yoga is in essence the union of the soul with the immortal being and consciousness and delight of the Divine, effected through the human nature with a result of development into the divine nature of being, whatever that may be, so far as we can conceive it in mind and realise it in spiritual activity. Whatever we see of this Divine and fix our concentrated effort upon it, that we can become or grow into some kind of unity with it or at the lowest into tune and harmony with it. The old Upanishad put it trenchantly in its highest terms, ' Whoever envisages it as the Existence becomes that existence and whoever envisages it as the Non-existence, becomes that non-existence; ' so too it is with all else that we see of the Divine,—that, we may say, is at once the essential and the pragmatic truth of the Godhead. It is something beyond us which is indeed already within us, but which we as yet are not or are only initially in our human existence ; but whatever of it we see, we can create or reveal in our conscious nature and being and can grow into it, and so to create or reveal in ourselves individually the Godhead and grow into its universality and transcendence is our spiritual destiny." (Sri Aurobindo : *On Yoga*, P. 670)

knows, has passed over to the other world, does any such enjoy possession ?[1]

Yes, say the seers in emphatic terms ; the man who has realised, who has acquired the saving knowledge, goes from felicity to yet greater spiritual felicity. But not so the man who has failed. Though this particular Upanishad does not say it explicitly, there are other texts which declare in unmistakable terms that what one is determines what he shall be hereafter.[2] The world here and the worlds beyond are not separate. All is a connected, seried manifestation of the One Brahman. What is

----

[1] उताविद्वानमुंलोकं प्रेत्य ।   कश्चन गच्छती ३ ।   आहो विद्वानमुं लोकं प्रेत्य ।   कश्चित् समश्नुता ३उ । (II. 6)

[2] इह चेदशकद्बोद्धुं प्राक् शरीरस्य विस्रस: ।   तत : सर्गेषु लोकेषु शरीरत्वाय कल्पते ।

If in this world of men and before thy body fall from thee, thou wert able to apprehend it, then thou availeth for embodiment in the worlds that He creates. (*Katha Upanishad* VI)

अनुसयन्ति यथाकर्मं यथाश्रुतम् ।

According to their deeds is their goal and after the measures of their revealed knowledge. (*Katha Upanishad* V. 7)

इह चेद्वेदीथ सत्यमस्ति न चेदिहावेदीन्महती विनष्टि : ।

If here one comes to that knowledge, then one truly is; if here one comes not to the knowledge, then great is the perdition. (*Kena Upanishad* II. 4).

इहैव सन्तोऽथ विद्मस्तद्वयं न चेद्वेदीर्महती विनष्टि : । ये तद्विदुरमृतास्ते भवन्त्येतरे दु:खमेवापियन्ति ।

Verily, while we are here we may know this. If you have known it not, great is the destruction. Those who know this become immortal. But others go only to sorrow. (*Brihad. Upanishad* IV. 4.14)

कर्मानुगान्यनुक्रमेण देही स्थानेषु रुपाण्यभिसम्पद्यते।...क्रियागुणैरात्म-गुणैश्च तेषां संयोगहेतु :

According unto his deeds the embodied one successfully assumes forms in various conditions...(each) subsequent cause of his union with them is seen to be because of the quality of his acts and of himself. (*Shvet. Upanishad* V. 11-12).

done or happens in one world or on one plane of existence is attended by its inevitable sequel on the other levels. The Upanishad then proceeds to drive home this truth of all existence being the formation of One Reality by describing the emanation of the Universe out of the Being of Brahman.

It is out of Brahman, the Supreme Reality, that the All has issued. Why did it issue forth? Why did the Spirit, the One Brahman put out the Many? It is because of its own urge for a varied play of its self-delight. Blissful in its soleness of being, the Spirit would have Delight in a manifoldness of expression. " The self-delight of Brahman is not limited, however, by the

---

" Indeed, it is understood that the physical life is not the sole life and that the human soul does not end with its end, but continues its existence in another state of consciousness, in another plane of being corresponding to the condition and level of being it has risen to in the terrestrial existence. If man is to survive the physical death with a spiritual status, he has to establish in himself in the period of his bodily life on earth, points of contact with the higher powers of the Spirit, must have awakened and opened in him the subtle psychic and spiritual centres of knowledge and will communicating with the higher planes of being in other fields of Consciousness, in the supraphysical and still subtler and higher worlds that are the constituents of this Cosmos. For, thus and not otherwise, when the hour comes for the material body to fall or when the physical life has no further use for the Spirit, he can switch on to the light of his highest level, betake himself to the escalator of the Yoga Force that gives him the lift to those regions of the Spirit with which he has already familiarised himself in a way under conditions obtaining in embodied life on earth. This is a general law that holds good even in the case of one who has chosen—rather who is chosen for—the way of dissolution or absorption, laya, in the Being or a return to the Beyond that is absolved from all relations and conditions of being anywhere in the created existence. For the question of the states of the soul and survival does not arise at all in the case of one to whom realisation of Brahman is the absorption where he is, in the Absolute, and the very thought of this world or the next is out of question. But the man in whom the fire is not kindled for a life of the Spirit, gropes in the dark after death, revelling in things he ran after in embodied life; but only he who is able to know before the fall of the body is competent for a subtle and spiritual embodiment in other worlds." (Sri Kapali Sastry : Lights on the Upanishads, Pp. 45-46)

still and motionless possession of its absolute self-being.
Just as its force of consciousness is capable of throwing
itself into forms infinitely and with an endless variation,
so also its self-delight is capable of movement, of
variation, of revelling in that infinite flux and mutabi-
lity of itself represented by numberless teeming universes.
To loose forth and enjoy this infinite movement and
variation of its self-delight is the object of its extensive
or creative play of Force." (Sri Aurobindo)[1]

*The Spirit desired of old "I would be manifold for the
birth of peoples."*[2]

And what was the means of His manifold begetting?

*He concentrated all Himself in thought, and by the force
of His brooding He created all this universe, yea, all whatsover
exists.*[3]

Tapas-taptvā, by doing tapas. Tapas is the ingather-
ing of all of one's consciousness and concentrating its
force upon the object in view; as a result of this heat
of creative incubation there is a release of energy,
a dynamis which goes to effectuate the purpose under-
taken.[4]   Now, the Upanishad declares, Brahman

---

[1] *The Life Divine* (Vol. I, Chapter IX)

[2] सोऽकामयत ।   बहु स्यां प्रजायेयेति । (II. 6)

This is the same Desire, *Kāma*, that is spoken of by the Seers of the Rig
Veda :

कामस्तदग्रे समवर्तत That moved at first as desire within. (Rv. X. 129.4)

[3] स तपोऽतप्यत । स तप्स्तत्वा । इदं सर्वमसृजत । यदिदं किंच । (II. 6)

[4] "Tapas means literally heat, afterwards any kind of energism, askesis,
austerity of conscious force acting upon itself or its object.   The world was
created by Tapas in the form, says the ancient image, of an egg, which
being broken, again by Tapas, heat of incubation of conscious force,
the Purusha emerged, Soul in Nature, like a bird from the egg. It may be
observed that the usual translation of the word *tapasya* in English books,
'penance' is quite misleading—the idea of penance entered rarely into the

concentrated his consciousness-force to effect a manifold manifestation out of his Being and the Universe was the result. It is not to be thought that having produced, He left it to itself. Creating the Universe, He made a dwelling of it and expressed himself there variously.

Now when He had brought it forth, He entered into that He had created, He entering became the Is here and the May Be there.[1] *He became that which is defined and that which has no feature; He became this housed thing and that houseless; He became Knowledge and He became Ignorance; He became Truth and He became falsehood. Yea, He became all truth, even whatsoever here exists.*[2]

He became all that is here. But in that process He did not cease to be the Beyond. He is both what He ever was and will be, the *Beyond*, and the Here, what He has become. He is all that is in creation ; not merely in what is conceived to be the inherent aspects of Brahman, e.g. the Infinity, the Knowledge, the Good, but also in what appears to be their opposites. For Brahman being the One and the only one Reality, there could be no other which has taken these forms and no form could be born or exist outside of it. He is both the determinate and the indeterminate ; the form as well as the formless;

---

austerities practised by Indian ascetics. Nor was mortification of the body the essence even of the most severe and self-afflicting austerities; the aim was rather an overpassing of the hold of the bodily nature on the consciousness or else a supernormal energising of the consciousness and will to gain some spiritual or other object." (Sri Aurobindo : *The Life Divine*, Vol. II Chap. XII)

[1] Or, He became the existent and the beyond-existence.

[2] तत् सृष्ट्वा तदेवानुप्राविशत्। तदनुप्रविश्य। सच्च त्यच्चाभवत्। निरुक्तं चानिरुक्तम् च। निलयनं चानिलयनं च। विज्ञानं चाविज्ञानं च। सत्यं चानृतं च सत्यमभवत्। यदिदं किंच। (II. 6)

knowledge and the absence of knowledge—Ignorance ;
Truth and its opposite, Falsehood.

All that exists, says the Upanishad, is He. He is the
All and the All is He.[1]

Therefore they say of Him that He is truth.[2]

---

[1] The Vedantic seers, it may be noted, make no attempt to explain away
the existence of Ignorance and its sequel, suffering and evil, by divesting God
of all responsibility either by positing the principle of an Illusive Power, Maya,
or a manichean Duality. They are unequivocal on the point. God is all that
exists. " Sachchidananda of the Vedanta is one existence without a second ;
all that is, is He. If then evil and suffering exist, it is He that bears the evil
and suffering in the creature in whom He has embodied Himself." (Sri
Aurobindo : *The Life Divine*, Vol. I. Chap. XI) " To put away the responsibility for all that seems to us evil or terrible on the shoulders of a semi-
omnipotent Devil, or to put it aside as part of Nature, making an unbridge-
able opposition between world-nature and God-nature, as if Nature were
independent of God, or throw the responsibility on man and his sins, as if he
had a preponderant voice in the making of this world or could create anything
against the will of God, are clumsily comfortable devices in which the
religious thought of India has never taken refuge. We have to look courage-
ously in the face of the reality and see that it is God and none else who has
made this world in his being and that so he has made it. We have to see that
Nature devouring her children, Time eating up the lives of creatures, Death
universal and ineluctable and the violence of the Rudra forces in man and
Nature are also the supreme Godhead in one of his figures. We have to see
that God the bountiful and prodigal creator, God the helpful, strong and
benignant preserver is also God the devourer and destroyer. The torment of
the couch of pain and evil on which we are racked is his touch as much as
happiness and sweetness and pleasure. It is only when we with the eye of the
complete union can feel this truth in the depths of our being that we can
entirely discover behind that mask too the calm and beautiful face of the
blissful Godhead and in this touch that tests our imperfection the touch of the
friend and builder of the spirit in man. The discords of the worlds are God's
discords and it is only by accepting and proceeding through them that we can
arrive at the greater concords of his supreme harmony, the summits and
thrilled vastnesses of his transcendent and his cosmic Ananda." (Sri
Aurobindo : *Essays on the Gita*.) How came it to be that in this Creation
of Brahman who is Sat-Chit-Ananda, Infinite Existence, Consciousness and
Bliss, there is found such a dominant strain of Ignorance and Evil, is a large
question that has been dealt with at length by Sri Aurobindo in the pages of
The Life Divine.

[2] तत्सत्यमित्याचक्षते । (II. 6)

The Universe, then, is born *of* and *in* the Absolute Brahman.

In the beginning all this was Non-being. It was thence that Being was born.[1]

Before all this Existence came to be, says the Upanishad, there was only a Non-existence. And Non-existence, we must note, does not mean a Nothing or a Nil or a Nihil. For as the Chhandogya asks, how can anything arise out of nothing?[2] It can only mean a primal state, an Un-manifest, to which none of the terms of manifest existence can apply. It is something beyond all our conceptions of Being; and to emphasise this transcendence of categories of phenomenal existence it is called *non*-Being or *non*-existence. Sri Aurobindo points out:

" Non-Being is only a word. When we examine the fact it represents, we can no longer be sure that absolute non-existence has any better chance than the infinite Self of being more than an ideative formation of the mind. We really mean by this Nothing something beyond the last term to which we can reduce our purest conception and our most abstract or subtle experience of actual being as we know or conceive it while in this universe. This Nothing then is merely a something beyond positive conception. We erect a fiction of nothingness in order to overpass, by the method of total exclusion, all that we can know and consciously are. Actually when we examine closely the Nihil of certain philosophies, we begin to perceive that it is a zero which is All or an indefinable Infinite which appears to the mind a blank,

---

[1] असद् वा इदमग्र आसीत् । ततो वै सदजायत । (II. 7)

[2] कथं असत: सत् जायेत । (VI. 2·2)

because mind grasps only finite constructions, but is in fact the only true existence." And he observes, further : " Another Upanishad rejects the birth of being out of Non-Being as an impossibility ; Being, it says, can only be born from Being. But if we take Non-Being in the sense, not of an inexistent Nihil but of an *X* which exceeds our idea or experience of existence,—a sense applicable to the Absolute Brahman of the Adwaita as well as the Void or Zero of the Buddhists, the impossibility disappears, for That may very well be the source of being, whether by a conceptual or formative Maya or a manifestation or creation out of itself."[1]

Itself created itself ; none other created it.[2]

For the simple reason that there was no other than Itself.[3] Even the Tapas, the concentrated consciousness-power, the Shakti which was spoken of earlier as the efficient agency of manifestation is only a self-nature of Brahman. Thus is the universe Brahman-created *par excellence.*

Therefore they say of it the well and beautifully made.[4]

It is shaped out of the Being of Brahman– the Sat-Chit-Ananda—and naturally carries the characteristic nature of that which forms its substance. It is Brahman as Ananda that plunges into manifestation and it is this Ananda that goes to form the base and essence of all that is projected into this existence.

---

[1] *The Life Divine* (Vol. I, Chap. IV)

[2] तदात्मानं स्वयमकुरुत । (II. 7)

[3] तस्माद्धान्यत्र पर : किंचनास—there was nothing else nor aught beyond it. (Rig Veda, X. 129.2)

[4] तस्मात् तत्सुकृतमुच्यते । (II. 7)

Lo, this that is well and beautifully made, verily, it is no other than the delight behind existence.[1]

At the root of all creation is Bliss. " The self of things is an infinite indivisible existence ; of that existence the essential nature or power is an infinite imperishable force of self-conscious being ; and of that self-consciousness the essential nature or knowledge of itself is, again, an infinite inalienable delight of being.   In formlessness and in all forms, in the eternal awareness of infinite and indivisible being as in the multiform appearances of finite division this self-existence preserves perpetually its self-delight.   As in the apparent inconscience of Matter our soul, growing out of its bondage to its own superficial habit and particular mode of self-conscious existence, discovers that infinite Conscious Force constant, immobile, brooding, so in the apparent non-sensation of Matter it comes to discover and attune itself to an infinite conscious Delight imperturbable, ecstatic, all-embracing. This delight is its own delight, this self is its own self in all ; but to our ordinary view of self and things which awakes and moves only upon surfaces, it remains hidden, profound, subconscious.   And as it is within all forms, so it is within all experiences whether pleasant, painful or neutral.   There too hidden, profound, subconscious, it is that which enables and compels things to remain in existence.   It is the reason of that clinging to existence, that overmastering will-to-be, translated vitally as the instinct of self-preservation, physically as the imperishability of Matter, mentally as the sense of immortality which attends the formed existence through all its phases of self-development and of which even the occasional

---

[1] यद्वै तत्सुकृतम्। रसो वै स:। (II. 7)

impulse of self-destruction is only a reverse form, an attraction to other state of being and a consequent recoil from present state of being. Delight is existence, Delight is the secret of creation, Delight is the root of birth, Delight is the cause of remaining in existence, Delight is the end of birth and that in which creation ceases. ' From Ananda,' says the Upanishad, ' all existences are born, by Ananda they remain in being and increase, to Ananda they depart'." (Sri Aurobindo)[1]

The Supreme manifests Himself in an utter over-flooding of His Ananda for a diverse play of his potentialities; it is again this Ananda that supports as its bedrock all manifestation of which the evolutionary movement in which we are involved is a significant part. Life forms, persists and grows in spite of all factors contrary to its blossoming because of this principle of Ananda which feeds and sustains it from within :

For who could labour to draw in the breath or who could have strength to breathe it out, if there were not that Bliss in the heaven of his heart, the ether within his being ?[2]

And the Goal towards which the entire creation moves is a full and conscious partaking of this Delight by each individual in union with the One and the All here in terrestrial life. This is the true character of creation

---

[1] *The Life Divine* (Vol. I, Chap. XII)

[2] को ह्येवान्यात् क: प्राण्यात्। यदेष आकाश आनन्दो न स्यात्।

" A transcendent Bliss, unimaginable and inexpressible by the mind and speech, is the nature of the Ineffable. That broods immanent and secret in the whole universe and in everything in the universe. Its presence is described as a secret ether of the bliss of being, of which the Scripture says that, if this were not, none could for a moment breathe or live. And this spiritual bliss is here also in our hearts. It is hidden in from the toil of the surface mind which catches only at weak and flawed translations of it into various mental, vital and physical forms of the joy of existence. But if the mind has once grown sufficiently subtle and pure in its receptions and not limited by the grosser nature

and the life therein. It is due to Ignorance and its vitiating sequel that this truth is veiled from us. And in proportion as we over-pass this limiting Ignorance and grow into the wider Knowledge which opens to us the gates of the Ananda coursing behind our surfaces, we begin to perceive and experience the creation as a product of Delight.

When he has got him this Delight, then it is that this creation becomes a thing of bliss.[1]

" Such then is the view of the universe which arises out of the integral Vedantic affirmation. An infinite, indivisible existence all-blissful in its pure self-consciousness moves out of its fundamental purity into a varied play of Force that is consciousness, into the movement of Prakriti which is the play of Maya. The delight of its existence is at first self-gathered, absorbed, subconscious in the basis of the physical universe; then emergent in a great mass of neutral movement which is not yet what we call sensation ; then further emergent with the growth of mind and ego in the triple vibration of pain, pleasure and indifference originating from the

of our outward responses to existence, we can take a reflection of it which will wear perhaps wholly or predominantly the hue of whatever is stronger in our nature." (Sri Aurobindo : *On Yoga*, P. 677)

Vide also :

A secret of pure felicity
Deep like a sapphire heaven our spirits breathe ;
Our hearts and bodies feel its obscure call,
Our senses grope for it and touch and lose.
If this withdrew, the world would sink in the Void ;
If this were not, nothing could move or live.
A hidden bliss is at the root of things.
A mute Delight regards Time's countless works :
To house God's joy in things Space gave wide room,
To house God's joy in self our souls were born.

(*Savitri* : Book X, Canto 3)

[1] रसं ह्येवायं लब्ध्वानन्दी भवति । (II. 7)

limitation of the force of consciousness in the form and
from its exposure to shocks of the universal Force which
it finds alien to it and out of harmony with its own
measure and standard ; finally, the conscious emergence
of the full Sacchidananda in its creations by universality,
by equality, by self-possession and conquest of Nature.
This is the course and movement of the world." (Sri
Aurobindo)[1]

When one realises in one's own being this fact of
Bliss as the true character of all life, when one identifies
oneself with Brahman as Ananda, one embraces all as so
many currents of the one Sea of Brahmananda. He feels
one with his fellow creatures. There is no effective sense
of 'others' in his consciousness, with the result that the
actions and re-actions which are normal in the interchange between men and men as separate selves lose
their edge here. One no more needs to protect himself
from the invasive movement which comes from another ;
he has no more fear that the 'other' will harm and
devour him. For fear comes only when there is the other,
dvitīyād vai bhayam bhavati.[2] In his self-awareness, his
neighbour is not the other, but only another centre in
his own expanded being which is one with the Universal
Self.

*It is He that is the fountain of bliss; for when the Spirit
that is within us finds the Invisible Bodiless Undefinable and
Unhoused Eternal his refuge and firm foundation, then he has
passed beyond the reach of Fear.*[3]

---

[1] *The Life Divine* (Vol. I, Chap. XII)

[2] *Brihad. Upanishad* I. 4.2.

[3] एष ह्येवानन्दयाति । यदा ह्येवैष एतस्मिन्नदृश्येऽनात्म्येऽनिरुक्तेऽनिलयनेऽभयं
प्रतिष्ठां विन्दते । अथ सोऽभयं गतो भवति । (II. 7)

But, warns the Upanishad, for one who fails to unify himself completely with this Eternal, the Brahman, for one who in his imperfect knowledge maintains a distinction—however small and in whatever form—between himself and the One, there is still room for fear. Separativity in consciousness, however slender, creates a gulf between him and others, between him and the One who is the source of All. The One Himself in His immensity of Consciousness and Power has an over-powering effect on the limited and self-limiting individuality.

But when the Spirit that is within us makes for himself even a little difference in the Eternal, then he has fear, yea, the Eternal himself becomes a terror to such a knower who thinks not.[1]

x   x   x

The One not only creates but He also governs. It is the Imperative of this embodied Spirit that is being executed by the Gods who are the cosmic powers and personalities put out by the Godhead to work out His purpose. In the poetic imagery of the Upanishad:

Through the fear of Him the Wind blows ;
through the fear of Him the Sun rises;

through the fear of Him Indra and Agni and Death hasten in their courses.[2]

x   x   x

Brahman has been described as the Fountain of Bliss. Sheer Ananda is His nature. It is indeed ineffable;

---

[1] यदा ह्येवैष एतस्मिन्नदरमन्तर कुरुत। अथ तस्य भयं भवति। तत्त्वेव भयं विदुषोऽमन्वानस्य। (II. 7)

[2] भीषास्माद्वात: पवते। भीषोदेति सूर्य:। भीषास्मादग्निश्चेन्द्रश्च। मृत्युर्धावति पञ्चम इति। (II. 8)

21

yet, some idea of its vastness and intensity can be rendered to the mind in terms of the joy experienced in normal human life. For even the incomplete and mixed joy and pleasure of the mortal living in ignorance, are derived ultimately from this Delight; they are a diminution, though a deformation of the divine Ananda. And this is what the Upanishad now proceeds to do in working out, what has been aptly called a Calculus of Beatitude. Starting with as full a human joy as possible as its unit, the text goes on, step by step, to describe the degrees of Ananda that are attainable on higher and yet higher grades of existence in the scale of evolution as conceived by the ancient Indian mind.[1]

Let there be a young man, excellent and lovely in his youth, a great student; let him have fair manners, and a most firm heart and great strength of body and let all this wide earth be full of wealth for his enjoying. That is the measure of bliss of one human being.

Now a hundred and a hundredfold of the human measure of bliss, is the one bliss of men that have become angels in heaven.

This is the Bliss of those who, at the close of their earthly life, have become angels in heaven by virtue of their merit. But, the Upanishad adds, this bliss can also be of him (while here on earth) who has imbibed the Knowledge (of the Self) in the Vedas and

whose soul the blight of desire touches not.[2]

---

[1] II. 8

The depth and range of the Bliss is proportionate to the knowledge that one attains. As the vistas of Knowledge open wider and wider in the ascension of the soul, so do the seas of Ananda.

[2] श्रोत्रियस्य चाकामहतस्य ! (II. 8)

The higher Bliss comes naturally to the man who has grown into the liberating Knowledge and who is not subject to the hold of Limitation and its issue—desire and struggle.

A hundred and a hundredfold of this measure of angelic bliss is one bliss of Gods that are angels in heaven.[1]

Again, this too

is the bliss of the Vedawise whose soul the blight of desire touches not.

A hundred and a hundredfold of this measure of divine angelic bliss is one bliss of the Fathers[2] *whose world of heaven is their world for ever.*

And this is the bliss of the Vedawise whose soul the blight of desire touches not.

A hundred and a hundredfold of this measure of bliss of the Fathers whose worlds are for ever, is one bliss of the Gods who are born as Gods in heaven.[3]

And this is the bliss of the Vedawise whose soul the blight of desire touches not.

A hundred and a hundredfold of this measure of bliss of the first born in heaven, is one bliss of the Gods of work[4] *who are Gods, for by their strength of their deeds they depart and are Gods in heaven.*

And this is the bliss of the Vedawise whose soul the blight of desire touches not.

---

[1] Not those who have arrived at the status of angels by effort but they who are angels by birth.

[2] The Manes.

[3] Gods in their generality.

[4] God-Manifestation for specific purposes.

A hundred and a hundredfold of this measure of bliss of the Gods of work, is one bliss of the great Gods[1] who are Gods for ever.

And this is the bliss of the Vedawise whose soul the blight of desire touches not.

A hundred and a hundredfold of this measure of divine bliss, is one bliss of Indra[2], the King in Heaven.

And this is the bliss of the Vedawise whose soul the blight of desire touches not.

A hundred and a hundredfold of this measure of Indra's bliss is one bliss of Brihaspati,[3] who taught the Gods in heaven.

And this is the bliss of the Vedawise whose soul the blight of desire touches not.

A hundred and a hundredfold of this measure of Brihaspati's bliss, is one bliss of Prajapati,[4] the Almighty Father.

And this is the bliss of the Vedawise whose soul the blight of desire touches not.

A hundred and a hundredfold of this measure of Prajapati's bliss, is one bliss of the Eternal Spirit.[5]

And this is the bliss of the Vedawise whose soul the blight of desire touches not.

Note the repeated affirmation by the Upanishad that a seeker, while he still remains a human being, can

---

[1] Of the Overmental heights.

[2] Lord of the Heavens of pure mentality.

[3] The Master who gives the Word of Knowledge to Indra and the Gods.

[4] The Creator.

[5] Brahman the Absolute.

realise in himself each of the states of Beatitude in the higher grades of being provided he strives and equips himself thatwise.   This possibility which is ever present before man is not open to the other orders in Creation. They are what Sri Aurobindo calls typal beings who are fixed in the frame of their own perfection.   If they want to enlarge themselves and progress beyond their status by acquiring the characteristics natural to other gradations of the manifestation, they have to come down and strive on the Earth which is the appointed field of evolution and progress.

And so, it is to this Bliss of Brahman that the man who knows arrives.   Here is the clear answer of the Upanishad to the questions posed earlier as to what is the state in which the man of knowledge finds himself after death and what of him who hath not the know-ledge.

One who realises in himself the truth that his own self and the self of the universe are One, the greater

---

Max Muller's remarks on this passage are interesting :

" In giving the various degrees of happiness, the author of the Upanishad gives us at the same time the various classes of human and divine beings which we must suppose were recognised in his time.   We have Men, human Gandharvas, Fathers, born Gods, Gods by merit, Gods, Indra, Brihaspati, Prajapati, Brahman.   Such a list would seem to be the invention of an indivi-dual rather than the result of an old tradition, if it did not occur in a very similar form in the Shatapatha Brahmana, Madhyandina Shakha XIV. 7, 1, 31, Kanva Shakha (Brih. Ar. Up. IV, 3, 32).   Here, too, the highest measure of happiness is ascribed to the Brahmaloka, and other beings are supposed to share a certain measure only of its supreme happiness....

" The arrangement of these beings and their worlds, one rising above the other, reminds us of the cosmography of the Buddhists, but the elements, though in a less systematic form, existed evidently before.   Thus we find in the so-called Garg Brahmana (Shatapatha Brahmana, XIC, 6, 6, 1) the following successions : Water, air, ether, the worlds of the sky, heaven, sun, moon, stars, gods, Gandharvas, Prajapati, Brahman.   In the Kaushitaki Upanishad 1, 3 there is another series, the worlds of Agni, Vayu, Varuna, Indra, Prajapati, and Brahman."

truth that it is the same eternal Spirit who is embodied in himself as well as in the universe, is not extinguished the moment he dies. Withdrawing from the world of physical matter to the subtle and still more subtle levels of existence, in an ordered manner, he finally arrives at the inmost Self that is of Bliss. And by implication it is clear that the man without knowledge fails to reach this consummation.

The Spirit who is here in a man and the Spirit who is there in the Sun, it is one Spirit and there is no other. He who knows this, when he has gone away from this world, passes to the Self which is of food; he passes to this Self which is of Prana; he passes to this Self which is of Mind; he passes to this Self which is of Knowledge; he passes to this Self which is of Bliss.[1]

o   o   o

A comparative scale of the various grades of Ananda, in the order of evolutionary ascension, leading up to the Bliss of Brahman was presented in the foregoing section. But that was only to bring home to the enquiring mind something of the vastness and intensity of the supreme Ananda. But truly, says the Upanishad, this Bliss of Brahman is ineffable. Like the highest, the utter Brahman, His self-nature too is unseizable in terms of thought or speech. The scope of the faculties of mind is too limited by its very constitution to grasp and the expressive power of human speech too narrow in its range to describe the nature of this Bliss ineffable. As

---

[1] स यश्चायं पुरुषे। यश्चासावादित्ये। स एक:। स य एवंवित्। अस्माल्लोकात्प्रेत्य। एतमन्नमयमात्मानमुपसंक्रामति। एतं प्राणमयमात्मान-मुपसंक्रामति। एतं मनोमयमात्मानमुपसंक्रामति। एतं विज्ञानमयमात्मान-मुपसंक्रामति। एतमानन्दमयमात्मानमुपसंक्रामति। (II. 8)

they approach near to it, they lose their functioning and tend to dissolve:

The Bliss of the Eternal from which words turn back without attaining; and mind also returns baffled.[1]

He who has realised his oneness with Brahman, and thus knows by identity of his being the Bliss of Brahman, has no fear from anywhere because to him all is one Bliss; there is no break in his extension which creates the 'other' giving room for fear.

He fears not for aught in this world or elsewhere.[2]

He has risen above the dualities of pleasure and pain, good and evil. Good and Evil are values that are pertinent as long as one's consciousness is in a state of development where they are necessary to educate and process it towards its self-development. Once the individual transcends the belt of Ignorance in which good and evil, right and wrong, are the necessary signposts, they cease to be. To quote Sri Aurobindo, while on the subject:

" In ancient Indian spiritual thought there was a clearer perception....the practice of truth, virtue, right will and right doing was regarded as a necessity of the approach to spiritual realisation, but in the realisation itself the being rises to the greater consciousness of the Infinite and Eternal and shakes away from itself the burden of sin and virtue, for that belongs to the relativity and the Ignorance. Beyond this larger truer perception lay the intuition that a relative good is a training imposed by World-Nature upon us so that we

---

[1] यतो वाचो निवर्तन्ते। अप्राप्य मनसा सह। (II. 9)

[2] न बिभेति कुतश्चनेति। (II. 9)

may pass through it towards the true Good which is absolute. These problems are of the mind and the ignorant life, they do not accompany us beyond mind; as there is a cessation of the duality of truth and error in an infinite Good, there is transcendence."[1]

The knower of the Eternal moves and acts directly from the Base of Brahman-Knowledge, the Eternal Truth, and whatever he does is the Right, whatever he expresses is the Truth. It is the flawless, self-effectuating Truth that acts in him in its undeflected Power.

Verily, to him comes not remorse and her torment saying ' Why have I left undone the good and why have I done that which was evil ? ' For he who knows the Eternal, knows these and delivers from them his Spirit; yea, he knows both evil and good for what they are and delivers his Spirit, who knows the Eternal.

And this is Upanishad, the secret of the Veda.[2]

---

[1] *The Life Divine* (Vol. II, Chap. 15)

[2] एतं ह वाव न तपति। किमहं साधु नाकरवम्। किमहं पापमकरवमिति। स य एवं विद्वानेते आत्मानं स्पृणुते। उभे ह्येवैष एते आत्मानं स्पृणुते। य एवं वेद। इत्युपनिषत्॥ (II. 9)

BHRIGU VALLI

The Knowledge is declared, the Brahma Vidya communicated. The Goal pointed out is nothing less than the Highest, *param*. And that one can reach only by knowing the Brahman. Brahman is that which is Truth, Knowledge, Infinity. Brahman is the ultimate as also the intimate basis and secret of all existence and one who would be master of life must needs know this veiled Reality of Brahman. All is Brahman because all has issued out of Brahman. All the constituents that make up the manifold creation not only of this material existence, the Earth, but of the several other planes of existence, have manifested out of His Being, and He himself has entered into every form, into each formation thus effected and presides over its career. He is the Strength which underlies the existence of every entity, the core of Bliss which is at the root of every life— whether in the individual or in the universal. The Spirit, the Self that activates both is the same Brahman who is also the supreme Transcendent.

And the Self, this Reality of Brahman is and should be the object of all wise seeking. Where is He to be searched ? He is to be sought, says the Scripture,—in a significant and cryptic passage which contains the seed and essence of a whole line of occult and spiritual discipline—He is to be found in the 'cavern heart of being', in the subtle spaces of the heart of things.

This is the teaching, the high knowledge that has been imparted. But all knowledge, unless it is translated into terms of one's own consciousness, made a part of being, in a word, unless it is realised, remains a

mental acquisition, an addendum to the store of
impressions and reflexes which are gathered by the senses
and other faculties of the mind or at best an enlightenment which gives a certain clarity to thought and serves
as a background to life-activity. However, "the knowledge we have to arrive at is not truth of the intellect; it
is not right belief, right opinions, right information about
oneself and things,—that is only the surface mind's idea
of knowledge. To arrive at some mental conception
about God and ourselves and the world is an object good
for the intellect but not large enough for the Spirit; it
will not make us the conscious sons of Infinity. Ancient
Indian thought meant by knowledge a consciousness
which possesses the highest Truth in a direct perception
and in self-experience; to become, to be the Highest that
we know is the sign that we really have the knowledge.
For the same reason, to shape our practical life, our
actions as far as may be in consonance with our intellectual notions of truth and right or with a successful
pragmatic knowledge,—an ethical or vital fulfilment,—
is not and cannot be the ultimate aim of our life; our aim
must be to grow into our true being, our being of Spirit,
the being of the supreme and universal Existence,
Consciousness, Delight, Sachchidananda." (Sri
Aurobindo)[1]

How to realise the Teaching, to make the Truth
effective in one's own being? The Upanishad proceeds
in the last section, named after its central figure Bhrigu,
to indicate the lines on which this most important, the
practical part of the Vidya, discipline, is to be carried
out.

---

[1] *The Life Divine* (Vol. II, Chap. XVII).

VARUNI VIDYA

Bhrigu, son of the celebrated Teacher Varuna, aspired to know Brahman, the Truth Eternal, and approached his father for the knowledge:

Lord, teach me of the Brahman.[1]

The Rishis of the ancient times, we have already noted, did not give any ready-made solutions to the problems of their disciples. They rather gave them verbal hints, pointed the directions in which the object was to be pursued and inwardly helped them with the needed guidance and strength, overtly acting only on indispensable occasions. Thus did Varuna, the Teacher, reply:

Food, Prana and Eye and Ear and Mind and Speech— even these.[2]

Yes, each of them is the Brahman; you have to look upon each as a formulation of Brahman; look into and through them to the Reality they veil.[3] *Anna*, Matter, *Prana*, Life, the very sense-powers, seeing, hearing and speech, the Mind which presides over them—all these are the doors through which one can enter Brahman. And, he added, in order to give the disciple a sure touchstone on which to test the results of his effort:

Seek thou to know that from which all existences are born; whereby born they increase and into which they enter in their passing hence.

---

[1] अधीहि भगवो ब्रह्म । (III. 1)

[2] अन्नं प्राणं चक्षुः श्रोत्रं मनो वाचम् ।

[3] *Vide* Kena Upanishad (I. 2): That which is hearing behind the hearing, mind of the mind, the word behind the speech, that too is the life of the life-breath, sight behind sight.

For that is Brahman.[1]

Bhrigu was enjoined to seek for That alone which would fulfil the conditions of an Ultimate Truth. Any principle, any truth which did not answer to these criteria was to be naturally ruled out.

These were the instructions with which Bhrigu launched upon his spiritual adventure. He did tapas, he concentrated all of himself in an intense movement of thought and directed the pursuit of his enquiry on the lines indicated by the Teacher.

As a result of his concentrated effort he discovered that Brahman is nothing else than Matter itself.

He arrived at the Knowledge that Matter is the Brahman.[2]

This perception seemed to satisfy entirely the conditions enunciated by his father.

For from Matter all existences are born; born, by Matter they increase and enter into Matter in their passing hence.[3]

But his satisfaction was short-lived. He doubtless realised that Matter could not explain everything; by

---

[1] यतो वा इमानि भूतानि जायन्ते । येन जातानि जीवन्ति । यत् प्रयन्ति अभिसंविशन्ति । तद् विजिज्ञासस्व । तद् ब्रह्म । (III. 1)

Vide also the definitions of Brahman in other Upanishads, notably:

That which is the Luminous, that which is smaller than the atoms, that in which are set the worlds and their peoples, That is This,—it is Brahman immutable; life is That, it is speech and mind. That is This, the True and Real, it is That which is immortal: it is into That that thou must pierce, O fair son, into That penetrate. (Mundaka Up. II. 2)

Releasing and maintaining all the worlds, He finally drew them back into Himself. (Svet. Up. III. 2)

[2] अन्नं ब्रह्मेति व्यजानात् । (III. 2)

[3] अन्नाद्ध्येव खल्विमानि भूतानि जायन्ते । अन्नेन जातानि जीवन्ति । अन्नं प्रयन्ति अभिसंविशन्ति । (III. 2)

itself Matter is inert and needs something else to vivify
it. Also, Matter is found to be, on closer analysis, a
result, a concretisation of energy which is a movement
of a Force, not an original substratum. So he approached
the teacher again and prayed :

Lord, teach me of the Brahman.[1]

He was directed to repeat the effort, to continue the
tapas :

By askesis[2] *do thou seek to know the Brahman,*

for the Guru emphasised,

askesis is the Brahman.[3]

Tapas, askesis, is really one end, a projection of a movement of consciousness which when sufficiently deepened
or heightened, merges into the Being of whom Consciousness is the very nature. That is to say, the self-
concentration ultimately resolves itself into the basic
origin of the entity in concentration which is nothing else
than Brahman itself.

Bhrigu engaged himself in tapas and

He arrived at the Knowledge that Prana is the Brahman.[4]

*For from Prana all existences are born; born, by Prana
they increase and enter into Prana in their passing hence.*

Again he perceived that even Prana was not all-
sufficient. It evidently needed a direction, an intelligence
to guide it. He once again came to the teacher and on
his instruction concentrated his energies still further, and

---

[1] अधीहि भगवो ब्रह्म । (III. 2)

[2] Energism of Consciousness.

[3] तपसा ब्रह्म विजिज्ञासस्व। तपो ब्रह्म। (III. 2)

[4] प्राणो ब्रह्मेति व्यजानात्…(III. 3)

He arrived at the Knowledge that Mind is the Brahman.[1]

For from Mind all existences are born; born, by Mind they increase and enter into Mind in their passing hence.

Still he felt a lacuna and waited upon the preceptor who counselled yet another term of tapas. The disciple persevered and discovered that a higher principle than the Mind, a Power of Truth-Knowledge, *Vijñāna*, was the key.

He came to know that Knowledge is the Brahman.[2]

For from Knowledge alone, all existences are born; born, by Knowledge they increase and enter into Knowledge in their passing hence.

Even so, he felt his discovery incomplete. The source of all knowledge, of all power was that indeed, but was that all? Where was the secret urge of all these manifestations? What was it that impelled these various existences? He once again pushed himself further on and at last

He arrived at the Knowledge that Bliss is the Brahman.[3]

For from Bliss all existences are born; born, by Bliss they increase and enter into Bliss in their passing hence.

Thus did Bhrigu progressively realise in his own being that each of the principles that base and organise the several planes of existence,—Matter, the principle of the physical plane, Prana of the life region, Mind of the mental, Truth-Knowledge of the Higher planes transcending the Mind, and above all Ananda basing not only

---

1 मनो ब्रह्मेति व्यजानात्...(III. 4)

2 विज्ञान ब्रह्मेति व्यजानात्...(III. 5)

3 आनन्दं ब्रह्मेति व्यजानात् । आनन्दाद्ध्येव खल्विमानि भूतानि जायन्ते ।
आनन्देन जातानि जीवन्ति प्रयन्ति अभिसंविशन्ति । (III. 6)

its own worlds of Bliss but the whole of the Manifestation, —is a Truth of Brahman, but not the whole of It. They are several self-expressive formulations of the Being of Brahman put forth by its innate Consciousness-Force, so many vibrant strings that strike the Symphony of the Creative Delight of Brahman.

This is the lore of Bhrigu, the lore of Varuna who has his firm base in the highest heaven.[1]

The striking feature of this Vidya,[2] it will be noted, is that to arrive at a real, i.e. full knowledge of the Brahman, one has not only to gain identity with the highest state of Brahman-Being, but also to realise and assimilate in oneself the truth of each tier of His manifestation; for each principle in the Manifestation has its own Truth in the Creator-Brahman. Each is to be sounded to its depths and their several realities are to be realised and integrated in oneself if one is to attain to the whole Truth of Brahman.

To sum up, we cannot do better than recall the words of Sri Aurobindo :

" All insistence on the sole or the fundamental validity of the objective real takes its stand on the sense of the basic reality of Matter. But it is now evident that Matter is by no means fundamentally real; it is a structure of Energy : it is becoming even a little doubtful whether the acts and creations of this Energy itself are explicable except as the motions of power of a secret Mind or Consciousness of which its processes and steps of structure are the formulas. It is therefore no longer possible to take Matter as the sole reality. The material

---

[1] Known after the Teacher Varuna who communicated it.

[2] सैषा भार्गवी वारुणी विद्या। परमे व्योमन्प्रतिष्ठिता।

interpretation of existence was the result of an exclusive concentration, a preoccupation with one movement of Existence, and such an exclusive concentration has its utility and is therefore permissible ; in recent times it has justified itself by the many immense and the innumerable minute discoveries of physical Science. But a solution of the whole problem of existence cannot be based on an exclusive one-sided knowledge; we must know not only what Matter is and what are its processes, but what mind and life are and what are their processes, and one must know also spirit and soul and all that is behind the material surface : only then can we have a knowledge sufficiently integral for a solution of the problem. For the same reason those views of existence which arise from an exclusive or predominant preoccupation with Mind or with Life and regard Mind or Life as the sole fundamental reality, have not a sufficiently wide basis for acceptance. Such a preoccupation of exclusive concentration may lead to a fruitful scrutiny which sheds much light on Mind and Life, but cannot result in a total solution of the problem. It may very well be that an exclusive or predominant concentration on the subliminal being, regarding the surface existence as a mere system of symbols for an expression of its sole reality, might throw a strong light on the subliminal and its processes and extend vastly the powers of the human being, but it would not be by itself an integral solution or lead us successfully to the integral knowledge of Reality. In our view the Spirit, the Self is the fundamental reality of existence; but an exclusive concentration on this fundamental reality to the exclusion of all reality of Mind, Life or Matter except as an imposition on the Self or unsubstantial shadows cast by the Spirit might help to an independent and radical spiritual realisation but not to an integral and valid solution of the truth of cosmic and individual existence.

"An integral knowledge then must be a knowledge of the truth of all sides of existence both separately and in the relation of each to all and the relation of all to the truth of the Spirit. Our present state is an Ignorance and a many-sided seeking; it seeks for the truth of all things, but,—as is evident from the insistence and the variety of the human mind's speculations as to the fundamental Truth which explains all others, the Reality at the basis of all things,—the fundamental truth of things, their basic reality must be found in some at once fundamental and universal Real ; it is that which, once discovered, must embrace and explain all,—for " That being known all will be known " : the fundamental Real must necessarily be and contain the truth of all existence, the truth of the individual, the truth of the universe, the truth of all that is beyond the universe. The Mind, in seeking for such a Reality and testing each thing from Matter upwards to see if that might not be It, has not proceeded on a wrong intuition. All that is necessary is to carry the inquiry to its end and test the highest and ultimate levels of experience."[1]

x   x   x

The Upanishad then proceeds to warn the aspirant that in his zeal for attaining to Brahman in His utter

---

[1] *The Life Divine* (Vol. II, Chap. XV)

Vide also :

' It is true that when Matter first emerges it becomes the dominant principle ; it seems to be and is within its own field the basis of all things, the constituent of all things, the end of all things : but Matter itself is found to be a result of something that is not Matter, of Energy, and this Energy cannot be something self-existent and acting in the Void, but can turn out and,

purity or absoluteness, the universe around, the material formulation of His creative Consciousness-Force is not to be despised; in the flight of the soul, the body is not to be rejected, *annam na nindyāt, annam na paricakṣita.*[1]

So too Prana, the Life-force and the other principles in creation. They are all put forth on purpose from the One Source and are mutually interdependent. *Anna,* Matter is to be accepted, fathomed, its truth *vis a vis* the other manifestations of Brahman to be realised, and its potentialities fully developed;

---

when deeply scrutinised, seems likely to turn out to be the action of a secret Consciousness and Being : when the spiritual knowledge and experience emerge, this becomes a certitude,—it is seen that the creative Energy in Matter is a movement of the power of the Spirit. Matter itself cannot be the original and ultimate reality..

It is true again that Life when it emerges becomes dominant, turns Matter into an instrument for its manifestation, and begins to look as if it were itself the secret original principle which breaks out into creation and veils itself in the forms of Matter ; there is a truth in this appearance and this truth must be admitted as a part of the integral knowledge. Life, though not the original Reality, is yet a form, a power of it which is missioned here as a creative urge in Matter. Life, therefore, has to be accepted as the means of our activity and the dynamic mould into which we have here to pour the Divine Existence ; but it can so be accepted only because it is a form of a Divine Energy which is itself greater than the Life-Force. The Life-principle is not the whole foundation and origin of things ; its creative working cannot be perfected and sovereignly fulfilled or even find its true movement until it knows itself as an energy of the Divine Being and elevates and subtilises its action into a free channel for the outpourings of the superior Nature.

Mind in its turn, when it emerges, becomes dominant ; it uses Life and Matter as means of its expression, a field for its own growth and sovereignty, and it begins to work as if it were the true reality and the creator even as it is the witness of existence. But Mind also is a limited derivative power ; it is an outcome of Overmind or it is here a luminous shadow thrown by the divine Supermind : it can only arrive at its own perfection by admitting the light of a larger knowledge ; it must transform its own more ignorant, imperfect and conflicting powers and values into the divinely effective potencies and harmonious values of the supramental truth-consciousness.' (*The Life Divine,* Vol. II, Chap. XVI)

[1] III. 8. 7

for that too is thy commandment unto labour.[1]

Matter, the physical form depends upon the life-force to animate and sustain[2] it even as Prana depends upon the physical organism for its individual station and action and feeds upon it as a fire consuming its fuel. Similar is the interdependence between the Waters, the streams of conscious energy and the Life-Force which effectuates itself through them.

Emphasising the mutual relation of the worlds and the principles governing them the Upanishad points out, that the very Earth which is the fullest embodiment of the principle of *anna*, matter, is buoyed up, held in position by Ether, *ākāśa*, the vast extension permeated with *Life-Force;* but also this outspread, the expanse of Ether bases itself upon the pedestal of the Earth and feeds upon it.

Verily, earth also is food and ether is the eater.   Ether is established upon earth and earth is established upon ether.[3]

Each sustains the other.

Food is established upon food.[4]

x   x   x

All is the Divine, the Brahman. He confronts the awakened eye wherever it turns. His is the force that moves in the characteristic activities of Nature, animate

---

[1] अन्नं बहु कुर्वीत । (III. 9)

[2] *Vide* Brihad. Up. V. 12, 1, पूयति वा अन्नम् ऋते प्राणात् , Verily Matter decays without Life. Also Chhand. Up. VI. 11. 3. जीवापेतं वाव किलेदं म्रियते, Verily, indeed, when life has left it, this body dies.

[3] पृथिवी वा अन्नम् । आकाशो अन्नाद: । पृथिव्यामाकाश: प्रतिष्ठित : । आकाशे पृथिवी प्रतिष्ठता ।

[4] अन्नम् अन्ने प्रतिष्ठितम् ।

and inanimate, and His the Presence that lends significance to every particle in creation. The aspirant should equip himself to receive Him on all the levels, in all the extensions of the Cosmic Manifestation. And as he seeks he shall realise; for Brahman reveals himself in the manner of the seeking. In the ancient language of the text:

Pursue Him as Mahas, thou shalt become Mighty; pursue Him as Mind, thou shalt become full of mind; pursue him as adoration, thy desires shall bow down before thee; pursue Him as the Eternal, thou shalt become full of the Spirit. Pursue Him as the destruction of the Eternal that ranges abroad, thou shalt get thy rivals and thy haters perish thick around thee and kin who loved thee not.[1]

He is everywhere, indeed! But in you also,—the scripture repeats:

The Spirit who is here in man and the Spirit who is there in the Sun, lo, it is One Spirit and there is no other.[2]

And he who has imbibed and realised this High Knowledge does not decay and wither away in death like other creatures in the Ignorance. On the other hand, —proclaims the sacred text in one of the most memorable and inspired perorations in Indian spiritual literature— he attains a sublime liberation. When the time arrives for him to leave the terrestrial life, he withdraws from it in a masterly manner, passing in controlled steps from

---

[1] तन्मह इत्युपासीत । महान् भवति । तन्मन इत्युपासीत । मानवान् भवति । तल्लम इत्युपासीत । नम्यन्तेऽस्मै कामाः । तद् ब्रह्म इत्युपासीत । ब्रह्मवान् भवति । तद् ब्रह्मणः परिपर इत्युपासीत । पर्येणं म्रियन्ते द्विषन्तः सपत्नाः । परि येऽप्रिया भ्रातृव्याः । (III. 10)

[2] स यश्चायं पुरुषे यश्चासावादित्ये । स एकः । (III. 10)

state to state, each perfected, within, during the life-
time, till he arrives at his rightful destination of ineffable
Ananda :

*He who has this knowledge, when he goes from the world
having passed to the Self which is of food; having passed to the
Self which is of Prana; having passed to the Self which is of
Mind; having passed to the Self which is of Knowledge;
having passed to the Self which is of Bliss....*[1]

In the utter beatitude that is now his natural state,
he realises an untrammelled identity with Brahman in
each of His varied statuses, the transcendent, the cosmic,
the individual and

*Lo, he ranges about the worlds, he eats what he will, and
takes what shape he will and ever he sings the mighty Sama.
Ho! Ho! Ho! I am food! I am food! I am food! I am the
eater of food! I am the eater! I am the eater! I am he who
makes the Scripture! I am he who makes! I am he who makes!
I am the first born of the Law; before the gods were I am, yea,
at the very heart of immortality.   He who gives me, verily, he
preserves me for I being food, eat him that eats.   I have
conquered the whole world and possessed it, my light is as the
the sun in its glory!*[2]

Thus he sings, who has the knowledge.

---

[1] स य एवंवित् । अस्माल्लोकात् प्रेत्य । एतमन्नमयमात्मानमुपसंक्रम्य । एतं
प्राणमयमात्मानमुपसंक्रम्य ।   एतं मनोमयमात्मानमुपसंक्रम्य ।   एतं
विज्ञानमयमात्मानमुपसंक्रम्य एतमानन्दमयमात्मानमुपसंक्रम्य ।

[2] इमान् लोकान् कामान्नी कामरूपी अनुसंचरन् । एतत् साम गायन् आस्ते ।
हा३वु । हा३वु । हा३वु । अहमन्नमहमन्नमहमन्नम् । अहमन्नादो ३हमन्ना-
दो ३हमन्नाद: । अहम् श्लोककृदहं श्लोककृत् । अहमस्मि प्रथमजा
ऋतास्य । पूर्वं देवेभ्यो अमृतस्य ना३भायि । यो मा ददाति स इदेव
मा३वा: । अहमन्नमन्नमदन्तमा३ द्मि । अहं विश्वं भुवनमभ्यभवा३म् ।
सुवर्न ज्योती: । (III. 10) य एवं वेद ॥ इत्युपनिषत् ॥

It is not to be concluded however that a complete
identity with Brahman is possible *only* after the death of
the physical body.   It is possible to attain it here even
while living.   There are texts which describe the state of
the liberated man while yet on earth, e.g. *the Song of
Liberation*[1] in the very Upanishad we have now considered; or, as in the Gita[2] where it speaks of the *Mukta*
and his way of life: *brahmārpaṇam brahma havih brah-
māgnau brahmaṇā hutam ; brahmaiva tena gantavyam
brahmakarmasamādhinā*, Brahman is the giving, Brahman
the oblation, by Brahman it is offered into the Brahman-
fire, Brahman is that which is to be attained by Samadhi
in Brahman-action.

---

[1] I. 10

[2] IV. 24

READINGS IN THE
BRIHADARANYAKA UPANISHAD

READINGS IN THE
BRIHADARANYAKA UPANISHAD
I
THE HORSE SACRIFICIAL

Brihadaranyaka, the Great Aranyaka, belongs to the Shatapatha Brahmana of the Shukla Yajurveda. The concluding portion of this Aranyaka, covering six chapters,[1] is the famous Brihadaranyaka Upanishad which is considered to be one of the oldest of the Upanishads. The Brihadaranyaka is so called because it is great in its size, *bṛhatvāt*, and also great in its profundity. Brahman is the subject-matter and the Upanishad is remarkable for the varied approaches it makes to the subject and the diverse methods it chooses to expound to the human intelligence the absolute and infinite nature of Brahman. The language it speaks is old, figurative and symbolic, reminiscent of the speech of the ancient Veda. The technique it adopts links the esoteric lore of the mystics of the Vedic age—with its outer frame of ritual—to the formulations of the Mind of a later era.

The Upanishad is divided into three Books, *Kāṇḍas:* Madhukanda, Yajnavalkya or Muni Kanda and Khila Kanda. Of these the first, Madhukanda, covering the first two chapters, enunciates the Doctrine of Brahman who is the One Sole Reality with which the Self, Atman, is identical and of whom All this is a manifestation. It posits the Teaching, *upadeśa*. The Second Kanda

---

[1] The Shatapatha is now extant in two recensions, the Kanva and the Madhyandina ; and this Upanishad forms the last six chapters (3-8) of the 17th Kanda of the Kanva Shakha and chapters 4-9 of the 14th Kanda of the Madhyandina.

The six chapters of the Upanishad are each divided into Brahmanas, of which there are in all 47. Each Brahmana is further sub-divided by Acharya Sankara into verse groups, *kaṇḍikas.*

comprising the (3rd and 4th chapters) establishes the teaching by Reasoning, *upapatti* : negatively repudiating alternate positions and positively arguing, in terms of the intellect, to carry home the Message. The last Khila (supplementary) Kanda (the 5th and 6th chapters) gives the Practice, *upāsana*, to realise in oneself the Truth of the Doctrine propounded.

The Upanishad opens with a striking imagery recalling—or more correctly, continuing—the language of the earlier Rishis of the Veda who used the most external physical objects as symbols of the deeper truths operating in the cosmos. The figure here chosen is the Horse, the Horse of the Ashwamedha, the pre-eminent Sacrifice of that age. The Ashwamedha commemorates, to the mystics of the Vedic tradition, a landmark in the inner evolution of man : it signifies his transcending the bounds of the ordinary material life in Ignorance and passing into the wider altitudes of the reign of Spirit. The Life-Force, the dominating Power in the being of man, *aśva*, is consecrated and delivered into the charge of the Gods who preside over the destinies of men and the worlds. The imagery is cast on a cosmic scale. The Horse, *aśva*, signifying strength, force and speed in the symbology of these mystics, is the Universal Force of Manifestation at work in Creation.

Of this Horse, says the text, Dawn is the head. The Dawn i. e. the beginnings of life-motion, the impulse towards manifestation, is the leading part, the front that first shows over our world. The sun is the eye with which he looks at creation and sustains it with his truth-light. The wind is the life-breath which he breathes into the world. And fire, the universal energy, is the open mouth through which he swallows and consumes the enjoyments of the worlds of his making.

The Horse is not a figure of this gross material universe alone. For Time is his body, his substance : the very texture of his being is made of Time which is non-material, though it manifests in physical Space as it does in the other extensions of Space. Earth is his footing. The material extension of Earth is the feet, the foundation created by the Power in manifestation. The Mid-region, *antariksa*, is his belly wherein all is seized and consumed. Heaven, the freer spaces of ether, the domain of purer Mind, is his back, the part on which this manifest creation rests. The four Quarters are the flanks and the intermediate regions the ribs; the stars, the stellar systems constitute the hard bones and the sky is the very flesh of his body. Periods of Time, the Seasons governed by the movements of the sun and stars are his members; months and fortnights set by the moon are that on which he stands. Thus does the manifesting Power cover in its self-extension all the three worlds of our creation in the dimension of Time moving in Space.

Further, the loose strands of the rivers are the undigested food in his stomach, the flowing rivers which carry the essential waters to the ends of the earth are his veins; the mountains with their invigorating air and the streams that spring of them, are his liver and lungs; the growths of earth, the herbs and the plants are the growths, the hair, on his body. The rising of the sun, the awakening of life into the move of ascension is his front and the sun-set which lulls all into rest is the hind, the disappearing portion of his Body.

When he extends and spreads himself there is the outbreak of light, the lightning in the skies : there manifests the light of Knowledge. When he shakes himself

out of rest and readies for action, there is the reverbera-
tion of sound, the thunder in the clouds : the manifestation of Power.   And when he rejects the waste-matter
from his body there ensues the downpour of life-giving
waters in the world.

His is the Voice that finds expression in the *vāk*, the
Word that is loaded with thought-content and creative
urge.

Great   as   he   is,   his   appearance   is   heralded   by   a
greatness, *mahimā*, in his front even as his passing is
trailed by a greatness behind.   Day is the grandeur
that appears with his advent, Night the grandeur that
follows his leaving—Day and Night being a constant
figure in this Thought, for the manifestation and
withdrawal into non-manifestation of the Eternal.
The grandeur that is the Day is born in the Eastern
Waters of the Infinite and the grandeur that is the
Night in the Western Waters.   The Cosmic Horse
stands in between linking both, the Manifest and the
Unmanifest, the Being and the Non-being.

Again, it is this Horse, this Universal Power that
carries on his back the several orders of creation
(represented by their typical beings) that are released
into manifestation, varying his strength, force and speed
to suit their different formulations of consciousness-
force.   He bears the Gods—fulfilled in their plentitude
—as the *haya*, one of delightful, abandoned and swift
movement ; as *vājin*, the horse of plentiful strength and
force, he carries the Gandharvas, beings of joy, beauty
and ease ; as *arvan*, the fighter-force, he bears the
Titans in their endless struggle for supremacy ; and as
aśva, consuming Force of strength, he adapts himself
to man, the creature who dies as he eats.

Finally, says the seer with great significance, of
this Horse the Sea is the brother and Sea is the place
of birth.[1] The Sea is the *sindhu* of the Veda, the
Upper Ocean, the *parārdha* from which derives this
lower ocean of ours, the *aparārdha*—figured here in the
image of the Horse of the Worlds—and whose Nature
is the same as the essential nature of his lower projection of itself, brother to it. And in this oneness of
Being and unity in Becoming lies the means of delive-
rance for the Horse of this Creation from subjection
to the *Hunger that is Death, aśanāya mṛtyu,* which is the
subject-matter of the next Brahmana.

To recapitulate this magnificent meditation as
rendered by Sri Aurobindo from the terse original in
Sanskrit:

"Dawn is the head of the horse sacrificial. The sun
is his eye, his breath is the wind, his wide open mouth is
Fire, the universal energy, Time is the self of the horse
sacrificial. Heaven is his back and the mid-region is his
belly, Earth is his footing, the quarters are his flanks and
these intermediate regions are his ribs; the seasons are
his members, the months and the half-months are that
on which he stands, the stars are his bones and the sky is
the flesh of his body. The strands are the food in his
belly, the rivers are his veins, the mountains are his liver
and lungs, herbs and plants are the hairs of his body;
the rising day is his front portion and the setting day is
his hinder portion. When he stretches himself, then it
lightens; when he shakes himself, then it thunders; when
he urines, then it rains. Speech verily is the voice of him.
Day was the grandeur that was born before the horse as

---

[1] The *aśva* i.e. Force, is always born of *āpah*, the Waters of Consciousness,
apsu yonirvā aśvah. (Taitt. Br. III. 8-4)

he galloped, the Eastern Ocean gave it birth. Night was the grandeur that was born in his rear and its birth was in the Western waters. These were the grandeurs that arose into being on either side of the horse. He became Haya and carried the gods,—Vajin and bore the Gandharvas,—Arvan and bore the Titans,—Ashva and carried mankind. The sea was his brother and the sea his birthplace."

HUNGER THAT IS DEATH

In the last section we spoke of the Force of Enjoyment which consumes while it enjoys, the characteristic
feature of this order of Creation. This Brahmana[1]
enlarges upon its role in the birth and the evolution of
the material world. Leaving aside the obviously ritualistic elements which are not germane to our present study
which is confined to the *Brahmavidyā,* the Science of the
Soul, the central burthen of the Upanishad, we shall now
follow the text in its account of the creation of the World
with which the second section commences.

In the beginning nothing whatsoever was here[2]. All
was covered with a Hunger, a Hunger that is Death. It
was a Hunger, a Desire[3] to spread out and enjoy in its
bliss, a Lust to manifest that was the origin of this world.
This Desire sought an embodiment; it needed a body
for the organisation and working out of its Impulse. It
dwelt upon itself i.e. upon the Truth in itself in an
adorative contemplation and there ensued the Waters,
the streams of Consciousness-Force which uphold all
creations.[4] From these Waters, following a process of
self-condensation, there came to be the Earth, the solid
base for the manifesting Force to stand upon and act.
And then came Fire, the Energising-Force at the centre
of the evolution of this creation. This force of dynamism,
the Agni, is the very life-essence, innate power of the

---

[1] I. 2

[2] Cf. *Asat vā idamagra āsīt,* In the beginning All this was the Non-Being.
(Taitti. Up. II. 7) *Nāsad āsīt na sad āsīt,* Then existence was not nor non-
existence. (Rv. X. 129)

[3] *Evam ime lokāh apsu antaḥ,* Thus do these worlds lie in Water.
(Shatapatha Br. X. V. 4-3)

[4] *Kāmah tadagre samavartata,* That moved at first as Desire (Rv. X. 129)

manifesting Godhead. And, says the Upanishad, this
Godhead active in the form of Desire or Hunger that is
Death, at the root of all creation divided Itself into three,
each a God presiding over a different formulation of His
Force : as Aditya, the Sun (presiding over the Heavens
of the Mind), Vayu (over the Mid-region of the Life-
Force) and Agni (presiding over the Earth—the Material
extension). He is not only at the base and the centre,
but He stands spread out entire in the cosmic extension,
manifest on each level in a different and appropriate
form, but active everywhere for the same end, for advanc-
ing and self-fulfilling career of the Divine Being on the
move.

He then desired to multiply. For this purpose He
activated His Word-Potential by the conscious force of
His Intelligence, And Time was conceived. Ere this
there was no duration of Time. He held the Time-seed
in incubation for a full period and then was Time born.
And out of Time errupted the Speech, *vāk*. Still there
was not yet a multiplicity for the enjoyment of a varied
manifestation and relation. So from the depths of this
revealed Word He brought out the whole world : the
creative rhythms of the Veda, the mode of Sacrifice to
sustain the world with its myriad creatures—men and
animals. And after this Creation of His self-projection
was complete, He commenced to eat it i.e. to enjoy it.
For indeed, all this is created, manifested, for His
Delight, for His Lila. Infinite, He eats infinitely, *sarvam
va atti it aditi.*

Again, He desired to sacrifice, to lend Himself for
further becoming. To the exclusion of His other self-
formulations, He concentrated and brooded upon his
developing body to render it fit for the great Sacrifice.

And with the maturity of Time He sacrificed His own Body to Himself the Godhead presiding over this creation. And lesser creatures He offered to the emanations of the Godhead, the gods participating in the Manifestation.

Thus are Fire, the Sacrifice (of the embodied World-Force), the Horse and Death one Divinity. He who *knows*, he who realises this truth in himself becomes that very God with death for his limb, a process of his living.

III

MEDITATION ON PRANA

Life, *prāṇa*, is the link between Spirit and Matter. It is the Life-Force that energises this manifestation and keeps it moving—*jagati*. And this Life-Force is not insentient, a product of matter. It is conscient, it is purposive in its operations. And that is so because the Life-Force is really a derivation, a projection of the supreme Consciousness-Force, Chit-Shakti of the upper hemisphere, the *parārdha*, in the lower triple world of mind-life-matter. As a facet of the Divine Shakti, the Life-Force, Prana, has been lauded again and again in the Upanishads and meditation upon Prana as born of the Self, indeed as the very Self, is a recognised means of attainment to the Supreme. We have seen in the first section of this Upanishad the importance attached to the consecration of the Life-Force, the Vedic *aśva*, to the Divine. This section[1] highlights the unique nature of this Force of Life and celebrates its glory by narrating a parable.

Of two kinds was the progeny of the Almighty Father : the shining ones, *devas* and the mighty ones, *asuras*. And what should be more natural than that the luminious children of light were outnumbered by the violent hordes of night! Both vied with each other for supremacy in the domains of manifestation of their Father. The Gods looked for a way to surpass the titans and in their innate wisdom saw that they could do it by resort to the *udgītha*, the chant of ascension, the vocal expression of upward aspiration, in a Sacrifice to the Supreme. Now the chant is to be vocalised by Speech

---

[1] I. 3

and so they approached *Vāk*, the organ of speech to give form to their common aspiration. Vak agreed and chanted. In so doing it provided the common enjoyment in the chant to the Gods but the rarer fruit of elegance it reserved for itself. The titans who were apprehensive of this move of the Gods, were on the wait for a loop-hole to strike and they got it in this egoistic self-reservation on the part of Speech and they smote it with Evil. This, says the text, is the evil that ever attaches to speech and becomes patent every time the improper is spoken.

Then the Gods approached the nose to chant. The nose chanted but it too appropriated the best for itself and gave room for the Enemy to strike ever tainting it with the evil of smelling the improper. Thus in turn the eye, the ear, the mind etc. were approached and each was found wanting and each was smitten with Evil by the Adversary. At last the Gods asked the Breath in the mouth, *āsanya prāna* or the Chief Breath, *mukhya prāna* of which all other pranas are functional operations,[1]

---

[1] " In the body of man there are said to be five workings of the life-force called the five Pranas. One specially termed *prāna* moves in the upper part of the body and is pre-eminently the breath of life, because it brings the universal Life-force into the physical system and gives it there to be distributed. A second in the lower part of the trunk, termed *apāna*, is the breath of death ; for it gives away the vital force out of the body. A third, the *samāna*, regulates the interchange of these two forces at their meeting-place, equalises them and is the most important agent in maintaining the equilibrium of the vital forces and their functions. A fourth, *vyāna*, pervasive, distributes the vital energies throughout the body. A fifth, *udāna*, moves upward from the body to the crown of the head and is a regular channel of communication between the physical life and the greater life of the spirit. None of these is the first or supreme Breath, although the prana most nearly represents it; the Breath to which so much importance is given in the Upanishads, is the pure life-force itself, first, because all the others are secondary to it, born from it and only exist as its special functions." (Sri Aurobindo : *Kena Upanishad*)

As the Prashna Upanishad puts it picturesquely : "As an emperor commands his officers and he says to one, 'govern for me these villages,' and to

to help them in their predicament. And this Breath of Existence gave the full-throated chant. The enemies rushed upon him. But like a clod of earth hurling against a solid rock, they were dashed to pieces. Shattered in all directions, the powerful enemies perished and the Gods, rid of their constriction, recovered their innate and original nature.

And the Gods naturally asked themselves, ' Where is he who has thus restored us to our Godhead ? ' They saw him in the mouth, *āsye antaḥ*, the Breath of the mouth, *ayāsya*, they perceived him to be the essence, the indispensable core of all the members of the body of manifestation—*angānām rasaḥ, āngirasa*.

This Life-Force is celebrated as the Deity *dur*, for Death is far from it, *dūram*, and far from one who knows it thus. It is again the Life-Force that thrusts the Evil, the very Death, far away from the Gods and casts it out into a region where none, neither Gods nor any other should venture lest one contact that Evil.

The Life-Energy, Prana Shakti, is the Dynamism that is capable of shooting across the belt of evil and death because it is in its very nature universal, infinite and by realising one's identity with it it is possible, through the inevitable shedding of the limitations of the individual ego-nature, to cross beyond death.

Once the Evil of death was banished, the Gods recovered their original nature. Speech became luminous[1] Fire, Agni ; for, Agni, forceful impulsion is

another, 'govern for me these others', so this Breath, the Life, appoints the other breaths each in his province." (III. 4).

Vide also : " I (Prana) dividing myself into this fivefold support this harp of God, I am its preserver." (Pr. Up. II. 3).

[1] Luminous above the reach of death.

what gives rise to the expressive Word, *vāk*. So did the Gods presiding over the faculties of smell, sight, hearing, come into their own, their uninhabited states of Air, Light, Ether or Space. And the mind recovered its innate Delight of the Moon, *soma*.

Then, continues the parable, the Prana sought and secured food for himself; for all food taken in by the body is really consumed by the Life-energy and food is indispensable to support its embodiment in the material frame. The other Gods asked for their share of nourishment. ' Gather round me ', said Prana and the Gods clustered around facing him. Hence the food eaten by Prana nourishes all the other Gods i.e., all the organs (over which the respective Gods preside). And that is so because it is on the strength of the Life-force that the life of the other organs depends.[1] They flourish with the waxing of Prana, the Life-Force, they decay with the waning of the Prana.

Not only is Prana the essence of all limbs, the feeder of all the Gods in the body, but he is also the Brihaspati. For Speech is the great Goddess, *bṛhati*, and Breath is the Lord, *pati*, of Speech. He is the Master of the potent Word that manifests all. He is also the Brahmanaspati, the conscious holder of the Creative word. And He is also the Saman, the Word of Harmonies. He is the one Life-Breath that extends equally in the tiny and the big, the white ant, and the elephant; it spreads over all the three worlds, over the whole universe. Indeed, he who realises this truth of the Supreme Breath attains union with it and extends himself wide with it.

---

[1] *Vide* Prashna Up. II. 4 : *tasmin utkrāmati athetare sarva eva utkrāmanti, tasmin ca pratiṣṭhamāne sarva eva prātiṣṭhanti.*

prāṇe sarvam pratiṣṭhitam. II. 6.

This too is the Udgitha, the upward chant of aspiration. It is this Breath that holds all aloft and impels all effort upwards. It is this Breath in the mouth that gives a full-throated expression to the will for ascent to the Divine. Perforce the Sound needs to be in rhythm with the Idea. And the voice that chants is impelled and held in flow by the Breath governing.

This is the true form of the Force of Life, Prana, and as such it should be meditated upon. One who realises the truth acquires the competence to receive and repeat in Japa[1] the Mantras to follow. This is the famous prayer embodying the ages-long aspiration of man to be delivered out of his petty life in Ignorance, out of its falsehood, darkness and death into the felicities of Truth, Light and Immortality:

From non-Being lead me to True Being, *asato mā sad gamaya;*

from darkness lead me to Light, *tamaso mā jyotir gamaya;*

from death lead me to Immortality, *mṛtyor mā amrtam gamaya,*

The life that is the mortal's is riddled with falsehood and perversion, it is an existence contrary to the real Truth of Being, a life in non-Being. All right effort is a tapasya to move from these moorings in the unreal, the Falsehood, to the one Existence in Truth, the True Being, Sat.

It is again the darkness of Ignorance and its issues of limitation and error that obscure the true purpose and

---

[1] termed *abhyāroha* because it makes one ascend towards the Divine, *ābhimukhyena ārohati anena japakarmaṇā evam vit devabhāvam ātmānam iti abhyārohah* (Shankara). One attains by this to the state of divinity, *devabhāvam anena ārohati* (Anandagiri).

functioning of life. All right effort is a tapasya to out-grow one's tutelage in Ignorance and emerge into the Light that leads and illumines.

Life is at every point denied by death which is the inevitable result of the falsehood and obscurity that clog its steps. All right effort is a tapasya to break through this thraldom to death and recover one's sovereignty in the deathless existence of the True Being, the Immortality of *Saccidānanda*.

This, verily, is the Meditation that wins the World Above.

IV

CREATION

Different Upanishads give different accounts of the Creation of the Universe. At times even in the same Upanishad there are more accounts than one. That is because of the different standpoints taken, the different Principles sought to be brought to the forefront and the various processes of Manifestation revealed to the spiritual experience of the Seers. Thus in an earlier section of this Upanishad, we were given an account of the Creation along the lines of certain fundamentals like Time, Sacrifice, Elements, *vāk* etc. In the present section[1] we begin in a different setting.

In the beginning was but the Self in the form of a Person. He looked around and found none else but himself. And he said, 'I AM'. That is why the Self came to be known as 'I' *aham*.

He was afraid. But then he asked himself : " Of what am I afraid ? There is none other than myself." And immediately he realised this truth, the fear was gone. For, what else was there for him to fear ? Fear can come only from another and there was no other.

When there is the other apart from oneself then there is room for fear from that other. Where there is no sense of other, the sense of separateness, but only a realisation of oneness, of the one 'I' throbbing everywhere, there is absolutely no fear, no grief. Says another ancient text : " How shall he be deluded, whence shall he have grief who sees everywhere oneness ? "[2]

---

[1] I. 4.

[2] " Being is one, Becomings are many : but this simply means that all Becomings are one Being who places himself variously in the phenomenal movement of His consciousness. We have to see the One Being...We have to

But he had no delight (of manifestation) and there-fore he desired a second.   He grew and grew as big as a man and woman together.   His own body he parted into two, the He and the She, who together make up the Whole.   From their union issued forth Mankind.

Then followed the game of hide and seek between the creative Person as the He and the She—the Lila of the Divine hiding Himself for the joy of discovering Himself.   She hid Herself becoming a Cow.   He became the Bull and the bovine creation ensued.   She concealed Herself as the Mare;   He became the Stallion and the horse race came to be.   Thus followed several orders of life creation down to the ant, each repeating the duality of Self-expression, the *mithuna*, on which all manifestation is founded.

Once the Creation thus came to be, He saw that He Himself was the Creation for indeed He had released it out of Himself.   To realise is to become : He became the Creation.   The Creation is He Himself.   And he who realises this truth of creation being none other than God Himself, says the text, becomes himself a creator for he is identified with the Creative Person.

---

see all becomings as developments of the movement in our true self and this self as one inhabiting all bodies and not our body only.   We have to be consciously, in our relations with this world, what we really are,—this one self becoming everything that we observe.   All the movement, all energies, all forms, all happenings we must see as those of our one and real self in many existences, as the play of the Will and Knowledge and Delight of the Lord in His world-existence.   We shall then be delivered from egoism and desire and the sense of separate existence and therefore from all grief and delusion and shrinking; for all grief is born of the shrinking of the ego from the contacts of existence, its sense of fear, weakness, want, dislike, etc. : and this is born from the delusion of separate existence, the sense of being my separate ego exposed to all these contacts of so much that is not myself." (Sri Aurobindo : *Isha Upanishad.*)

Next, the Creator proceeded to manifest Agni, the flaming Force that brings all into being, sustains them in existence and carries them forward on the strength of his impulsions. He is the God in charge of this creation based upon the Earth[1] peopled with its multitude of inhabitants, mobile and immobile. He was manifested and is ever manifest in the power of Speech issuing from the mouth and in the power of activity flowing from the hands. And it is because they are the sources of dynamic Agni, that both the hands and the mouth are free from the covering growth of the shoots of inertia and inconscience—the *hair*.

Like Agni, the other Gods that have come to be and govern the Creation, are all the manifestations of this Master Creator. Their very food of immortality, the Soma, is produced from the essence of His own Body. As Soma He forms the food ; as Agni He eats the food. Both the eater and the eaten who constitute the universe are Himself. Though He has subjected Himself to the conditions of mortal existence in the course of His manifestation, He has yet emanated out of Himself the Gods who are above the state of mortality, immortal. Such is His great Creation.

Naturally, in the beginning all was an undifferentiated mass. Nothing was distinct ; it was an indeterminate creation. It was only later in the course of the manifestation that there appeared Name and Form marking out and determining each from the other.

Nevertheless, in spite of its wondrous variety of Names and Forms the whole Creation is One. For its sustenance and support is One. It is the One Self that

---

[1] *agniḥ pṛthivīsthānaḥ*

has entered into these bodies up to the very tips of the finger-nails, like a razor lying in its case, like Vayu in the body (or like fire which sustains the world lying hidden in its source). Dwelling within, It can be seen only in its functional forms each of which can only give a partial picture of It. When It courses as the vital energy, It is named Prana; when It speaks, It is named the organ of speech; when It sees, It is the eye; when It hears, It is the ear; and when It thinks It is called the mind. All these are merely names according to Its functions. Seen only in one aspect or function, the Self is revealed but partially and to concentrate upon any one or other of these and meditate upon it as the sole truth is to miss That of which all these are merely operations. What is to be meditated upon is the Self, the Self alone, *ātmā iti eva upāsīta*; for in it, verily, all become one, all recover their unity. Once That is known, others are known through It, as they all derive from It and in a manner constitute It in its functional aspect. Therefore the Self alone is to be meditated upon, *ātmā iti eva upāsīta*.

And dear is this Self to every one. For it is the innermost in each. Being the most intimate core of oneself, this Self is dearer than a son, dearer than wealth, dearer than everything else. Everything else is subject to mortality, to the rule of death. But not so the immortal Self. That is why, knowingly or unknowingly, one clings to it, directly or indirectly. Meditate upon this Self as the Dear. Approach It as the lover nears his beloved. To one in love with this Self there is no loss for he is given to what is Imperishable.

And this Self, Atman, is none other than the Supreme Reality that is Brahman. To realise this identity between the Atman and the Brahman that is All, is surely to gain oneness with All. This is the eternal secret of becoming one with the All, the Universe, whether for men or for gods or for seers like Vamadeva whose cry broke forth: " I was Manu, I was Sun ".[1] Against such a one not even the gods can prevail for he is become their Self.

With this identity with the Self that is One in All, there is freedom, there is autonomy. But should one forget this truth and fall into a separative state, feel himself 'other' from another, then, verily, he becomes a *creature*. One who so worships a God thinking ' He is one, I am another', does not truly know. He loses his identity with the gods and lapses into servitude to them. And the gods, says the Upanishad with lofty irony, love to have men in slavery. For such men are like so many animals of service and who would like to lose them? That is why, perhaps, the gods prolong this disabling ignorance of men by lavishing petty gifts to keep them content with their lot. The gods do not like that man should awaken to the liberating knowledge and surpass them.

The Upanishad then proceeds to give an account of the Creation from another angle, the fourfold order of manifestation of the Divine Creator in His puissance : the Divine as Knowledge, the Divine as Power, the Divine as Production and Interchange, the Divine as Work and Service. It is this quadruple order of self-manifestation that truly bases the fourfold division of humanity into the man of knowledge, the warrior, the producer and the serf : Brahmana, Kshatriya, Vaishya, Shudra.[2] Not

---

[1] Rig Veda (IV. 26.1)

[2] There is a 'Wisdom in the supreme consciousness of the Divine that conceives the order and principles of things; there is the Power that sanctions

only in the collectivity of men is this broad classification universal, but these four Powers of divine Self-expression are also to be seen in each individual. "In the soul-force in man this Godhead in Nature represents itself as a fourfold effective Power, *caturvyūha*, a Power for know-ledge, a Power for strength, a Power for mutuality and active and productive relation and interchange, a Power for works and labour and service, and its presence casts all human life into a nexus and inner and outer operation of these four things." " Our life is at once an enquiry after truth and knowledge, a struggle and battle of our will with ourselves and surrounding forces, a constant production, adaptation, application of skill to the material of life and a sacrifice and service." (Sri Aurobindo)

In the beginning was Brahman alone, the premier embodiment of all Knowledge. But being alone he did not flourish, the manifestation could not get into the stride. So he created the glorious form of the Kshatriya, and these are the Kshatriyas of his creation : Gods Indra, Varuna, Soma, Rudra, Parjanya, Yama, Mrityu and Ishana. These are the King-gods who rule supreme and in whose discharge of royal duties none can question. Of course the Kshatriya derives from the Brahmana (one who is the becoming of the Brahman) and he acknowled-ges it in his general demeanour.

The projection of the Kshatriya was not enough. Creation still did not flourish. So were created the

and upholds it; then there is the Harmony that effects the proper arrangement of its parts and the Work that executes the direction given by the rest.   These Cosmic Principles are in their origins, character and functionings Divine and are ever present in the very body of the creative Spirit.   We can indeed view them as, the Divine as knowledge, the Divine as power, the Divine as production, enjoyment and mutuality, obedience and work.' (Sri Aurobindo)

Vaishya, those species of gods who are designated in groups : Vasus, Rudras, Adityas, Vishwedevas and the Maruts—the legions that work in association in furtherance of the object of Manifestation.

That too did not suffice and Brahman proceeded to create the Shudra : Pushan. Pushan in the Veda is the increaser, the fosterer who 'advances our chariot by his energy'. And that Pushan is this Earth, for it nourishes all this that exists.

Even the creation of gods did not prove sufficient. Brahman projected that glorious form, Dharma, the Law that holds and sustains, the Law of Truth which governs *all*, governs the mighty Kshatriya, protects the weak from the strong and ensures the right ordering of creatures. Note the supremacy of the Truth and its Way of becoming, the Law of Truth, over the very gods that are the direct issues of Brahman.

Having created these archetypes of the fourfold order among the gods, Brahman went on creating in that mould the four classes among men : they are the Brahman, Kshatriya, Vaishya and Shudra. Agni among the gods, He became the Brahmana among men. As Brahmana he conducts the pilgrim-sacrifice among men and as Agni he reaches their offerings to the gods. Through the divine Kshatriya was manifest the human Kshatriya, through the divine Vaishya the human Vaishya and through the divine Shudra the human Shudra. What was worked out first in the higher world was projected in the human as the general mould for manifestation of the Divine Being.

Such is the Self that has projected Itself. Upon this Self and its Becoming one should meditate and know It.

Should one depart from this world without this saving knowledge of the Self and its manifestation, he goes un-protected; all the acts of merit done during life-time cannot stand by him for long, for they too have an end. That is why it is imperative to meditate and know the Self and its manifestation. The fruit of this meditation knows no end ; it is permanent. One gains an identity with the Self and because of it wields a power also to project what one wills. He shares in the natural power of the Self to create and to manifest.

Whatever the number of the orders constituting the universe, whatever the multitudes in each class of creation, there is underlying all a common oneness, not only a oneness of origin but also of life and sustenance, even as of Goal. Throughout there is a comprehensive bond of mutuality in creation. By his self-offerings and sacrifices man is in communion with the gods. By his absorption of the Knowledge of the Veda and his chant of their Word, he draws upon the Rishis of yore. Offerings to the ancestors who have made his physical existence possible and desire to continue their line in his progeny relates him to the Manes. To men around he is ever a source of shelter and support. Not only to members of his own kind, but to other creatures of earth, water and air, he is a provider. All round there is a community of interests. And to him, says the Upanishad, who is conscious of this Oneness of creation and owns fealty to his fellow members, all—from the gods to the ants—wish well and do well.

This is the character of this multiple creation that has come to be from the One Self. The Self was verily Single, alone. It was moved to multiply itself by Desire, *kāma,* the sempiternal Desire to manifest what It held in

Itself.　It moved into the creative poise of He and She and cast Itself into an abundance of Name and Form—progeny and wealth—setting up the law of interchange, *yajña*, to promote the Creation.　Thus was laid the foundation of Desire which actuates, in varying forms, all activity.　Thus is all manifestation constituted of the originating Self, the creative executrix—the Wife, the Truth manifested—the progeny, the effort of exertion—*karma*, and plenteous sustenance to draw upon for the purpose—wealth.　Anything short of these means an incompleteness.　These are the five essential factors in creation.　Even personally, each man has these five components constituting his individual manifestation : his mind that leads is the self ; his speech that follows is the wife ; his life-force that multiplies is the progeny ; his vision is his human wealth[1] and his audience the godly wealth[2]; his body embodies his effort as it is the body that makes all effort possible.　And this quintuple Truth governs not only the *yajña*, Sacrifice, that under-lies this Manifestation but bases also its orders of animals, of men, indeed of all that is.

---

[1] for by sight he comprehends and apprehends his share in whatever is.

[2] for by his ear he receives the Word of Rhythms which ushers in the Plenty of the Gods.

V

THE SEVEN FOODS

Creation has come into existence. The worlds have been released. The Gods have been manifested. The Elements have been brought into being. The various classes of beings, gods, titans, men and animals, male and female, have come to be. The Upanishad now proceeds to describe[1] the creation of Food for the created, the means by which the creatures maintain themselves in existence.

By His power of concentration and the light of His Knowledge, the Almighty Father produced seven kinds of Food. Of these one is the food that is common to all eaters. It is the food universal which man shall not attempt to eat alone for himself. It is to be offered first to those Universal Powers to whom it belongs by right and then partaken as their leaving. No to do so is to contaminate oneself[2] with the evil of stealth.

The other two He apportioned to the Gods. These are the oblations in the fire and the offerings made otherwise to the Gods. Therefore it is meet that men should perform these acts of consecration, offering the best of themselves in the fire of godward aspiration and the dedication of everything that they do to the Gods above. Whether in times of prosperity or adversity, whether at the flow or at the ebb of the tide of life, the work of dedication and self-offering should continue. Only, desire shall not pollute this act of consecration.

---

[1] I. 5

[2] *kevalāgho bhavati kevalādi,* he who eats alone sins alone (Rv. X. 107. 6).

27

One He gave to the animals : it is milk, the fine product of life that builds up life at all levels of animal creation.   It is the yield of embodied life that sustains and furthers the growth of other embodiments. All that exists, articulate or not, lives on this yield of life. To merely offer milk in ritual is not to conquer death. One must be conscious of its character as the sap of all sustaining food and in offering to it to the Gods one offers the essential sustenance of his own life to the Gods and secures it (his life) in their hold. Indeed, in offering this 'milk' of life to the Gods one offers all food in essence.

And such food that is consecrated and offered to the Gods before it is partaken does not decrease. For it feeds and nourishes him who takes it as the sacred leaving of the Gods, altered in its character by their acceptance. He is nourished in his several bodies and in its strength and vigour he produces more food.   Thus it is that food eaten truly well multiplies itself. If it is not so eaten i.e. if it is not raised to its full potential by consecration and offering to its rightful owner and then received in the aspiring system, if it is simply appropriated to oneself and swallowed up in the manner of the animal, then food loses its strength and decays.   And with its decay, the man who eats it.

One who knows the true character of food, its just use and function as the means for the transmission of the substance of the Gods to man, he alone partakes of it in the pre-eminent way, the masterly way. In offering it to the Gods he offers himself; in receiving the consecrated food from the Gods he receives in himself their own godly substance.   He attains identity with the Gods and lives on their strength of deathless nectar.

And there were the Foods the Creator designed for Himself.   They are the Mind, Speech and Life-Force, *prāṇa.* They are the three means by which the Creator constantly draws upon, feeds himself in the Universe and they are also the means by which He grows and throws Himself in the manifestation.

Mind is the one factor that acts constantly behind the senses and their activities. One hears because of the mind behind the ear; one sees because of the mind behind the eye. Similarly, desire, resolve, doubt, faith or want of it, steadiness or want of it, shame, intelligence, fear—all these are but the formulations of the mind. Even when the senses are not active or otherwise engaged, the mind perceives and knows directly.

Speech, *vāk*, is another such ubiquitous Food of the Creator. Sound, *śabda*, is the Potential out of which all, *artha*, emerges. And every sound is but the *vāk*, of the Creator which gives form, shape, determines what is and what is to be. Essential food that it is, it can produce, reveal and determine but itself it cannot be determined.

The third omnipresent Food of the Creator is *prāṇa*, the Life-Force, the Consciousness-force active in the form of Life in creation. This Force that sustains life and multiplies life organises itself in five currents for the purposes of its functioning : *prāṇa*, the upper breath that is concerned with inspiration and expiration of the universal Breath, with the chest as its normal base of operation ; *apāna*, the lower breath engaged in the expulsion of what is not assimilated or not necessary in the system, functioning below the chest; *vyāna*, that which regulates both the *prāṇa* and the *apāna* and keeps them in harmony, the breath which sustains when *prāṇa* is held in abeyance as in actions requiring effort ; *udāna*, the breath that raises, goes up, rising from the feet to the head, the breath by which one can take one's stand above the body in meditation or the means by which one shoots above the head at the time of death ; *samāna* is what is concerned with digestion of what is taken in and has its seat in the stomach ; *ana*, is the general combined function of all these several activities and is spread all over the body.

The Self in manifestation bases Himself on these three Foods and acts. In fact they are only self-formulations of Himself for the purposes of manifestation. He constitutes Himself as Speech, as Mind, as Prana.

Manifestation proceeds on the basis of these three Foods, basic substances, on different levels. The Upanishad has described them as directly related to the Self, the *ādhyātmik*. It now analyses their emergence as related to the Elements, *ādhibhautik*.

First, the Worlds three in number : Earth, the field of evolution is the manifestation, the working out of *vāk*, the dynamic Power of expression. The Sky-world, vast in extent and subtle in substance, is the formulation of Mind whose range knows no material limits and whose texture is almost intangible. The illimitable Heavens above, beyond the confines of both earth and sky, is the world of Prana, the Force of Life irresistible.

So are the three Vedas that uphold the three worlds with their Law. Vak, the Power of the Word of Invocation to the Divine, embodies itself in the Rig Veda, the Veda of hymns of adoration. Mind with its organising intelligence bases the Veda of Action, effectuating process, the Yajus. Prana, the soaring force of Life is the sustaining and energising soul of the Veda of Harmonies, the full throated chants of human aspiration to the Godhead, the Sama.

So are the three Types of Beings, Gods, Manes and Men. Vak, the creative Word constitutes the Power of the Gods; subtle Mind freed from the tethers of matter provides the stuff of being for the Manes beyond the bounds of earth; and boundless Life-energy, Prana, organises the being of Man in embodiment.

So too are Father, Mother and Progeny. Vak, is the creative agent, father; Mind, the subtle receiving stuff that it is in its true character, is the mother; and the Life resulting from the action of the one upon the other is the progeny.

So are what is known, what is to be known and what is not known forms of Vak, Mind and Prana. Vak, Speech, the revealer assumes the form of what is known, that is to say the form of what is revealed and guards him who knows this of Vak as the real knower and the known. Mind the enquirer who probes into everything in its quest for knowledge takes the form of what is to be known. And Mind itself is something to be explored and seen in its true form. He who knows that this is so and approaches the Mind as such comes to be saved by the Mind. Prana, the Life-force that has no limits and whose real range of power and effectivity remains unfathomed, takes the form of what is not known. And as the unknown it calls the spirit of man to adventure, adds zest to his life and ensures its growth.

Next comes the manifestation of the Three as related to the Gods, *ādhidaivik*. Of Vak, the dynamic power of manifestation, the Earth, *pṛthwi* is the body, for all manifestation here is based upon the pedestal of physical matter which constitutes the earth. And Agni, the flaming force of ascent is its luminous form. Both the gross form and luminous form, the Earth and the Agni, are governed in their range by the Power of Vak.

Of Mind the subtle power intelligence, the Heaven is the body and the Sun the luminous form. Both the gross form and the luminous form, the Heaven and the Sun, are governed in their range by the Mind. With the mingling of the two luminous forms, Agni and Aditya (Sun), Prana was born. When the luminous Intelligence of the Sun acted upon the burning form of Agni there issued Prana, the supreme Force dominating, brooking no rival. Prana has no rival because there is no other Force but himself; he is sole. And the man who realises this truth of Prana in himself partakes the same character of supremacy from Prana.

Now of this Prana, Water is the body; Prana flows through the Waters which are the flowing streams of Consciousness. And its luminous form is the Moon of bliss. Prana at its shining intensity bubbles with an inexpressible delight. Both the gross form and the luminous form, the Waters and the Moon, are governed in their range by the Prana.

These are the three Great Foods. They are equal in extensity; they are truly infinite. He who conceives them as limited and resorts to them as such, limits his destiny to that extent. But he who realises them as infinite expands his own being into infinity.

The Almighty Creator manifests Himself also in the form of Time symbolised by the Year. His manifestation in Time is characterised by periods of light and darkness, Day and Night, the bright half of the month and the dark half. The nights, hours of apparent inactivity, are truly His periods of assimilation and preparation for what is to be manifested anew during the next Day. Life is in incubation and the darkest night is the most pregnant hour when the slightest assault of violence on life is to be desisted from. In fact it is then that He is most active with his inmost Truth. This is the constant Factor which is unaffected by these variations of conditions. The man who knows this should conceive himself in the image of the Creator-Time and realise his self to be the constant factor which stands unaffected by the rise and fall of his fortunes in the material world. His essential being is the nave of his wheel of existence and his circumstances are its felly and spokes.

Three are the worlds spoken of : the world of men, the world of manes and the world of Gods. The means to win each world is different. This world of men is won through the Son. The son of one's body in the Veda, *tanūnapāt*, stands for Agni, the Force of aspiration shaping itself into the leader of the journey. It is he who makes the path and leads to the goal. It is through this Son that the battle of life on earth, this field of labour, is won.

Also it is through the agency of his physical son that the father ensures his continuity on earth. At the time of departing, says the Upanishad, the father calls his son and consciously transfers to him all the knowledge he has built up, all the technique and the fruit of action he has done, developed, all the mastery he has acquired over things in creation. The son receives the father in his own consciousness and the father lives in the son, in so far as it relates to this world of men. Having so relinquished his human lagacy to his progeny, he soars above unencumbered to receive the divine counterparts of what he has parted with viz. divine Speech, divine Mind and divine Prana. The divine Speech with its infallibility, the divine Mind with its ceaseless joy and the divine Prana which is imperturbable in whatever condition, mobile or immobile.

The next world, the higher world of the manes, is to be won by qualifying oneself for it while here by means of appropriate action. The Action performed here and the state of consciousness attained thereby in the body while on earth determines the state of man in the worlds after death. Similarly entry into the highest world of all—the world of the Gods, can only be secured by *vidyā*, by assiduous study and application in the Science of the Self. This is indeed the most difficult and therefore is this prize to be won declared the highest.

One who knows this truth, the truth of the three Foods of Speech, Mind and Prana being none other than his own Self, becomes the Self of all beings, adored of all, but not touched on that account by their evil or grief. For their grief sticks to them alone who are identified with it. Only their merit, their good—not their sin—goes to the Gods, to him who is one with their Self.

Are all the three, the Divine Speech, Mind and Prana equal in every way? It was said that the Speech, Mind and Prana are all equal in extensity, *sarva eva samāḥ* (V. 13). The Upanishad discusses it by means of a parable. Prajapati, the Almighty Creator, first projected these organs (of speech and others). As they were projected, they strove with each other. Vak, Speech, said 'I shall go on speaking (only)'. The Eye said, 'I shall see'. The Ear : 'I shall hear'. So did other organs decide to go each its own way. But Death in the form of fatigue overtook them and put them under hold. Thus it is that the organ of speech gets tired and so too the eye, the ear etc. But Death could not touch the central Prana. So the rest of the organs resolved to know it. 'He is the greatest among us; whether he moves or does not move, he is not vexed nor is he injured. We shall indeed all assume his form.' And they all assumed his form. Hence it is that they are called by the name Prana, they cannot function without the presence of this Prana.

So much with reference to the material embodiment. Now to the embodiment in Gods.

Similarly, says the Upanishad, there was an attempt at self-assertion among the Gods. Agni vowed : ' I shall go on blazing '. Aditya, the Sun : ' I shall go on heating '. The Moon : ' I shall go on shining '....And so did other Gods decide to go each on his own way. But each one has had to set, has had to cease at some time. Not so God Vayu who is among the Gods what Prana is among the constituents of the body. God Vayu never sets, never ceases. He alone was supreme. So it is that like the organs in the body viz. speech, mind etc. which work and cease from work in the force of *prāna*, the Gods also rise and set in their functions in the sea of Vayu.[1] Both Vayu and Prana are the same Force of Brahman and man should learn to put himself in rhythm

---

[1] " When a man sleeps, his organ of speech is merged in the vital breath and so are the mind, the eye and the ear. And when he awakes, these again arise from the vital breath. This is with reference to the body. Now with reference to the Gods : When the Fire goes out, it sets in the Air. Hence they speak of it as having set. It indeed sets in the Air. And when the Sun sets, it enters the] Air and so does the Moon. The Quarters too rest in the Air and they again rise from the Air." (Satapatha Br. X. 3. 3. 6-8)

with the flow of Prana in order that, first, he may not
be overcome by the fatigue that arises because of resis-
tance to the current of Prana or because of insufficient
support derived from Prana; and next, that he may
gradully acquire an identity with this Master-Force in
creation and partake of its nature of universality and
immortality. This is the meaning of the *upāsanā* of
Prana, the *Prāṇa Vidyā* of the Upanishads. It would be
relevant here to quote a few passages from the authentic
writings of Sri Kapali Sastriar on the subject :

> " Prana (is) an image, however gross and dark
> and refractory, of the Supreme Prana the Tapas in
> its highest form. For the Original Prana is the
> Supreme, founding its forms in the lower manifesta-
> tion, supporting its own fragments, reflections, or
> radiations in the living beings here, so much so that
> the Upanishads speak of two kinds of Prana. The
> *Mukhya Prāṇa* is the basis for individual life here,
> hence is called the Chief; all activities of the main
> life, of what we would call the sense-mind, are
> spoken of as Prana. For the Upanishad which
> starts with concrete objects in Nature using them as
> symbols for *upāsanā*, it is easier to advise the use of
> any of the Pranas—voice, seeing, hearing, all are
> termed *prāṇas* here—by special means known to the
> sadhakas of the age, for effecting their union with
> the *mukhya-prāṇa*, their Chief from which they
> branch out for their different functions. It is the
> *mukhya prāṇa* which is the individual centre here of
> the Supreme Prana, that has to become its true
> image. The culmination of the Prana Vidya is the
> correct expression, the ideal formation of the Life
> Supreme in the individual that is at once a real
> reflection, a substantial figure, a canalised current,

a focussed and focussing centre and vehicle in constant and conscious union with its Source, the original
and Omnipotent Prana of the Creative Self, the
Tapas of Ishwara....

" Of all the Vidyas of the ancient Vedanta, the
Prana Vidya is the most powerful, for in the higher
and wider reaches of the sadhana, it is Brahma
Vidya, par excellence. It is the living Breath of the
Purusha, the Puissance of the Creative Consciousness, the Power of the Sole indivisible Spirit that is
the basis of the Prana Vidya ; its aim is not *laya*,
absorption or going to the Beyond,—there are other
sadhanas that aim at it—but the realisation and
successful formation of the individual Life—a Life
that carries out its function as the function of the
Life Universal, having no divided will of its own,
but the One free Will and Tapas of the Ishwara,
and extends its activity as part of the Life of the
Supreme Spirit to a wider range, quite naturally..."
(*Lights on the Upanishads*).

VI

THE TRIPLE MANIFESTATION

This, then, is the Universe. It is a creation of the Divine, an ordered manifestation in Names, Forms and Movement, Action. It is a self-cast in the mould of a Triad of this triple truth of expression viz. Sound, Light and Power.[1]

Of all names, Speech, Shabda, is the source. Each term of call, each word which stands for a thing and summons it in our consciousness the moment it is uttered, is derived from the basic Shabda which throws itself in a million jets. It is not only their source, but forms their community. All names partake of the fundamental truth of Shabda which endows each with its characteristic nature of creative stress. Shabda again is what bears them up in existence.

In the order of creation, according to the ancients, the first to appear is the vibration of Sound, the *nāda* that vibrates and sends throbbing the waves of creative Impulse. The manifestation of Sound, Shabda, is followed by what the Shabda stands for. Shabda is followed by Artha. Sound by Form, *nāma* by *rūpa*. "What is this name? It is word, it is sound, it is vibration of being, the child of infinity and the father of mental idea. Before form can be, name and idea must have existed." (Sri Aurobindo : *The Upanishad in Aphorisms*)

Thus the second in the Triad is Form.

If Sound is the basic source of Name, Light, *tejas*, is the source of Form, Shape. Or as the Upanishad puts

---
[1] I. 6.

it poetically, the Eye is its source. For the principle that actuates and sustains the Eye is Light. It is *tejas* that makes possible distinct forms to outline themselves against the indeterminate and illimitable background of the Brahmic Vast and it is again the *tejas* that makes it possible for us to seize the form. Thus all forms, all shapes in line and colour, partake of the fundamental truth of *tejas*, the Eye, which endows each with its characteristic nature of luminosity. Thus the Eye, the Light that vivifies it, is the source, the community and the sustainer of all forms.

Both Form and Name, it must be remembered, are self-concretisations of the Divine for purposes of manifestation. " Forms are manifestations, not arbitrary inventions out of nothing; for line and colour, mass and design which are the essentials of form carry always in them a significance, are, it might be said, secret values and significances of an unseen reality made visible ; it is for that reason that figure, line, hue, mass, composition can embody what would be otherwise unseen, can convey what would be otherwise occult to the sense. Form may be said to be the innate body, the inevitable self-revelation of the formless, and this is true not only of external shapes, but of the unseen formations of mind and life which we seize only by our thought and those sensible forms of which only the subtle grasp of the inner consciousness can become aware. Name in its deeper sense is not the word by which we describe the object, but the total of power, quality, character of the reality which a form of thing embodies and which we try to sum up by a designating sound, a knowable name, *Nomen.* *Nomen* in this sense, we might say, is *Numen;* the secret Names of the Gods are their power, quality, character of being caught up by the consciousness and made conceivable. The Infinite is nameless, but in that namelessness all possible names, *Numens* of the gods, the names and forms of all realities, are already envisaged and prefigured, because they are there latent and inherent in the All-Existence." (Sri Aurobindo)[1]

However, Names and Forms only do not complete this Creation which is a manifestation in movement, *jagat.* There needs be activity, a movement to work out the purpose for which the numberless Names and Forms are projected. In a sense this working, Action, is more fundamental to the creation than anything else and that is why it is actuated by the very Atman who is at the centre of all creation. The basic urge for action comes from the central Self of the Universe. It is that Self which gives a common character to all Movement and it is the support of this Self that keeps all activity going.

In truth, not only Movement, Action, but even Name and Form are manifestations of this Central Divine that constitutes the Self of the Universe and of each individual. All the three derive from it and find their oneness in It. And the One Self formulates itself into these three fundamental modes of expression.

So all is divine. The Self within is the Divine unsullied in its immortal nature. The expression (triple) without is a formulation of the same Divine; it is the *satya*, Truth in manifestation. The Force of life, the dynamism that expresses itself into action springs from this core of immortality at the heart of creation. The Names, and the Forms answering to it, are equally thrown up by the Divine Truth at Work. Beneath the

---

[1] *The Life Divine,* Vol. II. Chap. 2.

multitude of Names and Forms buoys up the deathless Force of the Divine carrying them on its bosom. The One Divine Soul moves into a Becoming of various extension in modes corresponding to the states of its Being. "All that takes form in itself will be the manifested potentialities of the One, the Word or Name vibrating out of the nameless Silence, the Form realising the formless essence, the active Will or Power proceeding out of the tranquil Force, the ray of self-cognition gleaming out from the sun of timeless self-awareness, the wave of becoming rising up into shape of self-conscious existence out of the eternally self-conscious Being, the joy and love welling for ever out of the eternal still Delight." (Sri Aurobindo)[1]

[1] *The Life Divine*, Vol. I, Chap. XVII.

VII

KNOWLEDGE OF BRAHMAN

Though Brahman, the Supreme Reality, unattainable by our senses, is ineffable and transcendent, He is yet revealed through His myriad manifestations. For He not only puts out so many forms from Himself but enters into them as their immanent Reality. Thus Brahman can be approached and realised through any of His formulations. Particularly through certain of His special forms which are, we may say, concentrated manifestations in which the Brahman is more gathered and more patent than in other forms, for purposes of the Manifestation. The Upanishad focusses attention on this aspect of the truth of Brahman in the form of a story which incidentally throws considerable of light on the social and cultural milieu of those times.*

Bālāki, son of *Balākā* of Garga descent, was a Brahmin who was learned in the knowledge and science of Brahman and was proud of his attainments. Those were the days when the kings bowed low to men of learning and askesis, gave away wealth, princesses and even kingdoms for the gift of the saving Knowledge. Janaka the monarch was celebrated for his devotion to such exemplars of enlightenment to whom he offered bejewelled cows in thousands. Not to be outdone, other members of the Royalty vied with each other in honouring these knowers of Brahman with gifts and owning allegiance to them.

So one day *Gārgya Bālāki*, proud of his knowledge, eloquent speaker that he was, called on Ajatashatru, king of Kashi, and said : " I will tell you of Brahman."

_____
* II. 1

Ajatashatru was indeed happy that he got an opportunity to hear of Brahman and also because it was an occasion to outmatch the more famous Janaka, noted for his endowments. He replied : " We shall give a thousand cows for such a speech. All people rush saying ' Janaka ' ' Janaka'."

Gargya Balaki spoke of the Sun in the skies and said : " The Person who is yonder in the Sun,[1] him indeed I meditate upon as Brahman." For the light which is concentrated in the physical sun is really the material garb of the Celestial Light, the supreme Form of the Divine which is *bhārūpaḥ*. The Being who ensouls this orb is none other than Brahman Himself and is to be worshipped as such.

But that was nothing new to Ajatashatru who replied : " Don't you speak to me of him. For I know and I already meditate upon him as the pre-eminent, the head of all beings and as resplendent. And he who meditates upon him as such becomes pre-eminent, head of all beings and resplendent."

For as the Shruti says, one becomes exactly as one meditates upon Him.[2]

Next Gargya spoke of the Person in the Moon[3] as Brahman. But that was not new either. The king had already known to meditate upon him as the Vast, the White-robed, radiant Soma who covered the whole creation in his immense spread of life-giving Delight which excelled in its radiance in the measure of the white purity of its forms. To one who so meditates, the

---

[1] and consequently in the eye, for the Sun has a presiding relation with the eye. The Spirit manifests both in the macrocosm and the microcosm.

[2] Satapatha Br. X, 5.2.20

[3] and in the mind

king added, the abundant yield of the essence of all life-experience, *soma*, is constant; his sustenance does not decay.

Gargya pointed to the Person in the flash of Lightning[1] as Brahman. But Ajatashatru already knew of this manifestation of Brilliance and knew also that he who meditates upon this Brilliance of Brahman becomes brilliant and his progeny too becomes brilliant.

Gargya pointed to the Person in the Sky[2] of self-extension as Brahman. But Ajatashatru already knew of this manifestation of the Full and the Immovable and knew also that he who meditates upon this Fullness and Immutability of Brahman is blessed with the progeny o opulence, an opulence that is never extinct from this world.

Gargya pointed to the Person in the Vayu,[3] the wind of Life-Force as Brahman. But Ajatashatru already knew of this manifestation of the Lord, the Irresistible and the unvanquished host of Maruts and knew also that he who meditates upon this Brahman becomes indeed victorious, invincible and conqueror of the adversaries.

Gargya pointed to the Person in Agni,[4] the effectuating Will, as Brahman. But Ajatashatru already knew of this manifestation of the Vanquisher and knew also that he who meditates upon this Brahman becomes himself a vanquisher and his progeny too becomes vanquishing.

---

[1] and in the skin

[2] and in the heart

[3] and in the prāṇa

[4] and in speech

Gargya pointed to the Person in Water[1], the stream of Consciousness-Force, as Brahman. But Ajatashatru already knew of this manifestation of the corresponding Form of Brahman and knew also that he who meditates upon this Brahman comes upon what is corresponding to him and not what is contrary ; what is born of him is also the corresponding.

Gargya pointed to the Person in the mirror[2] as Brahman. But Ajatashatru already knew of this Shining manifestation of Brahman and knew also that he who meditates upon this Shining Brahman becomes himself shining, his progeny too becomes shining and he outshines all company.

Gargya pointed to the Sound[3] that follows after one as he goes, as Brahman. But Ajatashatru already knew of this sound as Life-manifestation of Brahman[4] and knew also that he who meditates upon Brahman as the Life lives a full length of life in this world and life does not leave him before time.

Gargya pointed to the Person in the Quarters of Space[5] as Brahman. But Ajatashatru already knew of this manifestation as the Double and Inseparable and knew also that he who meditates upon this manifestation of Brahman as the Double Inseparable has always a companion and his company is not separated from him.

Gargya pointed to the Person who consists of shadow,[6] as Brahman. But Ajatashatru already knew of this dark figure as the Brahman in the form of Death

---

[1] and in retas (vital fluid)

[2] and in what is bright

[3] and in life which sustains the body

[4] because of Life he walks and the sound issues

[5] and in the ears

[6] and of the veiling ignorance within

(following Brahman in the form of Life) and knew also that he who meditates upon this manifestation of Brahman lives a full length of life in this world and death does not come to him before time.

Gargya pointed to the Person who is in the body,[1] as Brahman. But Ajatashatru already knew of this manifestation of Brahman as the Embodied One and knew also that he who meditates upon this manifestation becomes himself embodied and his progeny becomes embodied.

Gargya remained silent.

For more he did not know.

Asked Ajatashatru: Is that all?

Gargya: That is all.

Ajatashatru: But Brahman cannot be known by knowing only that much.

Gargya realised that he had not known all about Brahman. There was evidently something more of Brahman which was not covered by the manifestations of which he spoke so proudly. He aspired to know what he did not know. But one can know of Brahman only from a teacher. So with becoming humility he said: Let me come to you as a pupil.

A Brahmin coming to a Kshatriya as a student to a teacher was not regular. It is the Brahmana who normally teaches. So Ajatashatru hesitated: Verily, it is contrary to the course of things that a Brahmana should come to a Kshatriya, thinking 'he will teach me of Brahman'. However, I shall cause you to know Him.

---

[1] and in the intelligence

So saying, declining to be the instructor who *makes one know*, he took him by his hand (as a friend) and rose.

Both went up to a man who was asleep. He called him out by various terms: "a Great one," "white-robed," "Soma," "king". But the man did not get up. Then Ajatashatru woke him up by pulling with his hand.

And Ajatashatru asked : When this man was asleep where was the conscious being and whence did it come back now?

Gargya did not know.

Ajatashatru explained : When the man was asleep, the conscious being taking in itself—the consciousness of the senses by means of its own consciousness, rests in the *sky* which is within the heart i.e. *within its own Self*. When thus is absorbed the *Prāṇa* (life-force), absorbed the speech, absorbed the eye, absorbed the ear, absorbed the mind, the being who so absorbs them is said to be asleep (lit. rests in his own Self, *svameva ātmānam apiti apigacchati*).

In the dream-condition, the being moves in these worlds of its making. Taking all the senses in itself, it moves about in its body as freely as a king in his domain with his subjects. It assumes different states, high and low as it pleases.

Now when it falls sound asleep and knows nothing, the being having crept back through the seventy-two thousand subtle nerve-channels (called *hita*) which lead from the heart to the pericardium, rests in the pericardium. As a baby or an emperor or a great Brahmana might rest when he has attained the acme of bliss, so the being now rests.

This is where the conscious being is when man sleeps. It rests in its own Self which transcends all the senses, all the organs, all their functions. It transcends all the modes of manifestation, aye, the very manifestation itself. And that too is Brahman. This that is manifest is Brahman. That which is not in manifestation is Brahman. Both are Brahman. One derives from the other.

As a spider moves along the thread[1] it produces and as from the fire tiny sparks fly forth, even so from this Self emanate all vital energies, all worlds, all gods, all beings.

The secret name[1] of this Self is the *Truth of truth*, *satyasya satyam*. *Prāṇas* (vital energies), verily, are the truth. And of them the Self is the Truth.

Life-currents are indeed real but these reals are put out by their One Real that is the Self which is no other than Brahman.

---

[1] Upanishad

VIII

FORM AND THE FORMLESS

Two are the deployments of the Eternal : The Eternal in Form, the Eternal as Formless.* When It determines itself in form, there arises naturally the possibility of de-determination, of freeing Itself from the form, dissolution of the form i.e. Death. When it is formless there is naturally no dissolution, no death, it is immortal. Again, what is so determined, is fixed relatively to the space it occupies; it is stationary even as what is not determined is not confined, is free in movement. Again, what is formed is concrete, palpable to the corresponding sense, it is identifiable as this; what is not so formed, the formless, is the beyond, beyond the range of actuality to the senses.

" These apparently opposite terms of One and Many, Form and Formless, Finite and Infinite, are not so much opposites as complements of each other ; not alternating values of the Brahman which in its creation perpetually loses oneness to find itself in multiplicity, loses it again to recover oneness, but double and concurrent values which explain each other; not hopelessly incompatible alternatives, but two faces of the one Reality which can lead us to it by our realisation of both together and not only by testing each separately." (Sri Aurobindo)

Thus is Brahman manifest on all the planes of Its Self-expression, cosmically as well as individually. Speaking of the cosmos, the Upanishad analyses the manifestation in both the aspects : the formed and the formless.

---

* II. 3

There are the five Elements which constitute this Universe. Of these, the air and the ether are more subtle than others. What is constituted of the other three Elements viz. earth, fire, water is the *formed* and it partakes of the characteristics of Form i.e. death, fixation and actuality. The essence, the core of this Formation of Brahman is the solar orb that emits heat. For the Sun is indeed the essence of the three constituent elements.

Turning to the Formless aspect of this cosmic manifestation of Brahman, the Upanishad posits it as the air and the ether. It partakes of all the characteristics of the Formless viz. it is immortal, it is moving, it is the beyond. The essence, the core of this manifestation of Brahman is the Person in the Sun, the Divine Purusha who ensouls the life-giving Orb in the skies.

As regards the individual aspect in creation, the Upanishad perceives the same truth—the formed and the formless.

All that is not the *prāṇa* life-breath, and not the ether, the subtle sky in the heart, is the formed Brahman in the individual scheme. This partakes of the characteristics of Form i.e, death, fixation and actuality. And the essence of this formed entity is eye. For it is the eye that precedes and directs the rest.[1]

Consequently, the manifestation of Brahman as the formless in this scheme is the *prāṇa*, life-breath, and the subtle sky in the heart. This partakes of the characteristics of the Formless i.e. it is immortal, it is moving, it is the beyond. And the essence of this formless individual manifestation is the Person in the right eye. This Purusha is the subtle being that is at the core.

---

[1] It is the eye that is first formed in the embryo, says the Satapatha Br. (IV. 2, 1)

This subtle Person is of variegated hue. As is the hue of the contacts, the impressions from outside that are impinged on the Person, so is the colour taken on by him. Now it is like a saffron coloured robe; now like white wool, now like the red beetle (Indragopa), now like a flame of fire, now like the white lotus, now like the flash of lightning.

The Upanishad has spoken of the two deployings of the Brahman—as the Formed and the Formless. Lest it should be assumed that these two categories cover the entire Brahman or exhaust it, the Seer goes on to add that even this does not adequately describe the Brahman. Whatever may be posited, the Brahman is still beyond it. It is neither this nor that, *neti*, *neti*.[1] It is more, It is other. It is Beyond all. And yet there is nothing which exists outside it. It is the Real of the real. All that lives is real, all the embodied beings are real; and of them the constituting Real is Brahman.

---

[1] "Brahman is the Alpha and the Omega. Brahman is the One besides whom there is nothing else existent. But this unity is in its nature indefinable. When we seek to envisage it by the mind we are compelled to proceed through an infinite series of conceptions and experiences. And yet in the end we are obliged to negate our largest conceptions, our most comprehensive experiences in order to affirm that the Reality exceeds all definitions. We arrive at the formula of the Indian sages, neti, 'It is not this' neti, 'It is not that', there is no experience which can limit It, there is no conception by which It can be defined." (Sri Aurobindo).

30

IX

THE DOCTRINE OF THE SELF

The Maitreyi Brahmana *of the Brihadaranyaka Upanishad is deservedly famous for its elaborate and picturesque exposition of the Doctrine of the Self. The dramatic setting in which the subject is introduced has a charm of its own, throwing light, incidentally, on the social conditions of those times underlining, among other things, the freedom claimed and given to the individual to adjust his social responsibilities to his inner needs and the general state of englightenment which set store by spiritual values in preference to material riches.

Yajnavalkya, a man of means and two wives—obviously assertive—announces his decision to leave his station of the householder and before setting out he wants to make a final settlement of his wealth between his wives, Maitreyi and Katyayani. When he breaks the news to Maitreyi, she asks, unexpectedly :

" Lord, if the whole earth full of wealth were to be mine, would I be immortal thereby ? "

" No," answers Yajnavalkya with feeling. "As the life of the wealthy, even so would your life be. Of immortality, however, there is no hope through riches."

" Then what shall I do with that by which I cannot be immortal ? " asks Maitreyi and prefers to hear from him what he indeed knows, the way of attaining to Immortality.

Yajnavalkya had always found Maitreyi endearing in the past and he is pleased that she should speak to him thus. He calls her to be seated by his side as he sets out

* II. 4.

to explain the precious truth and enjoins upon her to be
attentive and ponder over what he is going to say.

Behind all the multitude of Forms and Names that
constitute the universe there beats but One Heart. There
is One Indivisible Reality that has placed itself severally
and expresses itself variously in so many individuations.
That Reality is the Atman, the One Self that is the
backbone of the whole Creation universally, and also
the basic Truth sustaining each unit individually. It is
this Self at the base of all that is the root of all feeling of
oneness, all attraction, all sympathy. The Self in me is
also the Self in you. When I see you it is this Self
within me that rushes out to greet itself in your form.
This flow of the Self in one form towards itself in another
form is real Love. This Love has no cause, no motive
to propel it into action like human love which is normally
a perversion of the true Love. This truth of the Self
repeats itself at every level in creation, masks itself in
innumerable forms of relations. To awake to this central
Truth of the Self constituting All, the Self greeting the
Self and the Self embracing the Self, and to give full
expression to this perception by taking steps to eliminate
the veil of ignorance that bars this vision and orientate
the being in the growing light of this truth so as to gain
complete identity with the Self that is within me and at
the same time within All, is the way to Immortality.

This is the truth Yajnavalkya declares and hammers
into the understanding of the seeker, represented for the
nonce by Maitreyi, the enlightened spouse. Employing
an imagery of immediate appeal, he speaks :

" Lo, not for love of the husband is a husband dear,
but for love of the Self a husband is dear.

Lo, not for love of the wife is a wife dear, but for love of the Self a wife is dear.

Lo, not for love of the sons[1] are sons dear, but for love of the Self sons are dear.

Lo, not for love of the wealth is wealth dear, but for love of the Self wealth is dear.

Lo, not for love of Brahmanhood is Brahmanhood dear, but for love of the Self Brahmanhood is dear.

Lo, not for love of Kshatrahood is Kshatrahood dear, but for love of the Self Kshatrahood is dear.

Lo, not for love of the worlds are the worlds dear, but for love of the Self the worlds are dear.

Lo, not for love of the gods are the gods dear, but for love of the Self the gods are dear.

Lo, not for love of the beings are beings dear, but for love of the Self beings are dear.

Lo, *not for love of all is all dear, but for love of the Self* all is dear."

The Self is the One Magnet on which all the routes of love converge.

Verily, it is this Self that is to be seen. Seen, not physically, but perceived by the inner eye, realised in consciousness.[2] And how is that to be done?

---

[1] Acharya Shankara observes in his commentary that the references to husband, wife, etc. are made in the order of the worldly attachments.

[2] Such is the real purport of this passage which has come in for frequent citation and facile misunderstanding. It is taken to mean, by many, that the husband (wife etc.) is dear not for his own sake but for one's own i.e. for the satisfaction of one's own interests. That *atmānah* in the context does not mean one's ignorant being but the divine Self within is clear from the injunction that follows viz. *ātma vā are drastavyah*, the Self, verily, is to be seen.

It is to be *heard*. Knowledge of the Self is to be received from a Source that is in possession of it, be it the Scripture or one who has realised the Self and in a position to communicate it to another.

Not merely heard but *reflected* upon. The mind should cogitate over it; analyse the contents of the Knowledge so received, reason them out as far as possible and familiarise itself with their truth-content.

That done, the Self which is the object of the Knowledge should be *pondered on*, meditated upon continuously till it yields itself, till the conviction ripens into a fact of realisation.

When the Self is so seen, so heard, so reflected upon and so well-grasped in knowledge, this All comes to be known. For, this All is only a Becoming of that Self.

The Self constitutes the very existence of the All, and he who fails to see the Self in anything whatsoever, misses indeed the whole truth of it. The Brahmanhood of the Brahmana lies in the Self. To seek the Brahmanhood elsewhere than in the Self is to miss it altogether. So with the Kshatrahood of the Kshatriya, the extension of the Worlds, the Godhood of the Gods, the Being of the beings, the Existence of the All. They are not apart from the Self; they are what this Self is.

This Truth of creation is lost to sight in the profusion of the multitude that teems before the eye. The truth is to be seized at the source. The sound that is caused at the beating of the drum cannot be grasped externally; it can only be grasped by grasping the drum or the beater of the drum. The sound that is caused by the blowing of the conch-shell cannot be grasped externally; it can only be grasped by grasping

the conch-shell or the blower of the conch-shell. The
sound that is caused by playing on the lute cannot be
grasped externally ; it can only be grasped by grasping
the lute or the player of the lute. Even so, the truth of
the external universe can be grasped only by grasping
the Mind or by grasping the Self which uses the Mind
as its instrument.[1]

All is an outbreathing of this Great Being that is the
Self. Like distinct columns of smoke issuing forth from
fire as it is lit up, there has been breathed out of this
Vast Being a whole Body of Knowledge formulated in
the Rig Veda, Yajur Veda, Sama Veda, Veda of
Atharva Angirasa, Itihasa (History), Purana, Sciences,
Upanishads, Verses, Aphorisms, Explanations and
Commentaries."[2]

Not only is the Great Being the source and origin of
all Manifestation, it is also the Ultimate resting place of
all that has gone forth. As all waters debouch into the
sea, all touches find their one receptacle in the skin, all
savours in the tongue, all smells in the nose, all forms in
the eye, all sounds in the ear, all determinations in the
mind, all knowledges in the heart, all actions in the
hands, all pleasures in the organ of generation, all
evacuations in the anus, all journeyings in the feet, all
Vedas in speech, the final abode of All is the Vast Being.

---

[1] Or, to follow another explanation : the Self is lost to the awareness of
man because of the incessant activity of his senses with their objects without.
In the bustle and noise of their goings-on, the real truth of things is lost to sight,
lost to consciousness. One has to check and arrest the senses from this outgoing
activity before the truth of the Self can make itself felt. It is the drum, the
conch, the lute or the beater of the drum, the blower of the conch or the player
of the lute, that are to be held if the sounds that emanate from them and fill the
air are to be stopped.

[2] *asya mahato bhūtasya niśvasitam etad yad r̥gvedo yajurvedaḥ sāmavedaḥ
atharvāngirasaḥ itihāsaḥ purāṇaṁ vidyā upaniṣad s'lokaḥ sūtrāṇi anuvyākh-
yānāni asyaiva etāni sarvaṇi nis'vasitāni.* (II. 4.10.)

This Vast Being in indeed everywhere, infinite, limitless, massed in consciousness. Like a lump of salt dissolved in water, it cannot be seized, but like the salt that pervades every drop of the water, this Being is everywhere. When things come up it is That which manifests. When things lapse, it is again That which withdraws. After death, after the withdrawal from this manifestation, what so merges in the Infinite Being has no separate awareness of its own. It becomes one with It.

" How can that be? " asks Maitreyi in bewilderment. " If the Vast Being is a mass of Consciousness, what goes into It shall also acquire that Consciousness. How do you say that there is no consciousness after passing? "

" Not so," replies Yajnavalkya. " There is nothing to bewilder in what I say. Sufficient, verily, is this for understanding." The consciousness that is not is the particular consciousness, the awareness of separativity that characterises the individual in the Ignorance. It is the consciousness of duality, awareness of ' another ', knowledge of a ' second '. When the individual being merges into the Vast Being and becomes one with it, that separate consciousness cannot be for the simple reason that there is nothing to be so conscious of. For it is only where there is a duality, as it were, that one sees another ; then one smells another ; then one hears another ; then one speaks to another ; then one thinks of another ; then one understands another. When, verily, everything has become just one's own self, then whereby and whom would one smell? then whereby and whom would one see? then whereby and whom would one hear? then whereby and to whom would one speak?

then whereby and of whom would one think? then whereby and whom would one understand? Whereby would one know him by whom one knows this All? Lo, whereby would one know the knower?

X

THE DOCTRINE OF HONEY

The Satapatha Brahmana has an interesting legend. Dadhyan, son of Atharvan, was taught the *madhu vidyā*, Doctrine of Honey, by Indra. After communicating the secret knowledge, Indra charged Dadhyan with complete secrecy over it with the threat that should he ever reveal the knowledge to others, his head would be cut off with the famous thunderbolt Indra-Vajra. Now, the Ashwins, the divine physicians, overheard this conversation and came to know that Dadhyan, son of Atharvan, had come into possession of a precious knowledge of Integrality. Swiftly they repaired to the sage and entreated him to give them the secret knowledge. But he demurred: he explained that Indra had asked him not to speak of it to another and had threatened to sever his head should he ever do so. That was why, he said, he was afraid.

'Oh', said the Ashwins, 'we shall save you from that.'

'How can you save me?'

"When you come to instruct us, we shall sever your head, conceal it elsewhere and replace it with a horse's head. You will speak to us through the head of the horse. And Indra will indeed cut off the head—the head of the horse. Then we shall restore to you your own.'

The sage agreed, his head was severed and replaced by the head of a horse; he instructed the Aswins through that special head of power. Irate Indra duly cut off the guilty head and the grateful Ashwins restored to Dadhyan his own. (S. Br. 14.1.1)

31

What is this Knowledge which was so much guarded by the lord of the gods and so prized by the Ashwins who heal the sick and make full the maimed?

The fifth section of the *madhu kāṇḍa*[1] devotes itself to an exposition of this Knowledge which is aptly called the Doctrine of Honey, the Knowledge that holds the secret of oneness of life, of interdependence among all forms of life, of the Truth of the One Self, of One Delight that bases and holds the innumerable Many on its bosom. As Sri Kapali Sastriar notes in his profound study of the *Vidyā*[1]:

"It gives fourteen illustrations to impress on us the truth that in this Creation everything and any part of it is Honey to the whole and the whole is Honey to every part of it; and that is because it is the Honey, the Secret Delight that abides in the whole creation and in every part and detail of it that manifests and makes possible the world-existence intact and enjoyable, *bhogya*."

This earth, says the text, is Honey for all beings and all beings are Honey for this earth. All that inhabits the mother-Earth draws its sustenance, its life-force from her. And the earth too is fed in a thousand ways by the energies flowing from its creatures. The one leans on the other, one draws from the other; and that is possible because the Inhabitant of both is the same. He who is in this earth, the effulgent, immortal Purusha and he who is within one's own being, in the body, the effulgent, immortal Purusha, are indeed the same—He who is this Self, this Immortal, this Brahman, this All.

---

* II. 5 The *Kāṇḍa* derives its name from this important subject of *madhu* dealt with in this section.

[1] Vide chapter on *Vedic Wisdom in the Vedanta* in the *Lights on the Upanishads*.

This is the basic truth of all existence, whether looked at in its universal aspect or the individual. There is one Reality underlying both, forming the bridge between both and enabling the one to draw on the other. And the essential nature of that Reality is Bliss, Honey. This Reality reveals itself in several poises. It is experienced and realised as the Self, the one backbone of all existence; it is the Immortal standing for ever unaffected by the currents of birth and death, change and decay, that criss-cross the sea of life; it is again the Vast Expansion, Brahman (*br.* to grow) of the Spirit covering every possible term of expression; it is All that is spread out. And whichever the aspect that is approached, it reveals itself at the core as Bliss.

Bliss, then, is the root-principle basing this manifold existence. For one who has this perception of the true nature of the universe and himself and orders his life-movements in accord with that knowledge, all is harmony, all is delight, all is Honey. But when we are not aware of this commonalty of support and sustenance between ourselves and the rest, we tend to regard ourselves as separate, as entities to be protected from the life-waves that continually rush on us from 'outside'. We shut ourselves from the larger life that engulfs us. There is strain, friction, suffering. To gain in mind a knowledge of this underlying oneness of all manifested life in the form of Bliss, Honey and to translate that knowledge into practical terms of one's own life so as to arrive at a progressive realisation of the true character of all life as Honey, as Delight, is the object of Madhu Vidya.

This is a fundamental Truth that obtains at every level of Existence, in each organisation of the different principles that are manifest in the universe. Thus, proceeds the Upanishad :—

These waters are Honey for all beings and all beings are Honey for these waters; and he who is in these waters, the effulgent, immortal Purusha, and he who is within one's being, constituted of semen,[1] the effulgent, immortal Purusha, are indeed the same—He who is this Self, this Immortal, this Brahman, this All.

This Agni (Fire) is Honey for all beings and all beings are Honey for this Agni; and he who is in this Agni, the effulgent, immortal Purusha, and he who is within one's being, constituted of Speech,[2] the effulgent, immortal Purusha, are indeed the same—He who is this Self, this Immortal, this Brahman, this All.

This Wind is Honey for all beings and all beings are Honey for this Wind; and he who is in this Wind the effulgent, immortal Purusha, and he who is within one's being, constituted of life-force,[3] the effulgent, immortal Purusha, are indeed the same—He who is this Self, this Immortal, this Brahman, this All.

This Sun is Honey for all beings and all beings are Honey to this Sun; and he who is in this Sun the effulgent, immortal Purusha, and he who is within one's being, in the eye,[4] the effulgent, immortal Purusha are indeed the same—He who is this Self, this Immortal, this Brahman, this All.

This Quarters are Honey for all beings and all beings are Honey to these Quarters; and he who is in these Quarters the effulgent, immortal Purusha, and he who is within one's being, in the ear, at the hearing, the effulgent, immortal Purusha, are indeed the same—

---

[1] Corresponding (in the body) to the Water-principle.
[2] Corresponding to the universal Agni Principle.
[3] Corresponding to the universal Vayu Principle.
[4] Centre of activity for the Sun in the individual body.

He who is this Self, this Immortal, this Brahman, this All.

This Moon is Honey for all beings and all beings are Honey to this Moon; and he who is in this Moon, the effulgent, immortal Purusha, and he who is within one's being, in the mind, the effulgent, immortal Purusha, are indeed the same—He who is this Self, this Immortal, this Brahman, this All.

This Lightning is Honey for all beings and all beings are Honey for this Lightning; and he who is in this Lightning, the effulgent, immortal Purusha, and he who is within one's being, constituted of heat, the effulgent, immortal Purusha, are indeed the same—He who is this Self, this Immortal, this Brahman, this All.

This Thunder is Honey for all beings and all beings are Honey for this Thunder; and he who is in this Thunder, the effulgent, immortal Purusha, and he who is within one's being, constituted of sound and voice, the effulgent, immortal Purusha, are indeed the same— He who is this Self, this Immortal, this Brahman, this All.

This Space (ākāśa) is Honey for all beings and all beings are Honey for this Space; and he who is in this Space, the effulgent, immortal Purusha, and he who is within one's being, in the ether of the heart, the effulgent, immortal Purusha, are indeed the same—He who is this Self, this Immortal, this Brahman, this All.

This Dharma, Law, is Honey for all beings and all beings are Honey for this Law; and he who is in this Law, the effulgent, immortal Purusha, and he who is within one's being, constituted of the Law of Truth, the effulgent, immortal Purusha, are indeed the same—He who is this Self, this Immortal, this Brahman, this All.

This Truth is Honey for all beings and all beings are Honey for this Truth; and he who is in this Truth, the effulgent, immortal Purusha, and he who is within one's being, constituted of Truth itself, the effulgent, the immortal Purusha, are indeed the same—He who is this Self, this Immortal, this Brahman, this All.

This Mankind is Honey for all beings and all beings are Honey for this Mankind; and he who is in this Mankind, the effulgent, immortal Purusha, and he who is within one's being, the human person, the effulgent, the immortal Purusha, are indeed the same—He who is this Self, this Immortal, this Brahman, this All.

This Atman, Self, is Honey for all beings and all beings are Honey for this Self; and he who is in this Self, the effulgent, immortal Purusha, and he who is within one's being, the self, the effulgent, immortal Purusha, are indeed the same—He who is this Self, this Immortal, this Brahman, this All.

And this Self, says the Upanishad, " does not merely represent the basic principle of Madhu, the Bliss that abides in the heart of things, but he is the Master and King of all things and Beings and holds together—as the hub and felly hold the spokes—all beings, all gods, all worlds, all lives, all selves." (Sri Kapali Sastry)

Such is the Honey underlying all existence, the *madhu*, which the Upanishad declares to be the same as "the Madhu whose secret Dadhyan revealed to the Ashwins and is the same as the creative Spirit, the Purusha who 'made the two-footed cities (bodies), who made the four-footed cities (bodies) and who having become the Bird[1] entered into them.' And it further removes possible misconceptions as regards the embodied souls as independent self-separate finite entities which they certainly appear to be to our experience, by an affirmation that 'This Purusha is the same as He who abides in all the cities (bodies) and there is nothing by which he is not enveloped, nothing by which he is not concealed.' The last part of the sentence is again significant, a reminder that this Purusha is immanent in everything as the secret *madhu*, the potent Delight that is wakeful holding in its basic unity all forms and things and beings, the *madhu* that is to be discovered in the smallest, in the biggest, in any part or whole of this manifested existence, which to instruct the section opens. And it gives a fitting close too. For in unequivocal terms it reiterates the Vedantic Truth that not only the Substance of all existences, the essential Delight in the all and in detail is the Ananda, Atman, Brahman, Purusha, but all Form also is himself, his creation, a mould of the Substance, a shape of his Being,—he is the supreme Lord, the Divine Being, active, many-formed he moves about, he is the divine counterpart of every form, his countless life-powers are set in motion for ever. Thus closes the section with a Rik of Bharadwaja : 'To every form he has remained the counter-form : that is his Form for us to face and see. Indra by his Maya powers (creative conscious powers) moves on endowed with many forms; for yoked are his thousand steeds.'." (Sri Kapali Sastry)

And this Self, verily, is the steeds. He, verily, is tens and thousands, many and endless. This Brahman is without an antecedent and without a consequent,

---

[1] Bird here symbolises the supreme Soul.

without an inside and without an outside. This Self, the all-perceiving, is Brahman.

To conclude with the words of Sri Kapali Sastriar :

" This is the Madhu doctrine of the Brihadaranyaka Upanishad. It is significant that it comes close upon the Maitreyi Brahmana which concludes with famous passages often quoted in support of the lofty Idealism represented in Shankara's exposition of the Advaita doctrine of later times. It serves as a corrective to the metaphysical excesses to which the closing lines of the preceding section are often interpreted to lend support. It reconciles the Absolute Idealism to which the Maitreyi Brahmana tends with the relative Realism of World-existence in which an all-embracing dualism is the dominant note. It teaches that the secret Honey, *kakṣyaṁ madhu*, is the same as the . Delight of the Purusha, the creative Spirit, the One and uncompromising Absolute of all dualisms, the unifying principle that balances, harmonizes and maintains its own variations for Self-expression.

" To realise the interdependence of things and beings, human and others, is a necessary step towards a knowledge of the secret Delight that maintains the diversity for Self-expression and therefore for variations in form of the essential Self-delight. If it were a question of arriving at the Supreme Delight, the Ananda Brahman or Atman, the Self-delight, the doctrine of Madhu would not be necessary and the quoting of Riks devoted to the Ashwins would signify less than nothing. But the Madhu doctrine teaches that the diversity in creation is the manifestation of a secret Delight, that all things, howsoever heterogeneous and warring they may appear, are held together by a secret harmony effected

XI

LIBERATION

It was at the court of Janaka.

Monarch of Videha, Janaka was a model man who had covered himself with glory both in the material and the spiritual realms. He was a sage in his own right having arrived at great heights of Brahmic realisation and yet ever avid for fresh gains of the Knowledge of the Infinite. He was known for the felicity with which he presided over the destinies of his kingdom in all pomp and regalia, keeping himself all the while steeped in the depths of the Self and radiating the light of the soul in the affairs of State. Legend has it that once when his attendants rushed to him to announce that the palace was on fire, he refused to leave the work on hand saying "even if the whole of Mithila were on fire nothing of me is burnt". He was revered and loved. Rishis, scholars, minstrels all flocked to his court, eager to participate, to drink at the fountain of his wisdom in his assemblies which were famous in those days. It was at one of such gatherings on the occasion of a great Yajna conducted by the king that learned brahmanas from states far and wide had gathered.[1] Eager to know which of them was the foremost among the knowers and inculcators of Brahman, Janaka announced that he who was most established in the knowledge of Brahman could claim the special prize of the day—a thousand radiant cows with their horns studded each with ten pieces of gold.

Who would come forward? None of the Brahmanas dared to stake a claim. Yajnavalkya, the celebrated teacher, was present. Casually he turned to his disciple

---

[1] III. 1

in them by the hidden creative Self-delight of the Supreme, who is the effulgent Self, the Immortal. The Upanishad perceives the Vedic truth of Madhu and the Ashwins and teaches here the seeking of Madhu in the manifestation of all things and beings and not the delight that is unrelated to the Cosmic Existence." (*Lights on the Upanishads*)

and addressed him: "Samasrava dear, drive home these cattle".

Samasravas drove the cattle home.

The whole assembly of Brahmanas was in consternation. "How dare he style himself as the most Brahman-knowing of us?" they asked in anger. Aswala, the high priest in the court of Janaka, challenged Yajnavalkya, "Yajnavalkya, you are the most Brahman-wise among us, aren't you?"

"We bow to the Brahman-wise, all that we want is the cows only", replied Yajnavalkya.

Aswala the priest then decided to subject him to severe questioning.

"Yajnavalkya," he asked "all this is pervaded by Death; all is subject to Death. By what means is the Yajamana, Sacrificer, liberated beyond the reach of Death?" Yajnavalkya is quick with his answer. Inheritor of the Vedic tradition that he is, it comes naturally to him to see the solution of the problem of life in the institution of Yajna, Sacrifice, which the Vedic forefathers had built up as the one means of linking up mortal life with the immortal. No doubt by the time of the Upanishads the real significance of the Yajna was already getting obscured to sight behind the growing paraphernalia of ritual. That is why Yajnavalkya does not stop saying that by sacrifice one crosses over Death. He is concerned to underline the inner truth of the ceremony and draw attention to the conditions under which alone the Yajna could be effective for the purpose in view. Now, as is well known, the Yajna is carried on with the help of priests, different kinds of mantras and particular offerings of wealth etc. That the outer ceremony is only the supporting and expressive symbol of an inner proceeding which forms the real life and soul of the performance is indicated by the names chosen

for these constituents of the sacrifice. As Shri Kapali
Sastriar points out in his Rigveda Bhashya:

"The Ritviks (officiating priests) carry out the
sacrificial function in the right place at the right
time and help the Yajamana (the individual living
soul with personality engaged in the sacrifice)
throughout from the beginning to the end of the
sacrifice. The meaning of its component parts is
apt signifying, as it does, the Sacrificers (*yaṣṭāraḥ*
means worshippers also) who worship, *yaj*, in due
season, *ṛtu*. There are four orders or groups of
these *ṛtviks* in the *somayāga* (worship) viz.: *hotṛ*,
adhvaryu, *udgātṛ* and *brahma*....The *hotā* recites the
riks. The summoning of the Gods by means of the
riks is accomplished by him. Hence the *hotā* is
same as Summoner, *āhvātā*. By uttering the riks
which manifest the Divine Word, he brings to
proximity the Presence of the Gods. The import
is clear in the inner sacrifice. Such a *hotā*
(summoner) is no human priest, but a Divine
Priest. The Brahmanas consider the Divine Being
Himself to be the real priest, *purohita*, placed in
front. The *yājñikas* speak of the three worlds,
Earth, Sky and Heaven, as the supporters in
front, and Agni, Vayu and Aditya as the Purohitas
(Priests) placed in front....That is why Agni is
lauded as the 'Divine Ritvik, Hota in the front',
in the first rik of the Rig Veda of which Madhu-
chhandas is the seer. And it is this Agni who is sung
hundreds of times in the Veda as the Messenger
of the Gods, the Immortal in the mortals.

"The second is the *adhvaryu* taking his stand on
the Yajurveda. He sees to the performance of the
yajña by means of the *yajus*, leads the other *ṛtviks* in

accordance with the manual of *yajña* and it is on him, the active and chief functionary, that the entire performance of sacrifice rests....Though the word *adhvara* has come to mean sacrifice, *yajña*, yet in the Veda following the meaning of its component parts—*adhvānaṁ rāti*, gives the path—*adhvara* is described as journey or pilgrimage. And the diligent *adhvaryu* is he who desires and takes to such an *adhvara*, journey. Among all the Gods in the form of *ṛtviks* it is he who carries out all the action in the journey—signified by the term *adhvara*.

" The Udgata chants the Saman. He delights the Gods by chanting the Saman. In the inner sense, he is God Aditya who reverberates with his chant of music by the Udgitha (lit. song lofty) pleasing to all the Gods, averts the many dangers, harms and lapses from the Yajamana, makes him self-restored and leads him on to Immortality, Truth, Ananda.

" The last is Brahma. He is the Witness of the entire sacrificial ceremony, gives his sanction for the commencement of the ritual, gives the word of assent, Om (O Yes) at the appropriate moment and place, moves not from his seat and always silent he guards the sacrifice, to the very end of its ceremony, against every sin of omission or commission, of deficiency or excess of mantra and action in the ritual. Such, in brief, is the function of the Ritvik Brahma. The inner sense is obvious; the symbolic meaning is unveiled and clear. He is the God of the Mantras and in the Veda the Mantra is known as Brahma. Hence the causal material of all metrical mantra is *praṇava*, known by the syllable *Om*, the word of assent. Tha manifests the original word which is the source of all mantra. So it is Brahmanaspati, the deity presiding over the Mantras of all Deities, which depend upon the aforesaid *pranava*, that sanctions in supreme silence the inner *yajña* of the *yajamāna* by a single syllable, at the beginning, at the end, all throughout".

A Yajna, says Yajnavalkya, in which the sacrificer is conscious of these inner significances, the true roles of the participants, is the sure means to cross beyond the reach of Death. He declares that the liberation is attained through the *hotā*, the priest (Ritvik), who intones the Word of call through *vāk*, the inspired speech of the Summoner, through Agni the ancient priest of call. For the *vāk* is the real *hotṛ*, summoner ; the *vāk* itself is Agni, not only in principle, *tattwa*, but also in its impulsion ; and Agni is the time-honoured *hotā*, the invoker supreme When this identity between the *hotā*, *vāk* and Agni is realised and made a living knowledge in the performance of the Yajna, then is attained liberation, absolute liberation.

Aswala proceeds to ask another question : " Yajnavalkya, all this is pervaded by Day and Night, all subject to Day and Night; by what means is the Yajamana liberated beyond the reach of Day and Night ? " How to get beyond Time, the swallower of all, the solar time measured by Day and Night ? Yajnavalkya replies that is done through the *adhvaryu*, the Ritwik who conducts the Yajna, through the eye that sees and holds all in its vision, through Aditya, the Sun-God who presides over the procession of moments and events ; for the seeing eye is the *adhvaryu* who performs ; the eye functions because of the source of light that presides over it, the Aditya ; and this Aditya is thus the real *adhvaryu* who makes possible the successful conduct of the sacrifice. When this identity between the *adhvaryu*, the eye, and the Aditya is realised and made a living knowledge in the performance of the Yajna, then is attained liberation, absolute liberation.

What about lunar time? asks Aswala, "Yajnavalkya, all this is pervaded by the bright-half and the dark, all is subject to the bright-half and the dark; by what means is the Yajamana liberated beyond the reach of the bright-half and the dark?" Through the Udgatri who chants the melodies that enspell the gods in their rhythms, through *prāṇa* the life-force, through *vāyu* the Air, says Yajnavalkya. For it is the life-force, *prāṇa*, that is the propelling power in the chant, the real *udgātṛ* of the Yajna; and this life-force is again derived from the cosmic Vayu, Air; and Vayu it is who is thus the basic strength of the *udgātṛ*. When this identity between the *udgātṛ*, the *prāṇa*, and that Vayu is realised and made a living knowledge in the performance of the Yajna, then is attained liberation, absolute liberation.

Aswala has another query : " Yajnavalkya, this mid-world is as if without a support. By what support then does the Yajamana attain to the world of Swar?"

Yajnavalkya carries the context of the sacrifice still further. He replies : "Through Brahma, the Ritwik who assents, through the force of his mind which receives the supreme direction, through the moon whose healing rays pour the balm of the Spirit." For the pure mind it is that is the real Brahma who receives and gives the password to proceed ; and this mind is presided over by the Moon with which it has a corresponding relation; and thus the Moon is in effect the Brahma. When this identity between the Brahma, the donor of the assent,

the mind which receives and transmits the Word, and
the Moon who presides over both is realised and made a
living knowledge in the performance of the Yajna, then
is attained the liberation, absolute liberation.

Thus far about liberation. Aswala then turns to
the subject of acquirements through sacrifice. For it was
understood that the hymns used at different periods of the
ritual, the various offerings made at different junctures,
all these operated in different directions to evoke
different results, secular and spiritual, all to the enrich-
ment of the seeker. It is not necessary for our purpose
to go into the full details of the dialogue of this subject.
Suffice it to say that Yajnavalkya points out that there
are three kinds of Riks, chanted by the Hotri, those that
precede the actual sacrifice ; those that accompany its
performance and those that are for purposes of eulogy ;
these three go to win the worlds of the living for the
sacrificer. There are also three kinds of hymns of eulogy
sung by the Udgatri,—introductory, accompanying and
the benedictory—which correspond to the three breaths
in the body—*prāṇa* (in-breath), *apāna* (out-breath) and
vyāna (diffused breath)—and win for the sacrificer the
three worlds of the earth, the atmosphere and the heaven.
Similarly, he refers to three kinds of offerings : those that
flame up in their brightness of force, those that reverberate,
those that sink down, winning respectively the shining
world of the gods, the looming world of the manes and
the lower world of men. By which gods is the sacrifice
protected? By the pristine Mind that is close to the infinite
and a veritable form of the cosmic godhead; by meditat-
ing on this truth of the infinity and divinity of the Mind
at work in the sacrifice one gains the world infinite.

XII

DEATH

So far regarding liberation from death. But what exactly is death? Is it just a sudden happening, an event that comes to be at a particular moment and terminates the bodily existence? No, says the Upanishad, death is not something that comes all of a sudden and ends everything. It is a continuous process of wearing down life and the body that houses it, and it is only the climax, the final precipitation into extinction of life that is known by the name. There is, in the life of man, a perpetual going forth and coming back of his energies on the impulsion of desire; the senses, through their organs, leap forth at every object that comes by, seize it and occupy themselves with it. Another object sails into view and again the process of seizure and appropriation. According as the object is one of like or dislike, there is augmentation or diminution of the nervous energy. Either way there is a spending, a constant outflow that depletes the life-energy and sets afoot a movement of steady disintegration. Death is slowly preparing itself. What are the doors of this outflow of life-force, the senses and their instruments, and what are the objects that overpower our senses thiswise? That is the question that is next asked of Yajnavalkya.[1]

Artabhaga, of the line of Jaratkaru, next, rises and asks:

Yajnavalkya, how many are the seizers and how many the overseizers? How many are the senses that seize the objects? How many are the objects that overpower the senses and drag them to themselves?

---

[1] III. 2

33

Yajnavalkya : Eight are the seizers and eight the over-seizers.

Artabhaga : What then are the eight that seize and the eight that over-seize ?

Yajnavalkya : Prana, Breath,[1] is the seizer ; and fragrance that is wafted on the breath that brings it[2] is the over-seizer. It is the fragrance that attracts the sense of smell and impinges itself upon it through the incoming breath. This is the first.

Speech is the seizer ; name—and what is denoted by name—is the over-seizer. For by Speech, indeed, are the names i.e. words (and their meanings, *artha*) expressed. This is the second.

The tongue is the seizer ; taste is the over-seizer. By the tongue, indeed, one knows the tastes. This is the third.

The eye is the seizer ; form is the over-seizer. By the eye, indeed, one sees the forms. This is the fourth.

The ear is the seizer ; sound is the over-seizer. By the ear, indeed, one hears the sounds. This is the fifth.

The mind is the seizer ; desire is the over-seizer. By the mind, indeed, one cherishes the desires. This is the sixth.

The hand is the seizer ; action is the over-seizer. By the hands, indeed, is action done. This is the seventh.

The skin is the seizer ; touch is the overseizer. By the skin, indeed, one feels the touches. This is the eighth.

These are the eight that seize and these the eight that over-seize.

If such are the constituent agents of death,—and they are ubiquitous—, is Death the final truth ? Or is

---

[1] standing for smell, organ of smell.

[2] *apāna, apānīyatvāt.*

there anything that is greater, what can overpower and swallow Death itself? Evidently there is Something. Otherwise life would not preponderate over death. That is the next question that Artabhaga addresses to Yajnavalkya.

Yajnavalkya, if all this is food for Death, what Deity is that to whom Death itself is the banquet?

Yajnavalkya replies that Death which swallows all is indeed Agni that consumes all. And even as this Agni is swallowed up by waters, so too Death is contained by the Waters of Life, streams of the Consciousness-Energy in which all creation is afloat. And he who meditates upon this truth and realises that death is not the last but that beyond it is Immortality which is in the keeping of the pure Waters of the Divine Consciousness, conquers further death.

What happens, in such a case of liberation, to the senses, to the personalities that are formed round them? This is the next question of Artabhaga. Do they go forth with the person when he leaves?

No, replies Yajnavalkya. They are all dissolved here itself in the embodiment. All the dead weight is left in the material body and only the liberated being, the soul goes to its destination, leaving solely his Glory behind.

But what of the ordinary man in ignorance? Surely, all is not dissolved. There is something that persists and summons the soul back to mortal existence. Asks Artabhaga :

Yajnavalkya, when on his death, his speech attains to its universal Cause—the stuff from which it derives— Agni ; when his prana attains to the wind ; the eye to the sun ; the mind to the moon ; the ear to the quarters ; the body to the earth ; the ether in the heart to the skies ; the hairs of the body to the annual herbs; the hairs of the head to the trees ; blood and semen to the waters; where does the soul, the purusha remain ?

Too profound a question to be discussed in the public,—so feels Yajnavalkya and takes Artabhaga by the hand elsewhere. And in secret they deliberate. We only know what they conclude upon : the soul rests on its *karma*, in the folds of the lasting, potent impressions gathered during its life-time. And according as this *karma* is good or evil, meritful or sinful, so will his next embodiment be, good or evil, meritful or sinful.

Artabhaga, of the line of Jaratkaru, had no more questions. He remained silent.

OTHER TITLES BY SRI M.P. PANDIT: